Blueish Stain
On top of page
09/18/2017
KRV<

W9-CCO-192

You know you're the parent of a middle-schooler when . . .

- You're convinced aliens have moved into your family room.
- A simple question—like "How was your day?" or "Are you ready to go?"—sets off a volcanic eruption.
- You're buying training bras when there is nothing to train.
- Your son has to have a razor . . . for his peach fuzz.
- "You're so weird" is the most common comment aimed at you, and you're beginning to think your child is right.
- You caught your daughter talking to herself in the mirror.
- You wonder where you can go to resign as a parent . . . until college.
- You scour the shelves at Walgreens for Light Days, Heavy Days, Rainy Days, With Rebar, Without Rebar.
- A simple pimple stops the earth from revolving around the sun.
- You think: *Oh, Lord, three daughters. Three . . . three weddings too!*
- Your son is fascinated by his underarm hair.
- That boarding school you heard about in Egypt is sounding mighty good, and you've even checked how much the airfare would be.

- You see your daughter dressed up in a fancy red dress with spike heels and think, *I am so not ready for this.*
- Your son likes to flex his nonexistent biceps.
- The word *whatever* has multiple meanings, none of them good.
- Your child can't walk through an archway without jumping up to touch it.
- You'd pay anyone a lot of money to have the sex talk with your kids so you don't have to.
- You had no idea a haircut could create the scene you just witnessed.
- You're in survival mode daily.

Planet
MIDDLE
SCHOOL

Planet
MIDDLE
SCHOOL

Helping Your Child through the Peer Pressure, Awkward Moments & Emotional Drama

Dr. Kevin
Leman

Revell

a division of Baker Publishing Group
Grand Rapids, Michigan

© 2015 by Dr. Kevin Leman

Published by Revell
a division of Baker Publishing Group
P.O. Box 6287, Grand Rapids, MI 49516-6287
www.revellbooks.com

Printed in the United States of America

All rights reserved. No part of this publication may be reproduced, stored in a retrieval system, or transmitted in any form or by any means—for example, electronic, photocopy, recording—without the prior written permission of the publisher. The only exception is brief quotations in printed reviews.

Library of Congress Cataloging-in-Publication Data
Leman, Kevin.
    Planet middle school : helping your child through the peer pressure,
awkward moments & emotional drama / Dr. Kevin Leman.
        pages cm
    Includes bibliographical references.
    ISBN 978-0-8007-2305-7 (cloth)
    1. Middle schools—United States. 2. Middle school students—United
States. I. Title.
LB1623.5.L46 2015
373.236—dc23   2015010386

Scripture quotations are from the Holy Bible, New International Version®. NIV®. Copyright © 1973, 1978, 1984, 2011 by Biblica, Inc.™ Used by permission of Zondervan. All rights reserved worldwide. www.zondervan.com

To protect the privacy of those who have shared their stories with the author, some details and names have been changed.

15 16 17 18 19 20 21   7 6 5 4 3 2

In keeping with biblical principles of creation stewardship, Baker Publishing Group advocates the responsible use of our natural resources. As a member of the Green Press Initiative, our company uses recycled paper when possible. The text paper of this book is composed in part of post-consumer waste.

To my grandchildren,
Conner and Adeline:
"I love you to the moon and back."

And to the parents of middle-schoolers:
Enjoy the ride.

Contents

Contents

Contents

Acknowledgments

To all my beloved Facebook fans, whose real-life questions spark book ideas such as this one—thank you.

To my wife, Sande, and kids—Holly, Krissy, Kevin, Hannah, Lauren—who made our own Planet Middle School such an intriguing time of growing and changing together, to form the loving connection we have to this day.

To my editorial team—Ramona Cramer Tucker, Lonnie Hull DuPont, and Jessica English—for their finely tuned skills, wisdom, and encouragement. We're all in this together to make a difference for families.

Introduction

You've Just Arrived
on Planet Middle School

They're up, they're down, they're floating in the stratosphere. But you can make these weird years the best and most fun age of all.

Have you ever wondered if someone left the door open in your house and let an alien into your family room? Suddenly that sweet son who picked a dandelion from your yard and presented it to you like a prize rose, and that precious daughter who snuggled by your side on the sofa and told you all the secrets of her heart, have morphed into middle-schoolers you can't recognize—complete with smart mouths and self-centered attitudes.

Just tell any mom on the playground that you have a child about to enter middle school, and you'll get a cluck of empathy. "Oh, you have one of *those*. Well, you'll get through it," she'll say and pat your hand in sympathy. To quote Sande, my dear wife, who has weathered (and enjoyed) raising four girls and a boy, "Preadolescent and adolescent girls are the worst creatures walking the planet."

Middle-school boys can be mean and are often clueless. Middle-school girls can be even meaner, not to mention catty as all get-out too. One glimpse of two preadolescent girls going at each other will send all but the toughest of men running for cover.

Entering middle school is like stepping onto a different planet for both you and your child—a time and an expanding universe where peer pressure, society, media, and technology influences, as well as hormone changes, can create havoc in your child's life and in your relationship. Your home environment can sometimes feel more like a red-hot planet about to spontaneously combust, especially if you have two middle-schoolers of the same gender cohabiting the same space. Solar flares of emotions are an everyday drama, and the sudden flashes can be blinding.

> Your home environment can sometimes feel more like a red-hot planet about to spontaneously combust.

These "expanding universe" years—ages 11 through 13—are when your child will do almost *anything* to fit in . . . yes, even if you've taught him to do otherwise and you're certain he knows better. With hormones swirling and body parts changing, all middle-schoolers are at risk for behaviors you wouldn't recognize as belonging to your son or daughter. Add together these influences:

- the continual bombardment flowing through their iPods, cell phones, and tablets;
- the interactions with their peers on a daily basis;
- the many schools that now use electronic textbooks; devices such as Chromebooks for assignments, tests, and research; and their own email systems;

- the popularity of Facebook and Twitter accounts, not to mention other social media; and
- the media messages of movies, YouTube videos and songs, and computer games;

and it's no wonder today's middle-schoolers are growing up faster than ever before.

What you can't change are those ever-present facts of life. But you can learn to be smart about them. The middle-school years don't have to create chaos in your family. Whether you're smack in the middle of them or nervously anticipating them, you can navigate the meteor-strewn universe with confidence and a steady hand. With a little knowledge and some key principles, you can steer your middle-schooler toward lifelong success.

Planet Middle School will help you

- understand your middle-schooler and her rapidly expanding universe;
- respond but not react to the solar-flare dramas (and keep your sense of humor);
- naturally model the single most important character quality of all—an attitude of gratitude;
- relate to his survival-of-the-fittest struggles every day;
- identify signs of at-risk behavior;
- grapple with the black hole of technology—a fact of life—that sucks your child in;
- learn how to safeguard your child in the midst of the swirling morass of information and online predators;

> These "expanding universe" years—ages 11 through 13—are when your child will do almost *anything* to fit in . . . yes, even if you've taught him to do otherwise and you're certain he knows better.

- teach your child the basics of sex (before someone else tells them their version) and why respect for themselves and others is so critical to their long-term physical and emotional health;
- talk in ways your middle-schooler will hear;
- harness the power of positive parental expectations in your relationship with your child;
- create an environment that keeps your child happily saying, "There's no place like home" (even if it's not to your face);
- encourage your child in his unique bent without being pushy;
- foster opportunities to broaden your child's world from "all about me" to "the importance of we."

Yes, your middle-schooler will still be weird at times. No doubt about it. But armed with the insight and practical principles of this book, you can make the middle-school years the best and most fun age of all. Someday, in fact, you and your grown-up kids will be sitting around the dinner table, laughing and swapping stories about these memorable years. Just like my beloved bride, Sande, and I do with our five children now.

I guarantee it.

1

Creature from the Black Lagoon

There's a new creature in your family room . . . that used to be your kid. Why your home and relationship can sometimes feel like a sci-fi flick, and what you can do to ease the transition.

"Not since the beginning of time has the world known terror like this! . . . Shocking and suspenseful," says the trailer for the classic 1950s sci-fi adventure *Creature from the Black Lagoon*.[1] In this monster film, fossil hunters travel down a dark, mist-shrouded river and enter the domain of a prehistoric, one-of-a-kind creature. But capturing the creature only kicks off the nonstop action, especially when the creature surprises them all, doing what they never could have expected, and creates an atmosphere of terror and chaos. "Out of the murk and mystery . . . up from the depths of unknown waters comes a creature to confound science and terrorize the world!"[2]

Does the creature from the black lagoon sound a little like your middle-schooler . . . on a good day? Does he or she sometimes create chaos in your home and confound your reasoning ability?

It seems only yesterday your 11-year-old son was eager to please you. "Would you mind bringing in the trash can from the street?" you asked.

"Sure, Mom." He flashed you a smile. "Could you drop me off at Sam's afterward so we can shoot some hoops?"

Now, when he emerges from his bedroom lair before school, even asking him, "Are you ready to go yet?" sets off a major tirade.

"Go? Do I look like I'm ready to go?" he spouts defiantly in your face. Then he stalks off toward the bathroom, muttering about how stupid parents are in general—and you in particular. For extra drama, he gives the hallway wall a little kick.

Your thoughts whirl. *So I suddenly got stupid overnight? Well, that was fast. And what was that outburst about, anyway? All I asked was . . .*

And what about your daughter, your 12-year-old who told you last summer, "Mom, I love spending time with you"?

Now when you ask her, "Hey, honey, want to go to the grocery store with me?" she simply stares at you. No, not stares exactly. She rolls her eyes and announces, "Like *that* is exciting." Without another word, she starts texting like a mad woodpecker on her blingy hot-pink cell phone and flounces off to her bedroom. You hear the door close with more oomph than you're comfortable with.

After each of those encounters, you stand shell-shocked in the kitchen. *Who opened the door to our house and let in that sassy-mouthed alien?* "Murk and mystery" doesn't describe your conflicted thoughts at that moment. Another *M*-word pops to the forefront of your mind . . . something Cain did to his brother Abel, launching many of humankind's problems. But after you are done seeing red and your skyrocketing pulse settles, you think better of it. Prison orange really isn't your best color. What exactly happened? You've just experienced your own creature from the black lagoon, and it does somewhat resemble your child on the outside.

> "Murk and mystery" doesn't describe your conflicted thoughts at that moment. Another *M*-word pops to the forefront of your mind.

A Murky, Mysterious World

I'll be blunt. The middle-school years are some of the hardest for parents, educators, and psychologists to get their heads around. That's because the age at which a child goes through puberty, that time when his or her hormones kick in, can vary so greatly. Children who are in *pubescence* or *preadolescence*—the two terms are interchangeable—experience the uncomfortable state of their bodies being in constant change. An 11-year-old girl can be a pubescent in May, but by September, whoa! You've got an adolescent on your hands. For some girls, if an unknowing bystander assumed she was 17, you'd be hard-pressed to argue the point. Some kids grow up that quickly. And in today's world, the age in which puberty kicks in is dropping lower and lower all the time.

During pubescence, there is a wide range regarding middle-schoolers' maturity levels physically, emotionally, relationally, and intellectually.

Take, for instance, the huge difference between a sixth-grade boy and an eighth-grade girl. The sixth-grade boy is likely to be a little boy in so many ways. He might be five inches shorter than the girl, and his voice range is still basically soprano. As embarrassing as his "girly voice" is to him, especially when he's in the same school with the more manly eighth-graders, the cracking to come next will be even more so. For that sixth-grader, the signs of male anatomy development are probably the same as those he had in elementary school.

But his hormones have already begun to launch a mental switch, even if his body hasn't caught up. In elementary school, either girls had cooties and he ran from them, or, if he liked a girl, he pulled her hair or tried to wrestle her. Now he finds his eyes resting in a particular place on a girl's shirt and on her beautifully sculpted behind. Mysterious shivers run through his body. But old boyish behaviors are still kicked into gear. If he likes a girl, he'll bump her with his shoulder. He's not clued in to the subtleties of male-female relationships. His approach is more like what you'd see on Monday Night *RAW. Cool*, he thinks. *If I want her to know I like her, I'll just do a wrestling move on her.*

As for a sixth-grade boy's intellectual development? Spiders are on his mind. His purpose? To find one and plant it in a girl's locker and watch her scream. That would make his day, and he'd get her attention too.

Contrast that to the eighth-grade girl. She may still look like a little girl; she may be a late bloomer. But she can also truly be a young woman, including having the ability to attract an older boy's attention with curves in all the right places, as well as the physical ability to conceive and carry a baby. She may have had her period since third or fourth grade. Even a touch of makeup can catapult her looks into the high-school category, making her very interesting to older boys.

But that eighth-grade girl doesn't have any idea how voluptuous she really is. She's too busy dealing with her own emotional ups and downs based on the changes in her hormones. For her, love and romance aren't about the physical act of sex; they're about the emotional connection. When a boy likes her, her world suddenly bursts into rosy color. Everything about life is good, just because that boy is paying attention to her and thinks she's special. However, when he turns his attention to someone else, or she even hears that he doesn't like her anymore, her world crashes down around her and everything turns bleak and gray.

> As for a sixth-grade boy's intellectual development? Spiders are on his mind. His purpose? To find one and plant it in a girl's locker and watch her scream. That would make his day.

If you peeked into her diary, here's what you would likely see: drawings of intertwined hearts, with her name and a boy's name inside, and scribbles that say, "I think I'm in love" and "I wonder if he likes me." She daydreams in math class and doodles a boy's last name after her first name, just to see what they look like together. She imagines that boy holding her hand, gazing into her eyes, kissing her . . .

So when the sixth-grade boy, who is gaga over that girl, shoulder-bumps her to get her attention, he gains her attention, all right. But it's not the kind he wants. "Boys are so stupid," she announces in a condescending tone in his general direction. Then, chin raised high, she links arms with a girlfriend and struts past him.

However, if a finely developed eighth-grade male specimen happens to be walking that same hallway, the girl's relational behavior changes drastically. A well-placed giggle, a flip of the hair, and a flirtatious glance out of the corner of her eye are only a few of the behaviors intended to draw the boy in, like a spider drawing prey into its web. Add a little extra hip sway in the walk, and that male won't know what hit him. He's a goner. He may look like a high-schooler physically, but he has no hope of matching wits with the eighth-grade girl. She'll always have the upper hand.

If you check out her favorite YouTube playlist, you'll have a clue as to what's on her mind and the state of her emotions. Many of the songs and videos will be about love and romance, as she's dreaming of finding her "one and only." Just as her body prepares to some-day become a mother, her mind launches into family mode. Ever noticed how eighth-grade girls suddenly think babies are cute and want to coo over them and hold them, when a year or two earlier they only gave babies a cursory glance or treated them as a noisy interruption?

> Ever noticed how eighth-grade girls suddenly think babies are cute and want to coo over them and hold them?

The eighth-grade girl's intellectual processing on just about any subject would run circles around that sixth-grade boy, making his head spin. No way can he keep up.

So instead, he continues to do goofy things to gain her attention, which only annoys her. When the girl screams at the spider in her locker, he's stupid enough not only to be close by but to look outwardly thrilled so she knows he's the one who did it. Even her yelling, "You're such an idiot!" means to him, *Hey, she knows who I am. She acknowledged me.* (See what I mean about missing the nuances?)

But if that girl cries? He's terrified at this alien act and runs for cover, unable to cope with a female's waterworks.

Other than muttering about his stupidity, however, the girl has erased the sixth-grade boy from her mind. She's mesmerized by the older boys strolling down the hallway in front of her and engaged in chatting with the girls in her exclusive clique. She's too busy trying to figure out life in general—and her life in particular and her myriad roles—to spend much thought time on a boy whom she clearly doesn't consider dating material.

Sneak up on that clique of girls at school after they pass one of those older masculine specimens, and you're likely to overhear something like this:

Girl 1: "Oh, he's soooo cute! You think he likes me?"
Girl 2: "Of course he likes you. He looked at you."
Girl 3: "Yeah, he wouldn't give you a look if he didn't like you."
Girl 2: "Especially *that* kind of look."
All three girls exchange their own look.
Girl 1: "Really?" She giggles and does a little dance. "You think?"
Girl 2 and 3 chime together: "Yeah, we think."
And the conversation continues down the hallway.

Now, would middle-school boys ever have a conversation like that? Not on your life!

Talk about a chasm! So if you feel like you're casting around in the mud from moment to moment to figure out your kids and what you can do to help them and yourself, you're not alone. They can't figure themselves out either.

Caught in the Middle

For the purposes of this book, I'm defining the middle-school years as those when your child is approximately ages 11 through 13—the turbulent years between elementary school and high school. I don't stipulate which grades are considered "middle school," because schools and state stipulations vary. *Junior high*, a term some still use for *middle school*, can cover grades six through eight or seven through nine. No matter the grades it covers, the term *middle school* is apropos indeed, since children ages 11 to 13 are truly caught in the middle.

On one end, they are still young children, craving the protection, comfort, and safe boundaries of parental guidance. On the other end, they are heading toward young adulthood and desire freedom and independence from parental constraints. The constant internal struggle between the two creates an "I love you/I hate you" tug-of-war that can change their response to you instantaneously. You know which side of the love/hate war is winning if your son allows you to walk by his side rather than 12 feet behind—his usual request when he's around his peers. But even when he's in that "I love you" mode, Mom, you never hug or kiss your son in front of his peers. And I mean *never*.

Kids who are caught in the middle are not only trying to fine-tune their relationship with you and what their role in your home is, they're trying to figure out their positions and jockey for roles among their peers. Competition there is fierce.

What Worked for Us

I'll never forget the day my daughter told me, "Mom, stop trying to talk to my friends. It's embarrassing." I was shocked. Our home had been a parade of her friends for as long as I could remember, and I always talked to them. Then my daughter hit seventh grade, and suddenly I was shunned. A longtime girlfriend reminded me of our junior-high years, when we were pom-pom girls. Our moms used to cheer loudly for us in the stands, and then they'd burst into our group of friends afterward and start hugging everybody.

"Wow, that was embarrassing," my friend said.

We both laughed.

I got the point. I'd done basically the same thing to my daughter that my mom had done to me. My daughter, though, had the guts to tell me to back off and let her have her own relationship with her friends. I never would have had the courage to tell my mom that. Yes, my daughter could have done it more nicely, but I got the point. I backed off because I don't want to lose what's most important to me—my daughter's trust and heart.

Francine, Connecticut

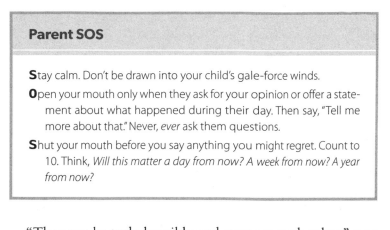

Parent SOS

Stay calm. Don't be drawn into your child's gale-force winds.

Open your mouth only when they ask for your opinion or offer a statement about what happened during their day. Then say, "Tell me more about that." Never, *ever* ask them questions.

Shut your mouth before you say anything you might regret. Count to 10. Think, *Will this matter a day from now? A week from now? A year from now?*

"They can be truly horrible and nasty to each other," says an educator who has worked in middle-school environments for over 30 years. "But some days they can be surprisingly charming and kind. You never know which behavior to expect until you're right in the middle of the situation and the mood of the moment plays out."

A middle-school principal reported, "Within a 30-minute period yesterday I dealt with a food fight in the cafeteria, sexting in the girls' bathroom, and bullying in the PE hallway. When I got back to my office, two sixth-graders handed me a plate of pink frosted cupcakes. Sometimes I have to shake my head at the widely varying behavior."

EGRS

Unless you UPS those middle-schoolers to Zimbabwe for three years, they will be living with you (or, if you're divorced, they'll likely be with you part of the time). So here's a bit of advice in a memorable acronym. Think of your middle-schoolers as EGRS, for *Extra Grace Required Sometimes*. Whether you roll through the middle-school years with only a few meteors here and there, whether your ride more closely resembles interplanetary war, or whether you're somewhere

27

floating in the stratosphere in between, your child needs you at his side . . . as well as all the grace you can muster.

What can you do to smooth the journey for both of you?

Expect the unexpected . . . and relax in between. When you expect almost anything to happen and it does, you can't be blindsided, can you?

With your "verbally skilled" children (a nice way to put it, don't you think?), when no meteors hit your living space, you can sit back, relax, and smile. Enjoy that temporary, beautiful view of the stars and the amazing quiet . . . at least for 15 minutes, until the next meteor ricochets into the room. Use the quiet times to gain long-term perspective and to strategize next steps.

If you have one of those quiet zombies living with you—who seem to stagger from school to the kitchen for food and back to their computer game with only nonsensical grunts in between—you may want to cautiously enter their space at times to make sure all is well. (Hint: Tantalizing aromas open any door, even one with "Stay Out—My Space" posted on it. Cinnamon or chocolate works especially well.)

Give them room to grow and change. Just because your child is up in the stratosphere one day doesn't mean he won't be on earth the next. And a single fight with a sibling doesn't mean they hate each other. In a few hours, those two will probably be sitting side by side, watching *NCIS*. The child you think is all about himself may surprise you by helping an elderly neighbor up the steps with her groceries . . . all on his own.

Every day your middle-schooler is experimenting with how life works and trying to figure out his role in it. Encourage those efforts when they are in a positive direction by saying things like, "I saw you helping Mrs. Dawson. That must have felt good to be able to do that for someone who has a hard time doing it herself. I'm sure she appreciated it." Secretly, he wants to please you. Knowing that works to your benefit . . . and the entire family's.

Remember what your own middle-school years were like. Flash back to your first day of middle school—what you were wearing, how you did your hair, how you felt the first time you stepped into the doors of that foreign place. It felt so huge, so alien, so overwhelming. Some of you may not be able to remember a thing, because middle school was so rough that you've blocked out all the bad memories. But taking a few minutes to reflect on the highs and lows of your middle-school years will drum up a little empathy for

You Know You Have a Middle-Schooler When . . .

- He does wild bird calls at the most inappropriate moments.
- She loves jeans with holes in them because they're popular. (Back in your day, you'd be embarrassed to wear them because everybody would think you were poor.)
- Every conversation is dotted with the words *always* and *never*.
- He used to hate taking showers, but now you catch him sniffing his own armpits. (That used to be your job as you caught him before he flung himself out the door for school.)
- Her day is made or ruined by one comment from one peer.
- He can't walk through an archway without jumping up to touch it.
- His baseball cap is usually at the five-o-clock position, and the crotch of his pants slides down to his thighs or knees.
- Jekyll and Hyde can't compare to her mood swings.
- He flexes his biceps in the bathroom mirror.
- One simple pimple becomes Mount St. Helens.
- He grew five inches over the summer.
- He or she defies gravity. She's always on the ceiling about something. With a running start, he can jump 12 steps in one leap, do a Michael Jordan–like 360, and then complete the last 8 steps with equal ease, all to announce, "I'm ready for dinner."

your kid. And for him, it's even more difficult, with all the social media influences pushing him to grow up faster.

Sift through mood changes for the real reasons behind the emotion, and don't take the mood switches personally. Your middle-schooler doesn't have a devious plan to make your life miserable, but you're the one who often catches the grief. Take that as a compliment. She's smart enough to know that if she rags on her friends, they'll ditch her. Teachers won't put up with it either, and she'll discover quickly that detention after school is no fun. So she comes home and gives her next candidate a go—a sibling, if she has one. But siblings aren't dumb either. They usually go running to Mama to narc on her, and her action backfires. Who do you think is next in the pecking order to fight with? You, Mom or Dad, because you're "safe," and she reasons, *They're stuck. They have to put up with me.* Depending on your parenting style, your child's attempt is either successful and thus worth trying again or halted in its tracks due to your dictatorial control.

Wise moms and dads use a different method. They learn how to listen, especially for what's behind her flurry of angry words—the real reason she's upset. Did a supposed "friend" circulate an embarrassing rumor about her? Did she fail a test because she spent her time texting instead of studying, and now she's mad at herself and afraid to tell you she failed? Did she find out in PE class that her BMI (body mass index) is 29 percent and she's considered overweight? Worse, the cattiest girl in her class overheard that?

Often the real reason won't be revealed until later, when the dust settles. If you maintain your calm, go about your business, and don't react to the emotion, you'll be surprised what you learn a few hours or a few days down the road.

Wise parents never, ever engage in a fight. Fighting is an act of cooperation that works only if both sides engage. Amazing how a fight loses its heat when one person withdraws. All the fun goes out of it too.

While you're giving your child that extra grace required, don't forget to give some to yourself. You won't always say or do the right thing when you're battling that creature from the black lagoon. But don't worry. Tomorrow's a new day, and your child is more forgiving than you might think. So lighten up!

Look on the bright side. You won't even have to spend a couple bucks renting the latest sci-fi flick. You've already got it in full color in your living room. All you have to do is sit back and watch.

2

Their Expanding Universe

What you need to know, and why you need to be along for the ride.

When kids are three or four, their universe is very small: Mom and/or Dad, Grandma, Grandpa, a few other close relatives, the dog, and the goldfish. Those same children hit kindergarten, and suddenly they've got these other kids in the mix who don't look or act like anything they've seen before.

Then comes elementary school, and things get a little bigger. They have a different teacher every year, kids in their class change, and they have to walk down a hall to get to gym class and the library. And the playground? With such a mix of ages and sizes of children, it can be a scary place.

Then your child hits middle school—the time when everything changes. A child who is used to a one-room class and a homeroom teacher might now have six to eight classes and just as many teachers. Even more, that child has to race from one floor or building to another and play "find the classroom" before the bell goes off that declares him late and gains him detention after school. No wonder many middle-schoolers come home with blisters on their feet from the miles they've walked that day. They feel exhausted, overwhelmed, and discouraged the first couple weeks of school. Wouldn't you feel a little cranky yourself with all that transition?

> All of a sudden, the king of the hill becomes the low man on the totem pole.

Up to this point, your child was fairly self-focused. He thought about things that affected him, and what was most important was how he felt about them. Now he's starting to notice others, especially the opposite sex. And he wonders what his peers think about him.

Take, for instance, the fifth- or sixth-grader. He rules in the K–5 or K–6 school. He's the big kid on the playground. Younger kids see him coming, and just because of his size compared to theirs, they let him go first down the slide at lunch or have the volleyball at recess.

That same kid who is used to ruling the roost enters middle school. All of a sudden, the king of the hill becomes the low man on the totem pole. In fact, he's so low he's on the bottom of the manure pile, and things can get pretty messy and stinky down there.

Meet Erin

Erin was a wallflower-type girl, whom few seemed to notice except for a small group of friends . . . until she got the lead role in the fifth-grade musical. Then suddenly she catapulted to the popular group. For the last three months of her fifth-grade career, the "hottest" boy in school flirted with her. She ditched her former friends and ate lunch with her new friends. They flattered her to her face but gossiped about her behind her back. When one of her former friends tried to warn her, Erin blew the girl off. "You're just jealous."

But when Erin entered sixth grade, nobody cared that she'd been the lead in a fifth-grade musical. In fact, when she auditioned for the middle-school play, she wasn't even chosen for one of the chorus roles. Erin lost her identity; she got lost in the middle-school shuffle. Her former friends didn't trust her anymore and no longer wanted to hang out with her. Her popular friends from fifth grade ditched her in a nasty exchange of gossipy texts and moved on.

Midway through sixth grade, Erin stopped even trying to make friends. Her widely expanding world had shrunk to a lonely circle of one.

The next year, rumors circulated that Erin's parents were home-schooling her because she was depressed.

The Influence of Peers, Teachers, and Coaches

"One of the most frightening things to me as a parent," Valerie, a mom of an eighth-grader, told me, "is that my son is away from my influence about 10 hours a day, if you include school and after-school activities. During that time, I don't know what his peers are saying or what teachers and coaches are telling him, and I have no control over it. I only learn about something if he tells me, and he's talking to me less and less."

It's true. Once your kids reach middle school, activities outside your home increase. Friendships become more important. In the natural struggle for independence from you, peer influence mounts.

"How can I know if the peers he's surrounding himself with are good for him?" Valerie asked.

An easy answer is, "How does your son treat you and his siblings, if he has them? If you see a complete 180 in behavior, chances are, peer influence is involved." I wish I could say that one positive child among a mix of badly behaved children can turn a group around, but it happens more often the other direction. The group your child chooses to interact with makes a huge impact on the direction he goes during these in-between years.

However, the kind of peers your child chooses has everything to do with what you've done up to this point. Have you set a moral compass for your family?

> In the natural struggle for independence from you, peer influence mounts.

Have you not only taught but modeled in your child's growing-up years that certain qualities, characteristics, and actions are positive and helpful, and that others are negative and harmful? For some additional reading, you might find my books *Have a Happy Family by Friday* and *Have a New Kid by Friday* helpful.

Even if you rear children to align with your family's values, will kids sometimes make mistakes about the friends they choose? Of course. Many of them learn the hard way, like Erin, when those supposed "friends" gossip about them or set them up for a big fall. That's what I call "reality doing the teaching." The things your child learns firsthand have an amazing ability to stick. Once burned by fickle friendships, hopefully your child will be smarter next time about the qualities she looks for in a friend.

So what can you do to assist your child during this turbulent tweener time when the stakes are mounting?

Be Their Lifeline

Think of your preteen as an astronaut floating in the blackness of deep space. But that astronaut is connected by a lifeline back to the mother ship—sort of like the umbilical cord that attached her to her birth mother before she was born. The child needs to float out in the world, to explore and learn, including discovering

> Think of your preteen as an astronaut floating in the blackness of deep space. But that astronaut is connected by a lifeline back to the mother ship.

some things the hard way. But she also needs to know she can tug on that lifeline, communicate with you—the person she trusts most—and say, "Hey, it's too scary out here. I want to come back in." And if you see imminent danger your child doesn't see because of her lack of experience, you too can alert her and use that lifeline to reel her back in.

That, parents, is your role for these "in-betweeners." If you have raised them to know right from wrong, you've given them a good foundation. Now you need to let them float out there. But you also need to be that lifeline they can count on.

Be an Active Parent

A good parent—note I didn't say a *perfect parent*, since none of us is perfect—is an active parent. A parent who knows what direction their kid is going in, and when they need to tug that lifeline back to the mother ship. That means staying in touch with your child's heart, which, at this tweener age, includes a lot of listening for nuances in your child's speech and having regular times around the family dinner table. An active, smart parent also knows that this is the age when girls still have dolls, yet some want to dress like they are 21 and, when pressured by peers, will do things you could never imagine. It's an age where many boys are exposed to pornography just by the click of a smartphone. It's an age where many kids are not only thinking and talking about sex but engaging in sexual behavior.

So let me ask you, parent. Do you know who your kids are hanging out with? Why they linger at school on Tuesdays and Thursdays? If you wonder, and your child isn't talking to you, go out of your way to make sure you attend your child's after-school activities and games. Show up at his football practice or track practice. Don't embarrass your kid by waving or calling his name. Simply sit there and let your presence do the talking. Believe me, your kid will spot you. As you watch the events, take in the teacher's or coach's philosophy, the interactions between the kids, how your child is treated, and how he interacts with others. Those are all clues as to whether life is going well and your child is making good choices, or whether you need to go the second mile in figuring out what's going on.

Be Your Child's Advocate

Do you know who your child's favorite teachers or coaches are, and why? Or who their least favorite are, and why? Make certain that during parent-teacher conferences, you sign up for a time with that particular teacher or coach you're wondering about. If you want to see how your child responds to that adult, bring him or her along. Many schools welcome a child's participation, and even if they don't, you're the parent here, right? And it's within your rights to bring your child with you, since it's his or her education you're talking about.

If your child is edgy about going with you, that's a flashing alert. If your child is all smiles, that's probably a good indication that the relationship is a positive, healthy one.

There are times, parent, when you need to step in. There are other times when you need to butt out. The key is discerning when to do which, then acting on that parental gut.

But never forget one very important thing: *you* are the best teacher for your child. No one else should or ever will replace you. What you do during these years—the way you treat your child and respond to your child, the values you teach and model in the home—will indeed shape your son's or daughter's life.

✓ What Worked for Us

When Mandy was in sixth grade, she raved about her science teacher, Mr. Dyck. She loved his class so much that she decided she wanted to be a research scientist when she grew up. But she wouldn't talk to me about her French class. At parent-teacher conferences, I met with both teachers, but this time I brought Mandy with me.

Five minutes into our time with Mr. Dyck, I knew why Mandy loved him and his class. He was passionate about the subject and treated her with respect, asking her opinion and encouraging her questions. He even shook her hand and thanked her for coming.

A different story with Ms. Fontane, the French teacher. The instant Mandy walked into the room, she ducked her head, and her body stiffened. Mrs. Fontane eyed her, then told me, "This is a *parent*-teacher conference. Your daughter can wait outside." She didn't even acknowledge Mandy by name.

All I said was, "Now I understand." I put my arm around my daughter, and we were outta there. Mandy cried all the way home. I went back to school, met with the principal, and insisted that my daughter be taken out of French class.

I'll never forget the look on Mandy's face when I told her she would no longer have Ms. Fontane as a teacher. It was a look of total relief. Trust. Gratefulness. In that moment I understood how important it is for a father to be his child's protector.

Joe, Virginia

Have you given your child opportunities early in life to make age-appropriate choices and discover the results of those choices? Have you held him accountable for what he says? What he does? Have you let reality do the teaching rather than trying to fix the situation or haranguing him?

Here's an example. When your child left his homework at home, did you rush to school with it to rescue him before the teacher found out it is missing? Or did you allow him to experience the teacher's stern response: "All homework is due by the start of the class period. You may turn it in tomorrow, but you will lose a letter grade." That would be letting reality do the teaching rather than you harping on him or rushing to school to smooth his pathway in life.

Every day, your child faces very powerful influences—peers, teachers, coaches, and the tantalizing lure of technology and the media (see chapter 6). But of all the forces tugging at your child, there's one that is greater—you. It's how you play your cards during these years that will make all the difference.

How do you communicate with your child? Do you show him respect in the way you dialogue with him? What is your demeanor when you send her off to school and when you see her after school? Do you listen to his processing as he solves problems for himself—or do you announce the answer to the problem? When her shortcomings are clearly visible, do you hound her about them or give her a free hall pass, knowing she's already learned her lesson the hard way?

> There are times, parent, when you need to step in. There are other times when you need to butt out. The key is discerning when to do which, then acting on that parental gut.

Use Food—the Miracle Drug—to Your Advantage

If you pick up your preteen after school, have food in the car. It can do wonders.

Angie's son had been surly for weeks. When I suggested she let food do the talking instead of asking him questions, she did just that. She thawed a few chocolate-chip cookies from her freezer so they smelled fresh-baked and handed them to him as soon as he got in the car. When he caught the whiff of chocolate, his spontaneous smile was worth the few extra minutes of work.

The next day after school, she brought him tacos. He'd inhaled them by the time they got home. That night her son said, "Uh, Mom, the guys were wondering . . . could you bring them some food after school too?"

This was the moment she'd worked for, but the smart mom kept it low-key. "Sure, no problem. The food would taste even better, though, if it was hot out of the oven. If you want to invite a few of your friends over after school, I'll have everything ready. I can drive them all home when you're done eating."

Angie got an earful of conversation from her son and his friends that clued her in to his world. Even more, the parade frequently made its way into her SUV and then her kitchen. She got to hear firsthand about her son's world, the struggles the boys faced, what

---

What Keeps You Up at Night? Round 1

Here's what parents of middle-schoolers say they worry about:

- That my child won't fit in.
- That he will get bullied.
- That she won't find a good group of friends . . . or even one.
- That he does whatever his friends do. It's like he doesn't have his own brain.
- That all she cares about is clothes, her friends, and texting. What happened to the compassionate girl who rescued the neighbor cat from bullies?
- That he's withdrawing from everyone, even us.
- That my ex and his live-in girlfriend won't be a good influence on my kids.
- That he's smaller than the other boys and they're picking on him.
- That she developed too early and boys are paying too much attention.

girls they liked, etc. And she gained points with her son when one of his friends said, "Your mom's cool."

Use whatever motivates your child. For a tweener, food often does the trick. Be shameless about using it to your advantage.

How to Ease the Transition for Your Middle-Schooler

Let's face it. Planet Middle School is a scary place. But there are three things you can do up front to ease the transition.

Do a Walk-Through

Many middle schools give incoming students an opportunity to visit the school, meet the teachers, and find their classroom and lockers a day or two before school starts. If your school provides such a time, fabulous! Make sure your kid gets there. If not, call the school and ask if you can bring your child to do a walk-through yourself. Even better, invite a group of kids who will attend the school to do it with you. Then have a pre-school party—provide food and scatter some games. Be present, but don't hover. It's better for the kids to face and break through some social awkwardness before school starts than to face all the changes the first day. There's nothing like making your way down a crowded school hallway of strangers and being greeted with a friendly smile.

Give Practical Tools for Dealing with Bullies

Bullies abound in every school. But your child needs to know the secret behind why bullies do what they do: they feel so insecure that they have to pick on someone in order to look bigger and scarier to others. They also come in packs, since they're not secure enough to do things on their own.

Rosa and her family moved into a new town only a few days before school started. Her father had heard from some of his work colleagues that the middle school could be a little tough. So he prepared Rosa for some bully tactics.

Good thing, because on the first day she was surrounded by a posse of girls who clearly were in charge. It didn't take Rosa long to identify the leader, who immediately started in on her. Rosa didn't flinch. She just listened, then said calmly, "Wow, you really don't feel very good about yourself, do you, if you need to pick on somebody like me, the new kid, the very first day of school."

The other girls' jaws dropped. The leader shifted nervously.

"So," Rosa said, "I'll see you later. Nice to meet all of you." And off she went down the hallway.

Now that's a girl with guts, even though she stands only four foot nine. Funny thing, the posse backed off, because she'd called the head bully's bluff. That leader didn't want to go head-to-head with Rosa again and risk losing her pecking order with her posse. The best thing is, Rosa did it all respectfully and, as a result, gained the posse's respect. All because of a dad who cared enough to address the issue up front and to give her the tools to deal with it, should it happen to her.

All parents need to prepare their middle-schoolers for bullies. Unfortunately, today's bullies can also carry knives and guns. If you live in one of those areas and can move to another locale, even if it means living with a grandparent or other relative, do so. Your middle-schoolers have enough to deal with in other areas; fearing for their lives can take their stress level and ability to adapt to their environment over the top for them.

If you must stay in that school, keep your eyes and ears open for the events your child isn't telling you about. If he suddenly comes home with bruises but says, "Oh, I just fell," chances are he isn't telling the truth.

When that happened to Robert, his father didn't grill his son. He just started leaving work an hour early to pick up Robert instead of having him ride the bus. When he saw a group of boys surround his son, Anthony got out of the car and walked toward them. He didn't announce that he was Robert's dad or call out to his son; he simply strode toward the boys with purpose. The bullies scattered.

The next day the bullies tried the same thing, and again Anthony simply walked toward them.

The third day, the bully circle didn't show up. They'd given up and found somebody else to pick on.

> Keep your eyes and ears open for the events your child isn't telling you about.

If your child is struggling with bullies and is too afraid or embarrassed to admit to you what's going on, take action. Don't wait. Your child's safety—both physical and emotional—is at risk.

Help Your Child Get Organized

Some children are naturally organized, and others are not. It's easy to tell which is which. Your organized child lined up LEGOs and shoes in a perfect row at an early age. Organization is easy for that child, but he isn't high on surprises. In fact, throwing him a curveball can catapult him into panic mode. He's the kid who has checked out the school hallway map, listed his classes from one to seven on that map in neat red circles, and has them memorized.

Other kids are whimsical and impulsive. For lack of a better term, I lovingly call them *messies*. In fact, I've got one of them in my family. These are the kids who walk across the school ground with their backpack unzipped and books falling out. If they make it to their first class on time, it's a miracle.

In middle school, getting organized is a key to your child's success. Even a normally organized child may be overwhelmed by the huge stack of books and notes protruding from her backpack the

How to Organize for School

Use a different color notebook and folder for each subject. Or get a single notebook that has color dividers that match the folders for each subject. Make a schedule and laminate copies of it.

- On the schedule, write out the days of the week, then list the classes in order underneath each day.
- After the name of the class, add the teacher's name, time of class, and location.
- Add after-school activities, with the teacher's name, time, and location.

If your child is naturally organized, encourage her to put the schedule in a pocket of her backpack where she always looks (some kids input their class schedule into their cell phones, if those are allowed at school). If your child isn't naturally organized, place a copy of the schedule on the front of each subject's notebook.

Work *with* your child to help her organize. Don't organize *for* your child. As your child gains confidence, she will be able to organize more each year.

first day of school. As she moves forward in school, she'll figure out new ways to organize herself that you probably haven't thought of. But you, parent, may need to step in during the first week of each year of middle school with some practical suggestions. It's important not only for your child to be organized at school but for you as a family to be organized at home.

My wife, Sande, is a master organizer. When our five kids were growing up, we had a big paper calendar that not only included all of their school activities but also integrated other family activities such as vacations, birthdays, and other special events. Each of our children was responsible to check it every week and implement into their own schedules anything on the family calendar that would affect them.

But I want you to notice something. Almighty Mom and Dad didn't do all the work. Each family member added their own activities, and when changes were made in the activity schedule, each child was responsible to update the master calendar. Everybody in the family worked together.

Right now, some of you are shaking your head. "If I left it up to my kid, Dr. Leman, I wouldn't have a clue of what event he had and when. We'd never get anywhere on time."

Whose problem is that, really? Yours or your kid's? If your child doesn't show up for basketball practice, I highly doubt the coach

How to Organize at Home

Invest in a file cabinet (one drawer for each child, if possible). It doesn't need to be expensive. Any garage sale cabinet or even plastic bins will do. Label hanging folders in that child's drawer with each subject.

Any paperwork for that subject (homework, projects to do) goes in the corresponding folder. Even paperwork for down-the-road projects can be stashed there. No more digging through piles and "Oh no, where did that go!"

Start a master family calendar—whether a large wall calendar or an electronic version. For example, create a calendar on Google Drive, invite everyone in the family to share it, and give them the ability to make changes on it. Every family member chooses one particular color font and enters his or her own events, including time and place.

Let's say your son gets a schedule for his basketball games. He then needs to enter all the dates and times for practice and his games on the master calendar. Your daughter gets schedules for her band concerts and community service events. She enters those dates and times on the master calendar. You check for schedule conflicts and overlapping events. Have a family meeting to discuss options, clarify who will attend or not attend what, and discuss who will talk to the person in charge of the event about the conflict.

These simple steps will go a long way toward a less stressful year.

is going to say, "Oh, that's okay, kid. Just try to remember next time." No, he's going to read your kid the riot act. It won't likely be something your child will easily forget.

The smart mom or dad will say, "Well, we won't be able to make that practice. You'll have to explain why to your teacher." You let the ball of responsibility fall right where it belongs—in your child's court. You don't bounce the ball back and forth or run with it to try to score the point.

> Do you want a kid who is responsible? . . . "You start with the end in mind."

Do you want a kid who is responsible? Then, as my friend, the brilliant business entrepreneur Stephen R. Covey, used to say, "You start with the end in mind." Yes, you can teach a kid through modeling responsibility, but you also have to give him the opportunity to be responsible.

Launching Your Little Bird

Think of your middle-schooler as a young bird with a little soft fuzz on his wings. He doesn't have the full set of feathers to fly at his peak, but he's in process. In the meanwhile, he's curious enough about the outside world to inch closer and closer to the edge of the nest. When he peers over the edge, the wide world looks a bit scary. So he'll take a step back. But curiosity will draw him to the edge again. This forward-back, forward-back motion is natural in the growing-up process.

The wise mama and papa do all they can to prepare their fledgling for flight. When he at last steps a tentative foot over the edge of the nest, you can bet Mama and Papa are right there by his side, encouraging him on the journey. Should a predator even dare to approach nearby, Mama and Papa will go after it with a vengeance.

If the fledgling's wings tire and he starts to fall, Mama and Papa are right there to shore him up and steer him back to the nest.

That, parent, is exactly what your tweener wants from you. Even if she would never, ever say it until years down the road, when she has her own nest.

3

All Flared Up!

Why solar-flare emotions are an everyday drama, and what
you can do to weather the sudden flashes of brightness.

Your daughter has been a breeze to rear—helpful and wonderful,
even assisting you with her younger siblings without complaint.
But now that she's a seventh-grader, that light and airy breeze of
her personality can morph to a hurricane wind sweeping through
your living room when you ask even one question. And she's got
a good dose of drama queen to boot.

An hour later, she's hunting for a snack and plops herself happily on one of the kitchen stools as you're preparing dinner. "Hey,
Mom, these cookies are really good," she says as she munches.
Before she leaves, she even cleans up her crumbs without you asking, puts away the package of cookies in the pantry, and gives you
a hug before walking away singing her latest favorite song.

You're stupefied. All you'd asked her earlier was, "Honey, would
you take your lunch bag out of your backpack and put it on the

kitchen counter before you go upstairs?" That simple request got the hurricane reaction, but now she's helpful all on her own?

Then there's your normally cocker spaniel–personality son, who entered the kitchen that morning, took out a mixing bowl, and rummaged around in your cupboard for cereal. "Seriously?" he exploded. "No Cocoa Puffs?" He peered into the fridge. "And no milk?" The mutterings that followed were indecipherable because you chose to close your ears.

You just bought three boxes of Cocoa Puffs on Tuesday, and this is Thursday. He ate three boxes in two days? The kid who picked at his food and shoved it around his plate his entire childhood? Now he's eating half a box of cereal in a mixing bowl that would make Duncan Hines proud. And the milk? Somebody must have broken into your home and stolen the two gallons you bought Tuesday.

Well, the milk and Cocoa Puffs thief was standing right in front of you, glowering. Worse, he got up late and nearly missed the bus trying to hunt for a different breakfast.

> The mood changes are meteorite-swift. Anything they do or say is jettisoned to a new level. Most of the triggers have nothing to do with you.

As soon as he went out the door, you heaved a sigh of relief and sank into a chair. Then you started to strategize. *I'll go to Costco and get those jumbo boxes and stash about 20 of them in the basement. And maybe we ought to invest in an extra fridge downstairs. . . .* You scowl. *But I still don't appreciate the attitude.*

Have you just entered the Twilight Zone? No, your children are in middle school, and the mood changes are meteorite-swift. Anything they do or say is jettisoned to a new level. Most of the triggers have nothing to do with you. Children who are normally even-keeled can exhibit behaviors that look like wavy seismographic lines and are spread all over the map. But even though it may not seem like it, there are reasons for what they do. And once you understand the reasons, those children who may drive you crazy can become easier not only to love but to tolerate, even at their worst moments.

Why You Should Never, Ever Ask Questions

You and your daughter have just had a fabulous day at the mall. You had such fun trying on makeup and soaking in the personal attention and your new looks. You stopped midday and had lunch at her favorite restaurant. You didn't spend much money, but you had a great time. As you exit the mall, you can't imagine a better day than this one with your preteen. *She's growing up*, you think, with both excitement and sadness.

As you're driving home and making conversation, you ask casually, "Hey, this kid you've talked about a few times . . . Robbie. Who's Robbie?"

Your daughter's response isn't even close to the dialogue you imagined. The heat from her volcanic eruption is melting everything in the car.

You drive on in shock. The only thing you can think is, *What just happened?* And then, *Whose house can I drop her off at on the way home?*

Half an hour ago, she was all smiles and enjoying the day with you. Now she's silent and glowering, angled away from you, arms crossed, staring out the car window. To top it off, she never answered your question about Robbie.

You don't find out until days later, from her nosy younger sister who still tells you everything, that Robbie is the first young man to ever pay attention to your daughter. He's two years older, and she's in puppy love. The last thing she wants is for Mama to go sticking her nose into that relationship. Simply stated, she's not telling Mama nothin'.

I'll never forget the day I peered out my living room window and saw one of my daughters kissing some guy I didn't know. I'd never met him. Didn't even know his name. Talk about a shocker. In the drive toward independence, your middle-schooler wants to keep some things to herself. That's why she doesn't like questions. If she wants you to know about something, she'll tell you. If she doesn't want you to know, she'll keep her mouth shut.

You see, she doesn't always want to share with Mom and Dad. That's part of her drive toward independence. But if that boy dumps her or slacks off in his interest and pursues someone else, then she's a puddle of mess who needs her mama. Funny how some things work, isn't it? Growing up one minute and a little girl the next. That's the "in the middle" of middle school.

When the Volcano Blows

So, she doesn't want me to know everything about her life anymore, you reason. *I get that. But she could tell me that nicely. She doesn't have to blow up all over me.*

Yes, that's good logic. But there's a problem. Your preteen is far from logical. She's spontaneously shooting from the hip, and her hormones and emotions are running her. That's even more true if your child is a budding perfectionist. The slightest deviation from how she plans for life to go can create a monstrous eruption, complete with a psychological lava flow that might last for a couple of hours or even days. Worse, it burns up everything in its path.

> The slightest deviation from how she plans for life to go can create a monstrous eruption.

But what's happening inside is like the building of a volcano. When Mount St. Helens blew on May 18, 1980, it didn't just all of a sudden blow. The pressure and heat had been building for a long time.

While your kids are at school, tension, stress, and pressure build. There's no place for those things to go, so they continue to build inside. A kid won't usually go off on other kids at school, so she saves it for her home turf. That's where she feels safe enough to let the lava go . . . and you and her siblings are the lucky recipients. She even morphs into an Italian—talking with her hands.

Middle-schoolers are undergoing tremendous physical and psychological change. On one hand they want you close so they can curl up next to you and put their head on your lap. They want you

✓ What Worked for Us

My stepson, Ricky, and I go head-to-head a lot. It's worse now that he's an eighth-grader. It seems like every time he sees me, he has to challenge me or make a snarky remark. I get really sick of it. After seeing us battle it out verbally one day, a friend told me about your principle "Don't sail into your child's wind." Not only was I sailing into it, I was letting it suck me in with gale force!

The next time he picked a fight, I said calmly, "If that's what you think is true, I guess it's true for you."

He looked confused for a second, then tried again to suck me into the fight.

I switched the subject. "I was thinking of taking the rowboat out on the lake this weekend. You're welcome to join me." And I walked away.

You could have heard a pin drop. When I peeked back after I went around the corner, Ricky was still standing there, resembling a lost puppy that didn't know which way to go.

We had to go through that same cycle two more times. It was like he was testing me. Finally, he got it. This stepdad wasn't going to fight anymore.

Ricky still gets angry easily, but when he does, he now goes into his room and deals with it before he takes it out on me, his mom, or his sisters.

David, Illinois

to scratch their back and stroke their hair like you used to. But another part of them is screaming, "Get away!"

The "I love you"/"I hate you" extremes can be wearying. But your kids wouldn't be blowing up at you unless they knew it was safe to do so—that you won't turn away from them when others might.

Preteens tend to slip into negative mode when battling hormones, changing circumstances, and problems in friendships. Most have not yet learned how to process through the problem to a solution without engaging their emotions.

The Worst Thing of All—Your Criticism

Middle school is such an awkward time. Boys are especially clumsy and accident prone. Many of them resemble growing puppies, where the size of their feet and the rest of their body parts don't quite match up. *Uncoordinated* is their middle name. The girls? They don't take kindly to comments about their body development. Believe me, they are acutely aware their breasts are growing; you don't have to point it out. Making mention of any weight gain or their broadening hips will send you to the doghouse for a long time.

> They care what you, of all people, think of them. *Do my mom and dad accept me? Love me? Think I'm worthy? Valuable? Interesting? Talented?*

Middle-schoolers are super sensitive and susceptible to any criticism, especially yours. If you make fun of them or laugh about anything they say, they won't come out of their bedroom for a long time. You know why that is? Because they care what you, of all people, think of them. *Do my mom and dad accept me? Love me? Think I'm worthy? Valuable? Interesting? Talented?*

When Being "Different" Isn't a Perk

Life is tough on middle-schoolers who are seen as different or think they're different. Jane, a sixth-grader, is called "strange" because she wears skirts and more old-fashioned clothing. The seventh-grade boys don't want to hang out with Sam because his brother is "weird" (their word). Sam's brother, Joey, has Down syndrome. He's affectionate and loves to hug people. That makes the other boys, who are trying to figure out what being masculine means, uncomfortable. Anastasia is adopted—you can't miss it because she's a different race than the rest of her family—so the girls gossip that her "real parents" didn't want her and "gave her away." Jarrod walks with a slight limp. Danny struggles with his complexion.

In the dog-eat-dog world of middle school, anyone who is different is easy to pick on. That's why these kids especially need you to be the steady one in their lives. They need to experience unconditional love—the kind of love that doesn't change, that doesn't judge them.

Avoiding the Hot Spots

Hot spots are planetary flare-ups. Flare-ups in a middle-schooler's life, when everything is a crisis, happen particularly before school, when they can't find that hairbrush or a particular shirt they have to wear that day. Flare-ups also happen after school, when a child is processing all the hot spots during her day and needs to be alone to sort them out. But she'll flare up at anybody she meets along the way until she gets to that quiet place. Why? Well, you've only seen the hot spots before and after school. She's experienced them all day long—the embarrassments and twists of events that inevitably occur. She's spent all her emotional energy controlling her feelings among her peers, where gossip about her can turn vicious.

✓ What Worked for Us

I've reared seven children who miraculously made it to adulthood with all their body parts intact. But the single best piece of advice I got about middle-schoolers was, "Always have food available, and plenty of it." With their bodies changing so fast, middle-schoolers are hungry all the time. Just think how you feel when you're hungry. Do you cope well with anything someone tries to tell you? So stock up your fridge and cupboard with lots of grab-and-go, healthy snacks. When you make dinner, think double, even triple. Leftovers won't be left over for long.

A veteran mom, Minnesota

The wise parent learns when to say something and when not to. Some kids won't talk in the morning at all. Others talk your ear off in the morning . . . until they hit pubescence. Then all of a sudden they clam up, and nothing is going to force their traps open.

There's a fine art to parenting a middle-schooler. You have to learn how to play 'em. Otherwise you'll get slam-dunked with whatever their mood of the moment is, and you'll wonder if you're having any positive impact on their life at all.

When You Encounter Solar Storms

The strongest observed winds in the universe are on the planet Venus, which, curiously, rotates the opposite direction of all the other planets.[1] Sound a bit like the middle-schoolers in your home on some days? They rotate a different direction than the rest of your family? And their opinions, likes, and dislikes affect your family life like hurricane winds sweeping over a planet?

At times their winds will be howling and fierce; other days their breezes will feel good and their happy moods will energize other family members. Then there are times when both happen in the same day. A middle-schooler's world is so tenuous that a good morning, free of storms, doesn't predict a good afternoon. Some solar storms will come your way where you'll feel like running for cover. You don't know how many more of the meteorites you can dodge. You're pummeled from above, from below, and from all around. But keep in mind that what you see on the outside is calm compared to what's going on inside your middle-schooler. The biochemical changes occurring in their bodies and the resulting gamut of emotions are downright painful.

In this tweener time, you may have to send up a weather balloon to test what the atmosphere is like before you engage your child in conversation. That means you check out their facial expression, body language, and whether their bedroom door is open or closed. Those are all good hints of their current demeanor.

So how can you best help your middle-schooler?

Be Predictable

Do what you say you'll do when you say you'll do it. Kids gain security through routine.

This is important to all children, but especially to children of divorced parents. These kids often travel back and forth between their parents' homes like Ping-Pong balls being whacked at high speeds across both sides of the table. Whether they switch every week, on the weekends, every couple weeks, during holidays, or in the summer, the point is that they have to pack up, leave their friends and what they know behind, and go to another home. They deserve and need all the empathy and support you can give them.

> Kids gain security through routine.

Help Them Explore and Discover What They're Good At

It's critical during these years that your child sees himself as good at something. He doesn't need to do everything—and in fact, he shouldn't. If your kid is involved in city soccer, baseball, band, and the swim team, that's too much activity for any middle-schooler to handle. A preteen needs downtime to dream, to think, to process, and to observe. But he also needs to know that he belongs somewhere—that he does have a gifted area. It might be playing piano or basketball, running cross-country, or volunteering at a shelter for abused animals. Help your middle-schooler find something he can enjoy and excel at, and where he can make a unique contribution. Following that dream and spending time with like-minded people will get him through more than a few of middle school's tsunami waves.

Focus on Your Relationship

Her words, her emotions, her blue-streaked hair will change. All those things are temporary. What will remain, when the dust of middle school settles, is the core of who that child is and who she is becoming as she heads into young adulthood. So dig into what's really important in life. Who do you want your child to be when she leaves home? What kind of relationship do you want with her?

> Be real. Be authentic. Be who you want your child to be when she leaves home.

The best thing you can do is be real. Be authentic. Be who you want your child to be when she leaves home. As my friend Josh McDowell says, "Rules without relationship lead to rebellion." Your children can spot a fake from 50 yards away.

Listen to Their Hearts

Be a listening ear. No matter how trivial or large a subject is, listening without judgment is critical to your middle-schooler's

---

10 Rules for Surviving Tweenerdom

1. Do what you say you'll do.
2. Accept them for where they are right now.
3. Don't pick at their flaws. They're too busy doing that themselves.
4. Make only one point at a time.
5. Respect their privacy.
6. Act your age. That means you apologize first when you blow it.
7. Give them choices and then respect their decisions, even if you wouldn't make the same ones.
8. Don't embarrass them by showing them off or making them perform like monkeys.
9. Talk about a potential problem before it becomes a real one.
10. Don't make icebergs out of icicles, or you'll turn your home into a frost zone.

---

development. When all is said and done, what qualities do you want your child to walk away from your home with? Loyalty? Honesty? Empathy? Kindness? If you listen to their heart, model the values that are important to you, and keep their actions in perspective (even the ones you think are stupid), with God's help you'll get where you want to be. No, not instantly, but you'll see progress that will keep you and your child moving along in the direction you want to go.

Taking the Long View

Caught in that pull between little kid and wanting to be independent, middle-schoolers can sometimes become snarly and distant. That's because they're beginning to break away from you, and that's a natural part of the growing-up process. If you know your middle-schooler's demeanor can change almost instantly, you can be prepared. And if you realize an outburst isn't personally directed at you, even if it seems that way on the surface, you can more easily deal with it. You can keep your cool.

You might even have a little fun with it. When my son, Kevin, wanted to get his ear pierced, I decided to give him a little taste of what that might look like. So, with my beloved bride's help, I showed up at dinner one night with one of her clip earrings adhered to my earlobe.

At first Kevin was too busy snarfing down his dinner to catch my new accessory. Then he looked up, caught a glimpse of it, and frowned. "Dad, you look absolutely ridiculous."

"Oh, really?" I fluffed up my hair. "Your mother likes it."

At that moment Kevin decided an earring was not for him. The best part? There was no arguing, no yelling, no "But Dad . . ." Problem resolved.

In all honesty, though, if Kevin had still wanted to hang a fishing lure from his ear, we wouldn't have stopped him. After all, they're his ears, and if he's determined to hang something from them, he's welcome to.

If you handle situations with a twist of long-range perspective and even a sense of humor, you'll be amazed at how the powerful solar flares diminish. Sure, they may still blind you sometimes. But in between, the spontaneity of middle-schoolers is actually fun to watch. I wish I had their energy!

Someday you'll look back at this time and have lots of funny stories to tell your grandchildren when their own time comes for middle school.

Like I'm doing with my grandson, Conner, right now.

4

Survival of the Fittest

Why your child will do almost *anything* to fit in, and what you can do to combat the intensity of peer pressure.

Twelve-year-old Janae was shocked to find out another girl was passing a rumor about her around their middle school. She called Janae a slut—just because Janae had talked to the other girl's boyfriend in the cafeteria.

Sam was an innocent 11-year-old when he entered a public middle school. "Hey, I've got something cool to show you," a new friend told Sam. The friend pulled out his smartphone and flashed the most shocking image Sam had ever seen. He didn't even understand what he was seeing, except that it had to do with a naked woman and a naked man. But he wanted so badly to be included in a group that he played along like it was cool, even though warning bells were going off in his head, telling him, *This is very wrong. . . . What is this stuff anyway? If I say I don't want to look at it, will these guys think I'm a wuss?*

You know all those television reality shows where people from different backgrounds are plunged into impossible situations together yet have to survive, and one has to come out the winner? Well, the best way to describe middle school is this: Welcome to the jungle. You better grab a vine. If you can't swing to safety once in a while, you're going to get eaten alive.

In middle school, winning is all about fitting in with the peer group. This is the time when children are forming relationships outside the family and, in essence, creating their own world. That's why friendships become more and more valuable to them. Being part of the group is a driving force and can push kids to do really dumb things. That's why, parent, your kid will do anything to fit in, to be one of the important people at school. He's playing the jungle game to win, because losers don't survive.

"Survival of the Fittest" Is Alive and Well

Charles Darwin, an evolutionist, first used Herbert Spencer's phrase "the survival of the fittest" in 1869, intending it to mean "better designed for an immediate, local environment."[1] That concept still rules middle school. Either children adapt to their own immediate, local environment, or they die a social death.

Who does your kid want to be in middle school? Anyone but herself. No matter what group she's in, or if she's a loner, she's just praying it's not her day to get picked on.

James moved to a small town just in time to start junior high. The first thing he noticed was how big all the other boys were and how much older they looked. He wondered if he was in the wrong school. Then, as he was searching for his locker, he saw something shocking. Two older boys slammed a younger boy's head into a locker, then walked away, laughing, as the smaller kid sprawled on the floor.

Do you know what James's first thought was? It wasn't, *Wow, that poor kid just got smashed by two big brutes.* It was, *Wow, I hope that never happens to me.* And he filed away the pictures of those two older boys in his brain, determining never to cross their path.

See how the survival of the fittest concept works? It turns your child into "the world is all about me and what I need to do to survive." There is no room for his heart to be fine-tuned with empathy.

> Who does your kid want to be in middle school? Anyone but herself.

If you're all about yourself, you're going to do whatever it takes to survive. If something—anything—is presented as cool by someone in the popular crowd, kids are going to follow it . . . unless they have a very good reason not to. Peer pressure rules. Kids fall in and out of "like" and "love" faster than I change my underwear. And due to the rapid expansion of their world through new adult and peer influences and technology, the stakes are raised.

It's Not Your Middle School

Some of you vividly remember your middle-school years, because they were a painful time of not belonging. Others of you were in the popular crowd and either stayed top dog or got knocked off your pedestal. You might remember the physical awkwardness of tripping over your own feet or your mortal embarrassment when you discovered you'd been walking around with toilet paper stuck to your shoe. You might have been introduced to weed, alcohol, or other drugs.

But the worst things that happened to you in middle school probably don't come close to what your child faces every day. Things have progressed, and it isn't for the better.

Take Brianna, for instance. She lives in a wealthy suburb that has beautiful parks, gourmet restaurants, and unique boutiques. If you're not wearing the absolute latest fashion and you didn't buy it from a specific selection of high-class stores, you're shunned. The birthday parties the girls have resemble Hollywood-style, glitzy wine-and-dine events, with both boys and girls attending. Want to try cocaine? All it takes is one trip down a side hallway for a snort—free of charge, of course, as part of the party.

Two days later, those same middle-schoolers and their parents are sitting in the pews of the local church.

> The worst things that happened to you in middle school probably don't come close to what your child faces every day.

Then there's Stephen, who lives in a rough urban neighborhood. He fights his way to school and fights his way home. He's always intense, scanning for potential danger. "In my world, kids get knifed. People get shot. At least once a week I see an ambulance come to one of my neighbors." Even now, when every person who walks into the school has to go through a scanner, he says it's still not safe. All it takes is a small bribe to get a weapon in, and someone is going down.

Your child, like Brianna, is plunged into a world where opportunities of all kinds—legal and illegal, moral and immoral, good and bad—will be spread right out in front of her. Without you by her side, what will your child decide to do?

Your child may not fear being physically accosted, as Stephen does. But every day he lives in fear of being socially ostracized and put down.

The Odd Boy/Girl Out

Every time your middle-schooler heads to school, she is thinking, *I hope today's not my day to be gossiped about or taken down.* Is it any wonder she might be a bit surly to you when she walks out

> Anything that is different about a kid is fair game to peers.

the door for the bus or your car? After all, she's steeling herself for battle and hoping she won't be the one caught in the line of fire today.

Preadolescents are fickle. They're vicious. Anything that is different about a kid is fair game to peers. It might be a child's ethnicity, hair color, height, weight, other physical features, clothing, or anything else.

Name-Calling

"Look at Four Eyes! Check out the new shades."

"Is it lunchtime already, Pizza Face? Look, everybody, we can eat off Justin's face."

"Isn't it time for you to go home to your tepee, Indian girl?"

The old adage "Sticks and stones can break my bones, but words can never hurt me" doesn't stand up in middle school. Words hurt, and they hurt a lot. In fact, they go straight to a kid's heart and lodge there, making the child feel unloved and unworthy of love.

Jon, who is now 28, says he still remembers the name he was called in junior high: Pus Face. "It didn't matter that my parents were taking me to a dermatologist to help clear up my face. What mattered was the moment. To them, I was ugly, and that made me think I *was* ugly. My skin is clear now, with no evidence of all the zits I struggled with. But when I look in the mirror, I sometimes still hear that ugly name, and it still impacts my confidence in relationships and my view of myself."

Name-calling can have a lifelong impact. Jon says he never told his parents about it because he was too embarrassed.

Shunning

"You're not going to sit here. This table is for cool people only, and girl, you're not it."

"Why don't you go back to where you came from? You're not welcome here."

"We all voted, and you're out."

Middle school is filled with cliques. Even if you're part of one, you still aren't safe. You have to fight for your role within the clique or you'll soon find yourself on the outside of it. Because you have to keep the current leader happy for as long as possible, even "nice" kids can turn mean. Anything different about you—your clothes, the color of your lipstick, the zit on your nose, you name it—paints a target on your back.

Eleven-year-old Suzie was a talkative, vivacious child who always made others smile and laugh. She was spontaneous in her actions, often not thinking through them. The summer before she entered middle school, she decided to get her nose pierced at the mall. Her mother, who was with her, just shrugged, figuring, *So what? If she doesn't like it, the hole will close and life will go on.* Suzie insisted she was ready for a new look for her new school.

The first day, Suzie showed up with her nose ring, black T-shirt, and ripped jeans, only to realize that wasn't the look the cool kids at the school were going for. In fact, hardly anyone talked to her the first day. They just eyed her like she was weird. That night, when she came home, she said, "Uh, Mom, do you think we could go get a clear nose ring?"

Middle-schoolers don't want to be caught with anyone who is "weird" because that makes them weird. Then they will be shunned themselves.

The Put-Down

"Guess you never met a food group you didn't like, huh? Ever heard of Weight Watchers?" (Snickering.) "Yeah, well, I guess you are watching your weight . . . grow." (Full-fledged laugh.)

"Check her out. Her clothes are so, like, 2010."

"Could you fumble the ball any worse? I mean, seriously . . ."

"Did you see her hair? Oh my gosh, looks like her mother cut it."

At their core, most preadolescents are insecure. If they put people down, that makes them feel better, more secure about themselves . . . in theory, at least. Do they know they're doing that? No, they wouldn't think that reasoning through. But it doesn't mean it's not true.

The Secret behind Bullies

When I was a kid, bullies abounded. One in particular seemed to have a bead on me. One day he threatened to rearrange my face and did a pretty good job. Later that day, I gathered my courage. I decided I was going to tell the kid's father and mother what had happened. So, on my own, I walked to the kid's house.

You know what? Those parents couldn't have cared less.

As I walked home, I remember thinking, *No wonder that kid is a bully. If his parents don't care about their kid beating someone up, they probably don't care about anything—or him either. Guess that's why he has to beat other kids up.*

I still didn't like that kid, but I no longer feared him. And I guess beating the tar out of me once was enough for him. He didn't touch me again. It might have had something to do with the black eyes and black-and-blue face that my schoolmates commented on the next day, which gained me the reputation of an "okay" or "cool" kid.

> I still didn't like that kid, but I no longer feared him.

There will always be bullies in the world, and they blossom in the middle-school years. "Boys are mean, and girls are meaner," a middle-school teacher told me. Today they bully not only through fists, knives, and guns but through Instagram, Facebook, handwritten notes, and texts.

But think about bullies for a minute. Do you ever see them standing by themselves? No, they've got a posse for support. And where is the leader standing? Right in the middle of them. Not on the edge, where somebody could take a shot at him. That's because bullies are not secure enough to act on their own. They need the energy and bulk of a group to make themselves bigger and their position more powerful than they actually are. Bullies are like a pack of wolves descending on a single individual.

It's always "fun" to be on the giving end of bullying in a peer group. But the receiving end is . . . not so fun. Nobody wants to be the centerpiece of Instagrams, texts, or innuendos that get passed around middle school. But every bully's day is coming. It may not be in middle school or in high school, but someday he or she will fall from the top-dog position. Trust me, it will be a hard fall.

Leaping from Vine to Vine

A middle-school principal told me recently, "Kids will do absolutely anything to fit in. And when I say anything, I mean *anything*. They will violate every sensible value they were brought up to believe in."

That's a scary statement, isn't it?

> "Kids will do absolutely anything to fit in. And when I say anything, I mean *anything*."

True, some kids will walk the other way and stay on the path you've planned for them. They'll grab that jungle vine, choose their direction, and go for it. But those are the strong kids, the confident kids, who rise above the pack. They're in the single-digit percentage of middle-schoolers.

The majority of middle-schoolers are like monkeys who grab any vine swinging nearby and then leap onto it without looking just because the others in their peer group are on that same vine.

Combating the Intensity of Peer Pressure

Every middle-schooler wants to fit in. It's a lonely time for all kids, even for those who seem "popular." How can you help your child not only combat the intensity of peer pressure but settle into a place that is positive, wholesome, and good? Here are a few tips.

Bring Long-Range Perspective to Competition

Competition in middle school is a given.

For boys, that means vying to be the alpha dog—whether of the group as a whole or of a subgroup. That's why they flex their muscles, swagger down the hallway, and play any sport competitively. They also compete for the attention of the popular girls, because gaining the attention of even one will increase their status. Funny thing is, many attempt to do that with squeaky voices that still haven't changed to more masculine ones.

The girls are working hard at positioning themselves to be popular, especially with the boys. They will do anything to gain that popularity, even temporarily. If they catch the attention of a high-school boy, look out.

Tell your child, "I know middle school is competitive. Everybody's trying really hard to be noticed, to be popular. But I want you to know something. You're unique, you're special. You don't have to become someone else to be appreciated around here. I love you as you are. If you're going to compete for something, compete to be the good guy who is a friend to everybody and helps others. Then you don't have to worry about who's in the popular crowd and who's not, since those positions will change fast anyway."

Your child may give you a nod or shrug, and you might not be sure he heard, but he did. Your words will come back to him when he needs them most.

Affirm Positive, Compassionate Behavior

It seems as if so many today have lost all sense of caring about other people's feelings. Everything is "all about me" and "I really don't care about you." So when you see your child doing anything to support and encourage another person, make sure you say something.

Margaret told her daughter, "I noticed that you were talking to the girl who's on crutches and were carrying her books. Honey, that says so much about you and your character. And you know

---

✓ What Worked for Us

My daughter, Emma, has always struggled with her weight. In sixth grade, she was constantly called Fatty and picked on. The comments got so bad that we pulled her out of school the last two months and homeschooled her. We met with a nutritionist and spent the summer learning different ways to eat and cook that could help both of us lose weight. We also established an exercise program.

As we were running together, Emma met another girl who'd recently moved nearby and also liked to run. They ran together, Emma lost weight, and the two girls became friends. Emma and Elise entered seventh grade together, so she had an instant friend at school. For a while the other girls gossiped about Emma, but soon they moved on to pick on someone else.

To me, what was most important was that Emma found a friend to do things with, and that she and I grew closer during that tough time. She gave me the best compliment yesterday: "Mom, thanks for being somebody I can always trust to be by my side."

Wow.

Marian, Wisconsin

---

what? I saw that girl smiling. You made her day because you paid attention to her when perhaps no one else did all day."

That smart mom was telling her daughter a lot of things in only a few words:

- I notice when you do good things.
- Helping others is a right and wonderful thing to do.
- I like who you are and who you're becoming.
- Others notice what you do.
- You make a difference in people's lives.
- Your actions stand above the rest of the crowd.

The daughter who would do something like this—support the underdog—and who has a supportive parent like Margaret isn't one who will be easily led by the nose into doing something she doesn't want to.

Give Them Tools

Twelve-year-old Shauna came home really upset when she saw a girl get picked on at school. "Mom, it was so wrong. Everybody ganged up on Melissa, and she's a really nice girl. She didn't deserve it." Shauna hung her head. "I know I should have done something to help her, but I was too scared to step in." She looked at her mother. "But isn't that—doing nothing—almost as bad as picking on her myself?"

Shauna and her mother had a long talk about all sides of the situation.

The next day, Shauna sought out Melissa in the hallway. Melissa was slumped next to her locker, trying to be invisible. But Shauna walked right up to her and said, "You know, Melissa, what went down yesterday made me sick. You have to feel terrible, being ripped like that in front of a bunch of kids. I don't know what to say. I wish I could apologize for their behavior."

By now she'd caught Melissa's attention, and Melissa dared to glance up. She looked startled, then confused. After a minute of silence, she said, "So why are you telling me this?"

"Because," Shauna said, "I want to apologize for not stepping in to help you. It was bad enough that you were getting picked on. But nobody stepped in to defend you. Neither did I. And for that, I am very sorry."

As Melissa's eyes filled with tears, Shauna added, "I'd really like it if we could have lunch together. I'd love to sit with you and talk."

Melissa could only nod.

"Okay, then," Shauna concluded. "It's a done deal. See you then."

So the two girls had lunch together that day. "A lot of kids were staring at us," Shauna told her mother later. "But I didn't care. I found out that Melissa is exactly what I thought—a really nice girl."

Fast-forward four years. Both Shauna and Melissa are now sophomores, attending the same high school, and the best of friends. That day when Shauna dared to support Melissa launched a friendship that has only grown stronger through shared interests.

"Shauna had guts," Melissa said, "and I admired that. I was feeling lost at school even before I got picked on. Shauna's invitation to have lunch sparked a hope that I might at last be able to make a friend at that school."

They both grinned and gave each other a spontaneous hug. "And make friends we did!"

I love a good ending to a bully story, don't you?

Shauna's mom did things right. First, she listened. Then she gave her daughter the tools and the language to use to share with Melissa what was in her heart. Shauna's mom also encouraged her to do the right thing, telling her, "It's easy to be a friend when things are good and easy. What's hard is being a friend when it isn't the popular thing to do. But when you are, something happens—first, in yourself. You become stronger, more confident, able to stand on your own. All the stuff the popular crowd does suddenly isn't important. And second, you are a friend to someone who needs a friend. You have no idea how a little kindness from you can change someone's life."

That conversation between a mother and daughter sparked a change in two girls' lives. Shauna and Melissa are strong, confident young women who go out of their way to welcome and include new freshmen at their high school, and they seem to have eagle eyes for kids who are struggling and need a friend. The skills they are learning and their compassion for others make them stand out above the crowd.

> "You have no idea how a little kindness from you can change someone's life."

As for the "popular kids" who picked on Melissa? The members of that clique changed multiple times over the remainder of middle school. A lot of girls were hurt in the process and their reputations ruined, including that of the clique's leader herself. What goes around eventually does come around.

You can give your middle-schooler tools that will help her win for the long term.

Encourage Connections with Like-Minded Kids

A certain camaraderie develops with those who have similar interests, whether it's sports, art, music, or rock climbing.

Ethan had an interest in music, but he hated to practice his trumpet. "We got on his case too much," his parents admit. "We made him practice." But when he saw all the exciting things that were happening in the junior high band, he decided to check out the band for himself. He wasn't big on sports but went to football games to watch the band and was impressed. The band members seemed to enjoy hanging out together and stood up for each other.

The Top Six Secrets Middle-Schoolers Need to Know for Relational Success

1. Treat others as you'd like to be treated.
2. Do what you say you'll do.
3. Consider long-term results before you open your mouth.
4. Be a friend to everyone.
5. Stand up for yourself.
6. Never share your secrets with your peers.

So Ethan decided to audition, and the director happily agreed to let him join mid-semester.

When the very first practice concluded, the other brass players welcomed him and invited him to eat lunch with them the next day. They didn't wait for him to show up in the cafeteria either—they sought him out at his locker.

Now in his eighth-grade year, Ethan has lots of friends—almost all band members. He even put together a brass quartet that practices in his garage. For the recent middle-school dance, where there was a lot of pressure to have dates, a group of guys and girls from the band dressed up and went together. "It was a lot more fun than the pressure of a date," Ethan said.

Realize Your Support Matters Most of All

Sweep your gaze across the crowd, and your eyes would likely land first on 15-year-old Petra. She's a beautiful girl whose face and form stand out from the crowd. To top it off, she's sweet and kind to everyone.

But she also knows what it's like to be teased and ostracized by her peers. You see, Petra is a longtime model with a top modeling agency, and when she was 13, her jealous peers caught wind of who she was outside of school. The pack leader walked up to Petra and flung at her, "So you think you're really special. A star or something!"

Petra was stunned. She didn't know what to say. Only her family and close friends outside of school knew she was a model.

After that, the boys ogled her and the girls snipped at her for much of the remainder of eighth grade. If it wasn't for her strong, supportive family and her close friends outside of school, Petra would have had a tough time. Instead, she has grown into a strong, positive, confident young woman who goes out of her way to spend time with the kids in her class who are disenfranchised. What made the most difference?

"My parents always listened," Petra says. "My mom hugged me—a lot—and shared her perspective. When I realized that the girls were being so horrible because they were jealous and needed to try to take me down, it wasn't as hard to take their snotty remarks. When my brother showed up one day to take me out to lunch, they thought he was my boyfriend." She laughs. "Suddenly I had 'status' in their eyes."

> What made the most difference? "My parents always listened."

It didn't hurt that Andrew was a "hottie," as the girls called him. When they found out through the gossip grapevine that Andrew was her brother, the leader of the pack tried to befriend Petra. But instead of getting sucked into the popular group, Petra stuck with the small group of quirky, straightforward kids she had learned to trust.

Today Petra is a sophomore in high school. Andrew, two years older and a respected athlete, has her back. Nobody is ever going to pick on his sister again, not on his watch.

Petra continues to gather and hang out with the quirky kids—ones who otherwise might be loners. Her group is greatly respected by the administration and also by students. Kids who are in trouble or getting picked on inevitably find their way to Petra and her friends' table.

It's a Jungle in Here

You're going to be in the jungle for three years, so pace yourself. Some days things will go well for you. You'll be swinging happily from vine to vine, on your way to your destination. Then, all of a sudden, the vine will break and you'll drop onto the jungle floor. It doesn't take long for predators to gather. Sometimes the predators are after your kids, and other times the predators resemble your kids. Suddenly the very kid you would have gladly sold the night before is the same kid you're backing and trying to help now. In the upside-down, wild time of middle school, the best thing you can do is grab a vine and enjoy the ride!

5

Walking on Polar Ice

All middle-schoolers are at risk, but some more than others.
How to identify and help the ones who need it.

Choices your kids make in middle school can cost them for a lifetime.

Ginger never could have guessed that her son would have his first experience with meth at 11 years old, right behind his school. But she vividly recalls searching for him when he wasn't in their usual pickup spot and finding him passed out on the concrete around the back of the school. Immediately she ran him to the ER. Once there, she was shocked to find out he had meth in his system—not a good combination with his asthma.

Jessica was stunned when she was served a summons for her and her daughter to appear in court. Her daughter was being sued for harassment and bullying. When she talked to another mom, the two discovered that their daughters had been posting on an alternate Facebook account that neither mom had known about. And the content? It shocked both moms to the core.

Janet remembers the mix of panic and anger she felt as she walked into a police station to pick up her 12-year-old daughter, who was caught shoplifting and now had a record.

The ways your children cope with changes in their home environment can also impact them for a lifetime. Gabe will never forget discovering how his seemingly calm 13-year-old was dealing with his parents' divorce—by becoming a cutter.

None of these parents would have predicted such trajectories for their kids. So how do you know when your child is simply being a "normal" preadolescent, and when they are walking on polar ice that's about to crack under them?

Warning Signs

When kids are heading into trouble or secretly in the middle of trouble already, there are always some red flags. Some are blatant. Others need a parent's eagle eye to spot them.

Extreme Withdrawal

All preadolescents will withdraw since they need time to process and figure out their world. Withdrawing to regroup and think is normal. That's why I emphasize the word *extreme*. If your child suddenly doesn't want to engage with the family at all and only wants to spend time in his room, something is going on.

It might be simple discouragement. He might feel like he's failing to live up to everyone's expectations. This can be especially true of firstborn children, who are perfectionists. If your son used to get all As, and now he struggles to get a B because the classes are much harder, he might be discouraged. Also, if you are a parent who tends to be critical when he doesn't succeed, he won't want to

> When kids are heading into trouble or secretly in the middle of trouble already, there are always some red flags.

talk with you. He already feels enough like a failure without your judgment or hearing, "You ought to do better."

If your child spends a lot of time on the computer, he might be drawn too far into the fantasy world of gaming. A hobby is one thing; a single-minded focus is entirely different. If not balanced with real-life relationships, too much computer and alone time are detrimental to forming healthy friendships.

Secretive Behavior

If you enter your son's room and he quickly changes the screen, that's a red flag. Simply asking, "Whatcha lookin' at?" won't get the answer you seek. But it's clear as day: pornography. If the kid was listening to a song on YouTube or browsing a clothes site or any other regular site, why would he have to hide it from you? (Unless, of course, he's gaming when he's supposed to be doing homework. Then again, that's his problem, not yours. He's the one who will have to deal with the unhappy teacher.)

Kids who view pornography are smart enough to have a backup plan of a "safe" image they can click on if anyone steps into the room. That's when, parents, you get good at checking out the history button on the computer to see what sites your child is visiting.

The same applies for your child's Facebook account and email. If you see a lot of secretive behavior, something beyond the norm is going on.

Jo noticed that her 13-year-old daughter was texting a lot. Whenever Jo was near, Trista would hide the phone or turn the screen away from her mother. So Jo asked her, "Who are you texting?"

"None of your business," Trista retorted.

"You're wrong on two accounts," Jo said. "You are my business, and I own the phone and pay for the calling plan. Since you couldn't give me a straightforward answer, give me your phone."

Her daughter looked shocked but slowly handed over the phone.

"Now I would like you to wait right here while I scroll through some of your recent messages."

At this point, Trista became visibly nervous. "Mom, you don't—"

Jo looked her daughter in the eye. "Yes, I do."

What Jo uncovered was a trail of emails from a guy named "Franco" and plans for Trista to meet him the next night after 10 o'clock, when a certain park was officially closed. Jo felt sick. All of Trista's emails were filled with romantic wording like, "I can't wait to finally meet you . . . and kiss you." Franco's messages were cluttered with innuendo that her sexually innocent daughter wouldn't have caught.

Jo, a single parent, was speechless for a minute. Then her mama bear side kicked into gear. "Sit right there, young lady." With her daughter's phone in hand, she called a friend of hers who was on the local police force and explained the situation.

> Kids who view pornography are smart enough to have a backup plan of a "safe" image they can click on if anyone steps into the room.

Trista was furious. "You're ruining my life!" she screamed. "Just because you can't get a guy, you don't want me to have one."

For the next 24 hours, Jo didn't let her daughter out of her sight, nor did she let Trista near her phone or computer. Trista didn't go to school, and Jo didn't go to work, even though she missed a key presentation. "I knew this was too important," she told me, "and my protective instinct was in full swing."

Around midnight, Jo's cop friend showed up. "Got him. Known history of child molestation, 47 years old."

Trista sat, shocked, listening to the story told by a man she respected. If Jo hadn't been a watchful mother, that situation could have had a very different, and tragic, ending. Trista is now 22 and, because of her early wake-up call, is pursuing law enforcement with a specialty in tracking sexual offenders.

Extreme Discouragement, Seething Rage, or Caring about Nothing

The poignant movie *To Save a Life* tells the story of two best friends who grew up together. Roger was crippled when he saved Jake by pushing him away from the path of a car. The two friends still did everything together until sometime in the middle of their freshman year. That year Jake became a basketball star and was thrust into the popular crowd, but Roger wasn't cool enough to be invited. Roger was bullied and became a loner. After school he emailed other kids who felt lost and discouraged. He and Jake lost contact.

Three years later, Roger entered the high school with a gun and began to shoot. Jake approached him, saying, "You don't want to do this, man."

Roger stared at him. "It's too late, Jake. You don't care." A split second later, Roger pointed the gun at himself and pulled the trigger.

The tragedy spun Jake into wondering, *Are there other kids out there like Roger that I'm not seeing?* He befriended the "unlovables" at school, including a cutter and a former cutter. And he started a website in memory of Roger, where he could dialogue with kids who were feeling desperate, to show them that living was worth it.[1]

When a child progresses from "I can't do anything right and nobody likes me" to

- intense flashes of anger;
- caring about nothing;
- making comments such as, "What's the use? Life's not worth it";
- spending a lot of time in his room, especially with the lights shut off; or
- listening to dark music about death, dying, and suicide,

you have reason to be concerned. Children who experience depression or intense rage often take the next step of googling ways to commit suicide. Again, if you have concerns, check the history button on your child's computer. When his life might be at stake, the invasion of his privacy is a much smaller issue. Kids who become angry against "the establishment," other students in general, parents, teachers, or other authority figures can decide that not only is their own life not worth anything, but others' lives aren't either. If you see such signs of discouragement, rage, or numbness and inability to care about anything, get your child help immediately. Don't wait.

Comments outside Your Child's Experience

Another way you can tell your child is looking at pornographic images or listening to sexually explicit songs is if you overhear him making comments or acting in ways beyond the sexual knowledge you know he has.

Trevor's science teacher asked to see his mother, Jennifer, after school. Trevor had told a girl, "Nice booty," and had been caught drawing breasts and nipples on his notebook. When the teacher handed the notebook to Jennifer and she leafed through it, she was shocked. Upon digging, she discovered a friend had introduced Trevor to an explicit rapper's songs, and that had led Trevor to google the phrases in the songs to find out what they meant.

✓ What Worked for Us

When Aidan was in seventh grade, I noticed a lot of changes. He fought more with his little sisters, stopped reading (he'd always devoured books), and suddenly wanted to lift weights. But when a teacher called to say he was in detention for fighting, I knew there was more going on.

What he finally told me made me sick. A group of boys had been calling him a homo because they saw him reading. They'd always been careful to do it when no adult was there. Finally Aidan snapped, and he was the one caught by the teacher.

I wanted to nuke those boys to kingdom come, but I also knew there would be more bullies. "This has to stop," I told him. "But you and I need to work together to make it stop."

Aidan was scared the other boys would discover he'd ratted them out and things would get worse. So he and I came up with a plan. When we explained to the teacher, she said, "That makes more sense. Now I understand." She'd been surprised to see that kind of behavior from Aidan. She looped in the principal, and all the teachers were put on alert.

Less than a week later, the bullies shoved Aidan against the wall, and an alert teacher outside the restroom overheard the scuffle and remarks. Two of the five boys were suspended, two were expelled, and the other received a month of detention. Other kids who had been bullied by the same boys told Aidan how relieved they were not to get picked on. He and some of the other kids started a "No More" group at school—to watch out for bullying and quietly notify the principal so he could take appropriate action. I'm a tough guy, but seeing my son turn a bad situation into one where he helps others choked me up.

Malcolm, New Jersey

Disruptive or Out-of-the-Norm Behavior

Your child has been a basically agreeable kid. Rarely a problem. Suddenly you start hearing about him being disruptive in class— throwing things, making inappropriate comments to the opposite sex, using bathroom passes to wander the hallway. Well, is your child behaving the same way at home that he is at school? Is he being disruptive across the board? If so, that behavior in general needs to be addressed. Bad behavior won't gain him friends or get him anywhere in life.

However, if you see the bad behavior in only one area, then there's something wrong with the environment itself, and you need to take a close look at the situation and people involved.

Let's say your family goes to Uncle Harold's every Sunday for a barbecue. But the last three weeks, your daughter, Betsy, has suddenly not felt well and asked to stay home. The pushy parent would say, "You've missed the last three weeks. So get in the car."

But the discerning parent would say, "Honey, is there some reason you don't want to go? Are you not comfortable at Uncle Harold's anymore? Did something happen there?"

Then out flows the story. Betsy tells you that a month ago, Uncle Harold made several comments about her developing body and stared at her in a way that made her uncomfortable.

Parent, this is where you have a big decision. Your daughter has just shared with you a big event in her life. If you blow it off and say, "Oh, he's only noticing how you're growing," you will have lost your daughter's trust. From now on, she won't tell you squat. Plus you may be helping a child predator reel in another victim. *So what he did isn't a big deal, I guess . . . even if it did make me uncomfortable*, your daughter thinks.

But kids who are innocent sexually do not make up stories like that. *Anything* that makes your daughter uncomfortable is a big deal. That prickle of discomfort is the red flag of warning built into us to tell us when something is wrong. You should never, ever suppress that instinct in your child.

> Is your child behaving the same way at home that he is at school? Is he being disruptive across the board?

The wise parent takes action. All kids in the family should stay home, and only Mom and Dad should go to Uncle Harold's to confront him and to tell him such behavior is not appropriate. As for future barbecues at Uncle Harold's? I suggest you find a new Sunday afternoon activity you can do as a family, minus Uncle Harold. Or, if you do visit him, leave the kids at home.

Before you get on your child's case for acting a certain way, think carefully. Is there something about this situation or the people involved that could be causing this behavior? Out-of-the-norm behavior deserves close scrutiny.

You get an email from your daughter's math teacher that he's giving her a 1 out of 10 in the area of cooperation. He says she's surly and refuses to speak in class. *My daughter?* you think. *She's an A student, and every other teacher talks about how sweet and helpful she is.* That's when you take a careful look at the environment and the teacher. Upon meeting with the teacher, bringing your daughter with you, you soon figure out why.

In that short meeting, the teacher is condescending, shares secrets about other students and what they're struggling with, and then insists your daughter tell him what some of her interests are and what she struggles with. Your daughter politely and wisely says, "I have a wide variety of interests," and leaves it there.

"See what I mean?" he says in disgust, sweeping a hand toward her. "She won't talk."

Sound like a caricature of a bad teacher? Well, it's not. This is the true story of what happened recently to good friends of mine at a Christian school. Long story short, the daughter wouldn't talk because she didn't want information about herself spread around, and the teacher's attitude toward her and all the students stunk. With one week left of the semester, the girl and her parents decided she would go ahead and finish the class, but the father met with the principal to tell him about the parent-teacher meeting. At the end of the semester, the daughter had earned all As in every class and a 10 in participation and cooperation in all classes except for one. In math, she got a 1. The father notified the principal, the grade was stricken from the school record because of their previous conversation, and the daughter was moved to a different math teacher for the next semester. Sadly, because the teacher had tenure, he stayed at the school.

If your child's behavior is consistent across the board—in other words, from home to school and back again—that's one issue. If the trouble seems to be only in one place, you'll find the answers in that environment.

Wearing Long-Sleeved Shirts in Summer

When I grew up, no one had ever heard of cutting. Today, sadly, it's become a huge issue for young people. *Cutting* describes a process where someone takes a razor or sharp knife and cuts their wrists, forearms, stomach, legs, or other places. Kids good at hiding cutting will cut areas normally covered by clothes.

When I asked former cutters why they used to cut themselves, here's what they said:

- "It was the only way I had any control over my life."
- "If I was causing the pain, then I could stop it."
- "Nothing in my life made sense. The only thing I could control was making the cuts and how deep I would make them."
- "Everybody in my life had control over me except me, and I hated that. Cutting was something I could do in secret and only belonged to me."

Cutting is a huge indication that life is not going well for your child. It's also an alarm bell for parents who micromanage their kid at every turn and for those on the other end of the spectrum who aren't active in their child's life. If your child is cutting, you have to get them some psychological help. This self-destructive, dangerous behavior is suicide, piece by piece. It harms their body and their mind.

> Cutting is . . . self-destructive, dangerous behavior . . . suicide, piece by piece.

So how can you tell if your child is cutting? Does she wear long sleeves even in summer? Shy away from wearing anything that reveals her middle? Does he have cuts he explains away as clumsiness or accidents? If so, please investigate.

For Girls, the Frantic Need for a Boyfriend

Melanie is an honor society student and the lead soprano in chorus, and she won first prize for her science project at the county fair. She receives continual accolades for her high academics from everyone . . . except her father.

An architect, he is demanding and perfectionistic and doesn't engage Melanie in any warm, caring way. She can't ever remember him saying, "I love you," and his energy isn't invested in his daughter's life. She tries hard to please him but gets the brush-off. He's a busy man—he is president of the local rotary, serves on the deacon board at church, and works 12- to 14-hour days at his job. But he has no time for his daughter or to affirm his daughter's femininity. If you took a psychological snapshot of her, you'd see a void in her heart—her daddy's missing.

Melanie has a classic case of father hunger. She has already dated eight different guys her eighth-grade year (three were high-schoolers), and she gravitates toward any male who will give her attention. The attention she can't get in a healthy way from her daddy, she'll seek elsewhere in male role models who will take advantage of her neediness. Melanie's story reveals that a girl doesn't have to be from a broken home to have daddy hunger. Girls whose fathers are absent physically, emotionally, or both play right into the hands of horny boys who show her affection to get what they want.

> The same girl who cuddles up with her blankie at home is capable of getting pregnant.

That's because, in the betwixt and between of middle school, insecurity reigns. Many of these kids still sleep with the blankies they've had since they were three years old, but they wouldn't want anybody at school to know. Yet the same girl who cuddles up with her blankie at home is capable of getting pregnant. Without her daddy meeting her need for love and affection, she's set up emotionally and physically to be used by guys.

A Fixation on Food, Counting Calories, or Dieting

When Shelly got to seventh grade, her mother noticed her daughter ate a lot less. *I guess she's stopping growing and isn't as hungry,* Amanda assumed. But a month later, when Shelly still barely touched the lunch her mother packed and only moved small portions around her plate at dinner, Amanda got worried. Shelly's explanation chilled her. Her daughter, who weighed 100 pounds, said she was fat and needed to go on a diet. Amanda knew from what she'd seen that this was more than a passing phase, so she made an appointment with a trusted counselor.

Feeling lost in middle school, Shelly had fallen into anorexia to control the only thing she felt she could—her food intake. Thankfully, because of a watchful mother who knew her daughter's eating habits well, the anorexia was caught in its beginning stages, before

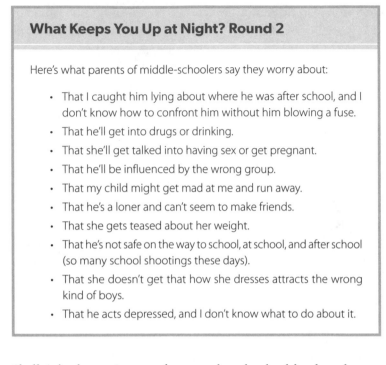

What Keeps You Up at Night? Round 2

Here's what parents of middle-schoolers say they worry about:

- That I caught him lying about where he was after school, and I don't know how to confront him without him blowing a fuse.
- That he'll get into drugs or drinking.
- That she'll get talked into having sex or get pregnant.
- That he'll be influenced by the wrong group.
- That my child might get mad at me and run away.
- That he's a loner and can't seem to make friends.
- That she gets teased about her weight.
- That he's not safe on the way to school, at school, and after school (so many school shootings these days).
- That she doesn't get that how she dresses attracts the wrong kind of boys.
- That he acts depressed, and I don't know what to do about it.

Shelly's body was impacted too much and unhealthy thought patterns were set.

With the focus on slender bodies in today's media, middle-school girls in particular can easily fall into anorexia (starving themselves to death) or bulimia (binge eating and then purging). Both are attempts at controlling an out-of-control world. If you see any such symptoms, get professional help immediately. You can't afford to wait.

Sudden Changes

If your child is suddenly dropping grades, withdrawing, being a real pain in the tail, and not going to the activities and events he used to love, such as sports practices, you've got a mountain to deal with. It's called *drugs*. Any child who does a sharp left-hand turn has discovered them, and you need to have an immediate discussion and intervention.

What to Do When You're in Crisis Mode

Sometimes a kid simply falls apart. His grades head south, and his attitude stinks to high heaven. She won't talk to you or ignores you when you talk to her. He picks fights with his siblings and won't come out of his room. Any small thing you ask her to do, she refuses to do.

You might think your kid is in space station A. But you might discover they're actually in space station B and starting to wall you off. They're building their own little fortress behind their bedroom door, with the door locked. So what do you do now?

Stop Everything

If your child isn't talking, and he's even moodier or more aggressive than normal, stop everything to find out what's going on. He doesn't go to school. You don't go to work or any other scheduled events. Your conversation might go something like this.

"From my perspective, things are not going well. I'm not sure what to do, but I do know that what's happening right now in our home can't continue. We are a family, and when one person is hurting, upset, or troubled, we all are. So some things have to change. We will not continue to do what we've done the first six weeks of the school year. You've been given a lot of freedom—time to hang out with your buddies, play games you like to play, text your friends, etc. But for whatever reason, that's not working. So now, when you ask to do things like that, you're going to get a stiff no, which will remain no until we figure out why you're behaving the way you are."

Everything stops in the family when you're in crisis mode. Your family can't and shouldn't move forward with any sense of normalcy until you address the issue.

Identify the Issue behind the Behavior

This is the moment, parent, where you have to wade right in the middle of the fray. If your child has been sassy or aggressive, clarify that you will not be used, abused, or taken for granted.

✓ What Worked for Us

My son, Seth, was what you'd call a messy. He couldn't open his locker without papers spilling out. And homework? As much as I nagged, he never did it on his own. He was always shooting hoops when I got home from work. Then I'd corner him and sit beside him (okay, I admit I helped a lot) so he'd get it done. When he brought his report card home with all Cs and Ds, and the notes from teachers said he wouldn't cooperate, I'd had enough. I'd also realized something about myself from one of your books: I was a permissive mom who was making my son's life easier out of guilt because he didn't have a dad.

Things had to change. I turned drill sergeant about his homework. He said, "Aw, Mom, why do you care? It's my homework."

"Exactly," I said. "It's your homework, and it says a lot to other people about who you are." I read the comments about him from one of his teachers, then asked, "Is that really who you want to be, Seth? A loser? Because I don't think you are. I think you're a smart kid who isn't applying himself because I've let you get away with it. But no more."

Six months later Seth is a totally different kid. He's getting As and Bs and helps me around the house—something he never did before without me begging. He's even made dinner for us twice—oatmeal and macaroni and cheese. You're so right, Dr. Leman. A family can turn completely around. We're living proof.

Anna, Oklahoma

You are done with Drama 101. You've moved on, and your child needs to move ahead too. Until you do those things, you can't have a profitable discussion that will get you anywhere or be able to brainstorm solutions to get your family back on track. When you push for the reason behind the behavior, you often find out more than you bargained for.

If your child is being picked on, empathize first to show you understand the pain and embarrassment. "I'm sorry. I know what it feels like to be laughed at, made fun of. I remember . . ." Tell about a time in your life when that happened.

But you don't leave things there. You add some Vitamin E—encouragement. "There are all kinds of things you could have said and done after that, but you didn't. You didn't strike back. You didn't use foul language in return. Even though you were hurting, you kept your cool. Inside you probably wanted to do terrible things to those boys—I would have too—but the good news is, you didn't. I went through some of those same things growing up. Though life has changed quite a bit, the basics remain, and that includes bullies. I remember feeling hurt and wanting to get back at those kids at the same time I wanted to avoid them. In fact, if I had my way, I wouldn't have shown up at the stupid school the next day. Do you feel that way?"

Your child nods.

You now solidify your partnership with your child. "But this is what you have to know. What those kids have done today and the other days they picked on you is very much against every rule in that school. Bullying is a big, hot issue, not only in your school but across the country. The good news is, there's a way to put an end to it, and I'm going to help you with that. You don't deserve

> When you push for the reason behind the behavior, you often find out more than you bargained for.

it; you don't have to put up with it. You're not a can to get kicked down the hallway at school every day. So we're going to put a call in to your teacher to alert her to the situation. Tomorrow you're going to go back to school and act like nothing has happened. I know you'll be nervous, and that's normal. If there is a recurrence of bullying, tell your teacher, and I'm sure she'll be able to take it from there."

Most of all, your child needs to know that you'll have his back and you'll get to the bottom of the issue. Stomping in to school, pounding on someone's desk, and declaring, "My son is being bullied, and you guys have to do something about it!" won't help your child. But when you come alongside, offer solutions, follow through, and keep your child informed as to what you're doing, you create a safety net for him. He knows you care, and you're not only willing but prepared to help.

If your child feels overwhelmed by activities, suggest solutions. If your child can't keep up with the difficult curriculum at school, hire a high-schooler for some tutoring or get additional help from the teacher. If your child is involved in too many activities, figure out ways to pare back. You may be stuck with commitments for this semester, but going forward, you can craft a plan: one activity per semester. Just knowing relief is coming down the pike will help your child handle the load better now.

If your child is in trouble for talking back and blaming others, the real issue is that she's working hard to keep herself out of the responsibility lane in life. Let's say she got a D on a paper because she didn't follow directions or handed it in on the wrong day. If her response is, "Well, the teacher wasn't clear when it was due," she's passing the buck. Worse, she's lying to you about it. Why else would all the other kids in the class have turned it in on time?

Kids need to learn responsibility, accountability, and respect. They need to own any blame that is theirs. If you take a careful look at someone who passes the buck in middle school, you'll often discover at least one permissive parent in the mix who covered that child's tail earlier in life and allowed her to be that way. Middle school is a critical time for learning responsibility. As soon as your child hits her freshman year of high school, the grades she makes and the notes teachers make about her character will influence the opportunities she has later in life. In fact, three or four years later, someone who doesn't know her will look at her grades on a computer screen and make all sorts of decisions about who she is, based on those grades.

> Kids need to learn responsibility, accountability, and respect.

If your child has become involved with drugs, alcohol, pornography, or a tough crowd, it's time to get out now. These are serious issues that need to be immediately addressed. Sometimes they will require a change of schools and a physical move. They also require a lot of tough love and many sacrifices from every member of the family. But the stakes are too high not to step in as soon as possible.

If your child is struggling with anorexia, bulimia, depression, or thoughts of suicide, she needs immediate help not only from you but from a trusted professional in the field. Your child's health and life are at risk. She is crying out to you in the only way she can—by exhibiting these behaviors. Don't let her down by being too busy to notice.

The Kid or the Environment?

Kids crumble for various reasons. Sometimes it's a fear of failing; sometimes it's a fear of success. *If I succeed, you'll always expect me to succeed, and that's too much pressure for me to handle.*

When I was in private practice, parents would bring me a troubled kid and say, "Here he is. Fix him."

"I want to talk to you," I'd say. "Not your son or daughter."

"What do you want to talk to us for?" the confused parents would ask. "Our son is the one who has the problem."

However, if the problem was with the environment, I needed the mom and dad in the room. In fact, the last person I needed was the kid. I wanted to see the child through his parents' eyes.

"Give me a description of your son. What was he like as a little kid?" I'd ask.

They would tell me, and then I'd ask, "So what's a typical day like now in your household? A typical morning?"

The parents would start to respond, and then I'd say, "Would you like me to give it to you?"

Startled, they'd nod.

I'd plunge in. "You're the human alarm clock. You warn, threaten, and/or bribe to get your kid moving. He drags his feet. You get on his case. He gets smart-mouthed. You exchange words. He goes off to school with a huff and a slammed door. You melt into a puddle of guilt."

> Want a change in your kid? Look at your home environment first.

"Wow," they'd say, openmouthed. "You just stepped into our kitchen."

Want a change in your kid? Look at your home environment first. If the coach and Scout leader say your daughter is wonderful and easy to get along with, but she's a pill at home, then her behavior is specific to your home environment, and something needs to change in the way you're interacting with your children.

If the problem is within your family life, that is something you can address immediately.

Andrea, an only child, had two firstborn parents. Terrified of letting them down in middle school, she went from being a straight-A student with a neat-as-a-pin room to a B and C student with a messy room that overflowed with clothes and papers. When she passed out in her room after a drug overdose, her parents found a note that said, "I'm sorry I couldn't be everything you wanted me to be," and rushed her to the hospital.

That was a wake-up call for two professional, driving parents. After an extended hospital stay in the psych ward and counseling for the entire family, Andrea came home to a completely different environment. Her mother had decided to work part-time and from home. Her father pared down his travels to once a month. He also realized that he'd been an authoritarian dad who barked out orders to his daughter but really didn't have a warm relationship with her.

Their family life did a 180. They trimmed down Andrea's activities, helped her catch up with school, and focused on family time. One weekend they spontaneously made brownie sundaes to celebrate her Bs in math and science. For that family, it was a huge turnaround. But best of all, Andrea was smiling again.

If you're an *authoritarian* parent—it's your way or the highway, and you bark out orders, being prescriptive and controlling—you're setting up an environment like the one Andrea lived in, where your child is afraid to fail. If you're a *permissive* parent—paving your child's path for him so he never fails and is always successful—you'll raise a child with a low level of responsibility and accountability. Either of these extremes leads to rebellion in your middle-schooler.

But if you are an *authoritative* parent—one who gives your child age-appropriate choices and responsibility and treats him as an important, unique, contributing member of your family—you'll develop an environment your child will always want to come home to.

For Parents of Prodigals

Nothing in life is a given. You can do everything right—work hard to instill your values in your child, bring him up in your faith—and still have a kid who shows every sign of rejecting what you've taught him. You might blow the whistle and have everything stop in your family to fix the crisis, but then your child sneaks out the back door to continue his behavior. He might throw you some lip service so you think he's changed, but behind the scenes he's playing you.

> Nothing in life is a given. You can do everything right . . . and still have a kid who shows every sign of rejecting what you've taught him.

However, if you've taught your child what is right, I guarantee that when he goes off course, he will feel guilty deep down. And he should. Some guilt is good guilt. It's the way our Creator has wired us—to make good, moral decisions. When we act otherwise, we violate our internal wiring. So your child knows the way things should be, yet he's making choices that derail him from that path.

Eventually his poor choices will catch up to him. But what should you do in the meanwhile?

Don't Snowplow His Roads in Life

Don't make it easy for him to continue on his wayward path. Don't give him money to support his drug habit. That means you don't give him money for anything else either, since you know he'll use it on drugs instead of lunch.

Let Reality Do the Talking

If he goes around your back and buys or sells drugs anyway, just wait for him to get nailed for possession of marijuana in school. Let reality do the talking—in the form of a stern judge who gives him the what-for. All the warning you can do in the world won't match up to the shock of going before a juvenile judge. Better for that to happen now than when he gets into high school or beyond, when he's considered an adult and offenses are taken to a new level and on permanent record. One of the hardest things a parent can do is show restraint in letting poor choices naturally unfold. Still love him, even if you don't like him right now. Someday that child's world will come crashing down. He might ignore you until that moment. But when that moment comes, he'll look up from the floor and want, more than anything, your love and support.

And of course you'll be right there. Not to pick him up off the floor, no. That he has to do for himself. But you will be there to encourage him as he gets up, dusts himself off, and makes plans for what he needs to fix and what he needs to do differently.

That's what being a parent of a middle-schooler is all about.

6

Confronting the Black Hole

Technology at Warp Speed

What you have to know to travel alongside and safeguard your kids.

Technology is moving at warp speed, and your middle-schooler is getting sucked into the black hole. If you don't think so, let me ask you:

- Do you have to pull your son away from video games to come to dinner?
- Does your daughter start texting as soon as you pick her up from anywhere?
- How did your child know a Hollywood star embarrassed himself only an hour after it happened?
- Does the earth stop spinning on its axis when your child can't find his cell phone?

- Is YouTube another member of your household?
- Have you ever wondered if your kid even hears you through his earbuds?
- How did Aunt Jenny know about your "surprise" trip that you just discussed with your child three minutes ago?

Welcome to the world of cell phones, video games, Facebook, YouTube, Twitter—you name it. In fact, in the time it takes this book to get to press, a lot will have changed. Landlines are disappearing in record numbers. What makes sense to you about technology, parent, will rarely make sense to your son or daughter because you grew up in primitive times, compared to them. If you don't know what a certain term is, ask your kid.

The other day, someone sent me a high-tech gizmo about an inch or two long. From the note that person sent, I knew it was a big deal and a wonderful gift, but I hadn't a clue what it was. All I knew is that I was supposed to like it. For now it's sitting in a little box on my desk until one of my kids comes home and identifies its purpose for me.

Even children who are three and four years old can function well in the high-tech world. That's because they're curious and have no fear about trying new technology out. But the emphasis on technology at our fingertips pulls a kid away from family at an earlier and earlier age. By middle school, it isn't so much what Mom and Dad say but whoever is topping the charts in the entertainment world. Culture rules and dominates. Much of it is self-centered and not in good taste.

> If you play in a manure pile all day long, at the end you're going to smell like . . . well, manure.

If you play in a manure pile all day long, at the end you're going to smell like . . . well, manure.

Have Appliance in Hand, Will Travel

Your middle-schoolers are in a time of spreading their wings. But once you put an appliance with internet access in their hands, they have wings like an eagle that can span the world. One simple click and your kid can look at anything anytime. And believe me, they are curious enough to explore. One family has an agreement with their daughter that she cannot click on attachments, send attachments, or download to her phone. But is that the answer? What about all the other images she can access?

Recently I was at Whole Foods, a classy supermarket. In the back they have a little bar where they serve burgers and other things. My wife, Sande, and I decided to stop and get a quick burger. She went to pick up something in the store and said, "I'll meet you in the back."

As I was passing one aisle, an employee told me, "Oh, be careful. Someone just hurled all over the floor." And there it was, in all its glory. I'm an adult, old and near death, but I couldn't get that horrible picture out of my mind or the stench out of my nostrils. Somehow the burger didn't sound that appealing anymore.

Children can see horrific things on the internet with the mere touch of a finger. Do you think they can get the hurling out of their minds? When you allow your kid to have a smartphone, you need to understand what you're really doing. Is your child emotionally and psychologically ready for the responsibilities of that phone? Have you trained him to discern which images are appropriate and which ones are not? Which sites are okay to go to and which ones are not? Have you trained him on safety protocol for the internet?

Think of a cell phone as a loaded gun. Once you pull it out of your holster, take the safety off, and hand it over to your kid, you've handed him an instrument that can be very destructive to his mind and soul. You've also given up a lot of your parental control. You're allowing your child to be exposed to a world that might be far removed from the values you hold dear.

As a parent, you have a right and a role to protect your child's innocence in an overexposed world. But while they're pushed outward, you're trying to bring them inward. That sets up a huge stage for conflict. Does that mean you should view technology as the enemy? Certainly not. Technology is a fact of life, and it's here to stay. It will continue to change at meteor speed. Some schools don't even use paper textbooks anymore; the students do all their homework on Chromebooks.

> Is your child emotionally and psychologically ready for the responsibilities of that phone?

When I asked a middle-school counselor at a public school in Arizona what percentage of their sixth- to eighth-graders had cell phones, he said, "Easily 95 percent. And all of them are smartphones." When I asked if the school had specific rules for the use of cell phones, he explained that the kids could use them before or after school but not during school. If a kid wanted to use it during the lunch break, even to call or text his mother, he had to go to the office to use it. Most kids didn't want to go to the office, so that was an effective control, except for rebels who sneaked their phones into the bathroom and used them there.

"Kids are better off without cell phones during the school day," the counselor stated, "because they are a distraction and an interruption. Kids shouldn't be texting each other during math to say, 'Have you seen this on YouTube?' And they certainly shouldn't be taking cell phone videos inappropriately in the restrooms, for 90,000 people to see the post."

When Should Your Child Have a Cell Phone?

I shake my head when I see kindergartners texting and playing games on cell phones. Why do kindergartners need cell phones?

They go from Mom or Dad's car to the kindergarten room and back to Mom or Dad's car. Hopefully Mom or Dad or at least a trusted adult is with them at all times. So do they really need a cell phone?

A good time to get a child a cell phone is when a child's activity requires it. Cell phones should become a reality when kids are active outside the home and are on their own. For example, your son plays softball and your daughter is on the stage crew for the spring musical. Both need to be picked up, but you're not sure of the conclusion time for either event.

Here's what I suggest, which might be unpopular, but hear me out first, okay? When you give your child a cell phone, don't start out with a smartphone. Get a basic phone that doesn't allow internet access. When a child is young, does she really need to be on YouTube? Sure, there are lots of fun and amusing videos, but there are also many things you don't want your child to see. Yes, you can filter what your child sees through subscription programs such as Covenant Eyes (www.covenanteyes.com) and get a report of where your kid has been on that phone, if you want to monitor it closely. But does your child *need* that kind of access to the internet in the first place?

When I asked parents of middle-schoolers how they handled cell phones in their family, here's what they said:

- "I get them in the hands of kids as soon as possible so they can learn the technology and be comfortable with it. I don't want them to be illiterate from a techie standpoint. But to me, there's a tremendous difference between a cell phone, a smartphone, and tablets. Smartphones and tablets depend on a child's maturity. I'd never give one to a child just because 'everybody else has one.'"
- "I check everything my children download—their songs, games, ..."

- "I warned my kids that they needed to use the internet wisely, or I would take their phones away from them."
- "Once a week I use their phone to check out where they've been and what they've viewed. I also go on their Facebook to see who their friends are, who they've added, and what they're saying."
- "We decided to pay for a basic package that doesn't have unlimited usage. Anything above the regular usage, the child has to pay for out of his allowance. We figure that will curb a lot of internet browsing."
- "We set up a password on our kid's phone so we can do a check anytime we want."
- "I had a frank discussion with my kids about the good things on the internet and also the dangers of technology."
- "We got our daughter a smartphone when she was in seventh grade but disarmed the internet feature. We agreed to turn it on after she graduated from eighth grade."

Many parents put all kinds of stipulations on the use of a smartphone, but some also paint themselves into a corner. Seriously, don't you think your techie child is smart enough to get around any restrictions you might set if he really wants to? Including changing a password you set up? (Then again, that certainly would be a red flag.) And if your child gives you the puppy dog eyes if he goes over his monthly usage, do you end up paying for it instead of taking it out of his allowance? Will you follow through with your threat to take away her phone if she doesn't use it wisely? And what is a middle-schooler's definition of *wisely* anyway? If you take away her phone, what happens when your kid can't reach you after school and the school office is already closed?

Perhaps it's time to consider a couple basics. What if you didn't give a child a cell phone until he needed it, and you didn't give him one with internet access until he needed it? Middle-schoolers vary widely in their age and maturity level. Some are ready for the rights and privileges of a cell phone. Others clearly are not.

To me, the simple questions are these: Do you trust your child to adhere to the family's values for what is okay to access and what is not? Have you shared your positive, high expectations with him about how you want him to use the phone? If you can't trust your

---

Cell Phones, Smartphones, or No?

Get your child a basic cell phone (not a smartphone) when she will be involved in activities where you aren't present.

Evaluate the maturity level of your child, the need for internet access, and the trust factor. Ask yourself: *Does my child adhere to our family values? Does he really need internet access? Can I expect the best of him in using a smartphone?* If the answer to all three questions is yes, consider getting him a smartphone.

Set up simple guidelines for the use of a smartphone before you give it to your child. Share your high expectations: "There are a lot of things on the internet that are good, and some that are very bad. We've reared you to believe in and follow certain values, and we trust you and expect that you will adhere to those values in what you choose to access with your phone. To keep you safe, we've set up a password that gives us immediate access to your phone at any time." This alerts the child in a low-key way that you will be watching but you won't be controlling.

Explain what will happen if your guidelines are not followed: "We expect you to make good choices. However, should you have a lapse of judgment, you can expect to lose the use of your smartphone until you have had sufficient opportunity to think about the guidelines you agreed to before we handed you the phone."

If areas of concern do arise—for example, overuse of internet minutes or secretive behavior—address them immediately. Always follow through on what you say you'll do.

---

child, why would you give him wider wings to be out in the world? It would be like giving your 16-year-old, who is a terrible driver and hasn't been able to pass her driver's license test yet, the keys to your car and saying, "Go enjoy yourself. Just don't kill yourself or anyone else along the way."

Technology might be new, but you're smart to use old, traditional discipline. If your child can't handle it, he shouldn't have it. It's as simple as that. A cell phone isn't a right; it's a privilege. And responsibility and accountability come with it.

Before you purchase that cell phone or smartphone, go to the phone headquarters and say, "Hey, I need some schooling on this thing." They'll take time to do it because they want to sell you a phone. Before you hand it over to your kid, get competent on the thing yourself. See what it can do. Tailor the privacy menu for what you and your family want. Believe me, your preadolescent will understand the phone better and faster than you do. You're going to be the one who needs to play catch-up, so why not get on the front end?

> A cell phone isn't a right; it's a privilege. And responsibility and accountability come with it.

The Influence of Media

At a time when 11- to 13-year-olds have enough to deal with simply in grappling with hormone changes, relational changes, and increased pressure at school, they are bombarded with media influences. Today's middle-schoolers are seeing and hearing things that people a couple of generations ago may not have seen or heard until they were in their twenties, if then. When kids hit the preteen years, exposure to the world in general looms huge. Some influences tell them how to be sexy, how to be cool. Those same influences whisper, "Being yourself isn't enough. You have to shock people—get people to see you differently—to matter in the world." What can you as a parent do to combat this influence?

Stay as Current as Possible Yourself

New sites pop up all the time. Many are good; others are destructive. If you want to take advantage of the good and steer clear of the worst of technology, you had better understand how media works.

The best person to ask is your child. "Hey, I'm trying to learn more about the internet and how it works. You know I stink at it, but I'm trying. Would you show me how to get to some sites and help me figure out how they work?" Playing a little dumb works wonders. Your child will naturally take you to sites he frequents. Since you typically hold all the cards in parental poker and know more than him, asking your child for help is like patting him on the back. I don't know a kid in the world who wouldn't be happy to help you out with that request and share his knowledge.

> If you want to take advantage of the good and steer clear of the worst of technology, you had better understand how media works.

In the process, you learn what sites he likes and can visit them yourself from time to time. Even more important, you gain insight into your child's world—what he's thinking, who he's admiring, what music he likes, and the cultural trends that intrigue him.

Be Aware of the Changes in Culture

In the late 1950s, the television show *Leave It to Beaver* was one of the first sitcom series written from a child's point of view. In every episode, young Beaver got into trouble for something. His parents would then correct him and set him on the right path. It was so popular that a series sequel released in the late 1980s called *The New Leave It to Beaver*. It focused on doing what was right, apologizing for or correcting what you did wrong, and making the family a strong unit.

Contrast that to today's innocence-lost world, where Hollywood stars pull in the young teen crowd through movies, YouTube, Facebook, Twitter, and all sorts of other venues. Then those same stars plunge into breakout roles in film, music, and their home life, displaying moral values both sickening and saddening. These are the types of role models who are influencing your children—the way they dress, the way they think, what their values are.

Know Who Your Kids Are Idolizing

It's human nature to idolize something, and your kids are human. What movie trailers are they looking at? What songs are they downloading? What Hollywood stars or indie musicians are they following? You might want to do some googling yourself so you at least understand part of the universe your children are exploring. Doing so will give you a window into what is important to them and how their values might be changing.

> It's human nature to idolize something, and your kids are human.

Be Aware of Your Child's Body Language

If your child is using his laptop, a strange emotion crosses his face, and he slams the cover of his computer down as if he's been startled, say gently, "You okay, honey? You seem upset about something."

The average child would say, "It's nothing."

You gently prod. "I know you're saying it's nothing, but I can tell by your reaction that something happened. I won't push now, though. I'll give you some time to think about it. You may not be ready to talk about it yet. But we will later."

Then make sure you revisit that discussion within 24 hours. Don't let the event pass without following up. Many parents are guilty of simply accepting the child's word: "Oh, it's no big deal." But it is a big deal. And if you're not there to help your child process the sexually explicit images he saw, curiosity will likely take him back to that site to view the image again, to try to make sense of it. Wouldn't you rather be in the driver's seat than allow your child to drive somewhere you definitely don't want him to go?

Nobody knows your child better than you. If you see a reaction, that's noteworthy and worth discussion.

Word Your Responses Carefully

What isn't helpful? Saying things like, "Hey, I noticed that So-and-So acted raunchy at her latest concert. Seriously, the girl's whacked out. And you want to listen to her music?" The only things this will accomplish are a glued-shut mouth from your kid and a permanent cutting off of the conversation when it comes to your child's taste in music.

What is helpful? "Hey, I just heard a song by one of the musicians you like, and it's pretty cool." Then go on to talk briefly about the lyrics that discuss real love and why you think it's an awesome song. Your kid is thinking, *Dad likes one of my songs? Maybe I'll show him the YouTube video I liked of that musician too.* And the exchange of ideas and the flow of information have begun.

The technology Goliath will always loom over your child's life. But if you formulate guidelines, prepare your middle-schooler, and expect the best of him, he's likely to remember your words long after you're gone.

I ought to know. When I was a young teenager learning how to drive, my dad drilled into my head that you never make a left turn until the car in front of you has already made that turn and you can see a clear lane. I'm now on social security and my dad is long gone from this earth, but when I get to an intersection I still remember his words. I've never turned left until I could see that the lane was clear. And as a result, I've never been in a car accident.

> Formulate guidelines, prepare your middle-schooler, and expect the best of him.

See how training works? Your training regarding the dangers of the internet might gain you an eye roll or two, but I guarantee your kids are listening . . . even if they do have their earbuds in.

What Your Child Needs to Know

Nate was a super tech-savvy kid. He wanted his own Facebook account, but his parents told him no and said, "We'll talk about it again when you're in high school." So Nate quietly took the reins in his own hands and created an account anyway. When other kids found out about it, they asked if he could do the same thing for them. Before long, there was a small network of secret Facebook accounts for kids at his middle school. Problem is, some of the kids were only 11 and 12, so Nate lied about their birth dates when he set up the accounts. (Facebook's current rule is that children have to be 13 years old to join the social network, though they are working on a way to allow users under 13 to have accounts.[1]) None of the kids had their parents' permission to set up an account.

It only took a couple of weeks before the jig was up. One sexually suggestive picture was posted, someone reported it to Facebook, and the account was blocked . . . but not before one of the parents became suspicious and started checking their child's internet activity. The parent confronted the child, who ratted Nate out.

To say Nate's parents—and all the other parents—were unhappy is a vast understatement. But Nate's parents also should have known better. Forbidding a kid to do something simply sets him up to attempt to do just that. It's part of the bid for freedom and independence during the middle-school years. It would have been better if Nate's parents had talked with him up front about the responsibilities of having a Facebook account and why they didn't want him to have one until high school, and then set a specific time when they would discuss it again.

> Forbidding a kid to do something simply sets him up to attempt to do just that. It's part of the bid for freedom and independence.

Before your child gets any social media or email account, here's what he or she needs to know.

Never Give Out Any More Personal Information than Absolutely Necessary

Yes, you might have a Facebook account with your name on it, but you don't have to make your file public and viewable by anyone. You also don't have to say how old you are, where you live, where you attend school, or any other specific details. Most teens post photos and videos of themselves; share their city, school name, and even their cell phone number and email; and talk about the places they typically go. You don't want to give child predators any head start. For example, if you say you live in a certain small town and you're involved in city soccer, how much detective work would it take for a predator to find your child?

We adults could take a lesson on this too. We can be just as naïve.

Take Megan, for example, who was excited to become a mom. When her son was only a day old, she snapped his picture—in which he looked somewhere between a turnip and a half-peeled onion—and posted it, along with all three of his names and his date of birth, on her social media account. Oops. All a child snatcher, con artist, or identity thief needs are those things to launch a campaign.

In general, we could all be a bit more careful about what we release to the public . . . and what we throw out in our trash and recycling bins. As Dorothy said in *The Wizard of Oz*, "Toto, I've a feeling we're not in Kansas anymore."

Carefully Screen Those You Allow to Become "Friends"

Your Facebook friends should only be people you know well—close friends and relatives. Never allow anyone into your network you haven't met in person. Not everyone is who he says he is. Online sexual predators look for innocent children who friend anyone. The children assume their new "friend" is the same age and often give away information that makes them an easy target for kidnapping and abuse.

Know That Anything You Text or Tweet Can Go Global in an Instant

The golden rule of social media should be: Don't say anything in written form that you wouldn't want to say in front of Grandma. With just one click, your "friend" can forward your message to a multitude.

Sarah learned that lesson the hard way. She shared her first sexual experience secretly with a "good friend." But, as friends often are in junior high, the other girl was fickle. She knew she had hot property and took advantage of it, tweeting it on her own social media account. Come Monday morning, "Slutty Sarah" was the focus of everyone's attention at school. Try living that reputation down as a 13-year-old.

As soon as you say something and hit the Send button, that message is portable. Anyone can forward it, and it becomes part of the permanent record on the internet. When Sarah applies to college, it's likely that someone will google her and come across that tweet. Your kids have to know that once something is out there, it's out there. It cannot be retrieved from all the places it goes. That means before they send a message, they need to stop and think it through. *If the person I'm writing this email about saw it, how would she feel?*

> The golden rule of social media should be: Don't say anything in written form that you wouldn't want to say in front of Grandma.

The best rule of thumb is never, ever say anything about another person unless it's positive and uplifting. As Thumper the rabbit said in the movie *Bambi*, "If you can't say something nice, don't say nothin' at all." That mantra sure would cut down a lot of the words flung around social media, now wouldn't it? And bring cyberbullying—the intentional decision to do harm to, embarrass, harass, or ridicule another—to a halt.

Educate your kid not only to be smart but to be nice. Then she'll never have to worry about anything she said leaking to someone else. Or if it does, it will make that person smile and feel good.

> Educate your kid not only to be smart but to be nice.

If your child is being cyberbullied, identify the source as swiftly as possible, and go straight to it. Demand that the bullying stop immediately and that posts regarding it be deleted. You can't stop the forwarding of that information, but you can at least get rid of the original posting. If a child is involved, contact his or her parents immediately. If you can't find the source, go to the police with the evidence in hand.

You must do battle with cyberbullying for your child's sake. There is a strong link between bullying, which includes cyberbullying, and suicide: "Bully victims are between 2 to 9 times more likely to consider suicide than non-victims, according to studies by Yale University. . . . 10 to 14 year old girls may be at even higher risk for suicide."[2] ABC News reported that "160,000 kids nationwide

---

What Worked for Us

Ashley, my 13-year-old, told me all her friends had a Facebook account. "Mom, I don't want to be left out," she said.

I didn't know much about Facebook accounts, so I talked to a good friend of mine about whether it was a good idea and, if so, how to start it. She gave me all the pros and cons and walked me through the setup if I decided to do it.

A week later, Ashley bugged me again, and I told her my concerns, especially that I didn't like the idea of information out there on the internet about our family. Finally I gave in, and we went through the start-up process. We were ready to click the button to make it live when Ashley got a shocking text. The parents of two of her friends had deactivated their Facebook accounts because they'd used school computers to log in and then had said mean things about a classmate. The comments had come to the attention of the school principal, and he'd taken action. The girls had been told they had to apologize to the girl, her parents, and the principal, then serve two months' worth of detention. If they refused to do so, they would need to leave the school.

Ashley was quiet for a long time. Finally she said, "I guess this is one time I don't mind being left out." She deleted her in-process Facebook account.

You're right, Dr. Leman. Reality can do the teaching. If my daughter ever decides to start a Facebook account someday, she'll be a lot smarter about how to use it and not use it.

Melanie, Illinois

---

stay home from school because they are afraid of being bullied."[3] See why your child needs your help?

Realize That a Picture Is Worth a Thousand Words

It only takes a simple click to attach a photo and another click to send it around the world.

Eleanor and Gary received a phone call from the vice principal at their daughter's school. "It would be helpful if you both could get here tonight. I'm willing to stay late if I need to. I'd like to talk to you about something that involves your daughter and is of a serious nature," Mr. Murdock said.

> What's happening today in social media can pack a wallop. A lifetime wallop.

Two hours later, the parents entered the office nervously.

Mr. Murdock pulled out a cell phone. "Before I show you this, I want to warn you. What you're about to see is shocking, graphic . . . in fact, pornographic. It will devastate you. But I don't know how else to deal with it except to show it to you."

When Eleanor and Gary nodded, he pushed the video button on the phone. The couple witnessed their eighth-grade daughter having sex with a young man. When it was over, they were speechless. Eleanor was crying.

"This phone was confiscated today in history class," Mr. Murdock explained, "from the boy who apparently took the video of your daughter and the other boy. Apparently many boys in this school have already seen the video."

What's happening today in social media can pack a wallop. A lifetime wallop.

Be Careful What Sites You Access

If you go on sites like Omegle, you are talking to a total stranger. That means your 12-year-old daughter might be talking to a

31-year-old sexual predator who says things like, "My parents treat me like a little kid. They don't let me do anything either." He uses language to develop a relationship with your daughter so she thinks, *He's my age, and he understands me.* That predator will work out a way to come face-to-face with her, and then, whether she's a willing or resistant partner, she's in harm's way.

It's imperative you educate your child about the dangers of the internet before you allow her to access it. Online predators know where to go and exactly what to do to reel in your child.

Think about this for a second. Millions of young people follow their favorite Hollywood stars' Instagrams. That ought to be frightening in itself, if you look at those stars' values and actions. But consider this: by way of Instagram, sexual predators have access to all those kids. That's why you must be familiar with the sites out there, the sites your child accesses, and your child's accounts and passwords.

> Listen to your gut as a parent, and act on it.

Yes, there is a fine balance between being an authoritarian parent who over-controls your kids and being a permissive parent who allows a child to go anywhere and do anything. Most parents who are actively engaged with their children know when something is amiss. Listen to your gut as a parent, and act on it.

Be Discerning about What to Post, Forward, Save, and Delete

Instagram is one of the top vehicles for young people to share pictures. There's also Snapchat, Skype, Vine, Twitter, YouTube, Tumblr, and lots of other venues. Once a photo is posted, it can go viral. If someone sees that photo, he has between 6 and 15 seconds to make a decision about whether he should forward that picture to someone else or take a picture of it himself so it's on his own device to share with anyone.

Most middle-schoolers don't have great discernment and wisdom about what is okay to forward, what they should save, and what should be deleted. Let's say an eighth-grade boy eggs on a girl to send him a sexy picture of herself. When he gets a picture of her with bare breasts, he shows it to his buddies like it's a medal he's earned. "Hey, check out what this chick sent me." Before long, it makes its way around the middle school.

Soon an immature sixth-grader gets it. "Oh, man, look at this." He gathers four more sixth-grade guys around to ogle it. Each of those boys has to decide what they will do with the information. If they are typical boys, they'll take a picture of the picture, if the first boy hasn't already forwarded it to them.

And the girl who originally sent it? She didn't dream that it would go viral or that anybody other than the first boy would ever see it. Yet, naïvely, she's allowed someone else to influence her future, because that picture will be forever floating around the internet. It's called *sexting*, and it's a huge issue with today's kids.

Not only that, but sexting and sex go hand in hand for middle-schoolers, according to *U.S. News & World Report*. "About 1 in 5 middle school students said they've received a sexually explicit message or photo. . . . Middle schoolers who reported receiving a sext were six times more likely to report being sexually active."[4]

> Naïvely, she's allowed someone else to influence her future, because that picture will be forever floating around the internet.

In addition, when researchers polled 1,200 students ages 10 to 15, they found out, "Students who texted 100 times or more each day were more likely to report sending and receiving sexually explicit text and picture cell phone messages, also known as 'sexts,' and be sexually active." Dr. Joe Austerman, a child psychiatrist at Cleveland Clinic Children's, says that preteenagers act impulsively,

---

Four Hot Tips for Parents Regarding the Internet

1. Become proficient yourself.
2. Talk with your kids about what they're seeing, watching, and listening to.
3. Be vigilant about checking the history button on your child's computer.
4. Be aware of your child's body language when he's using social media.

---

so "it's very easy to send a text out without thinking about the ramifications."[5]

Know That What You Put Out There Now Influences Your Future

I'm a football nut. Whenever I can, I go to football practice at the University of Arizona. Scouts often show up from professional teams to check out the players. One day an NFL scout told me, "See that guy over there?" He pointed.

"Yeah, I know him," I said.

"Well, we were interested in that kid until we took a look at his social media. We're no longer interested."

You see, the NFL is a huge business. They're not looking for knuckleheads, people who are going to embarrass the franchise. Any employer or organization that denotes success, a team, or a scholarship will google a person to see their track record. They'll check to see how responsible you've been in your comments and shout-outs that you put on social media. Passing on inappropriate information and pictures on the internet can cost you your future and end some of your dreams. Your kids need to know that up front.

But here's what a lot of parents don't think about. If your child splashes someone else's genitals all over social media, and

117

that child's parents decide to get an attorney, who do you think is really in the hot seat? It's you, parent. You're the one who has the contract and paid for the phone, not your 13-year-old. Does that make you rethink putting such a loaded weapon in the hand of your child? It should.

States differ in the ways they handle sex crimes. Some handle the child perpetrator as a minor and give them grace; some don't and treat them as adults. That means if your child has sent child pornography across the wire, he or she can become a sexual offender and be put on the sexual offender list.

As soon as you allow your child to have access to a smartphone, you are giving your permission for that child to make decisions that will affect not only their life long-term but your life and your bank account as well. Those decisions will be made in a split second, in the heat of peer pressure and "Hey, look at this."

If your child is at a friend's house and that friend wants to show him an off-color video, what will your child say? Will he say no because you've reared him to know that's wrong, or will he cave in to the peer pressure? The sooner you solidify with your children what is okay to look at, post, forward, and save, and what should be deleted or never posted in the first place, the better off you'll be.

It all comes down to training and trust. Do what you can to prepare your child for the broader world of social media. Become proficient yourself, since that's a huge part of your child's world. But at some point you have to let go, trust, and pray that the training you've done over the years—about what is right and what is wrong—will emerge even under intense pressure.

7

Growing Up Way Too Fast

Why the ABCs—acceptance, belonging, and competence—
are critical to keeping you and your child in the same
stratosphere.

It's the middle-school dance. Your daughter comes down the stairs
in a gorgeous dress and is wearing high heels. Not only that, but
her makeup makes her look like a high-schooler. You swivel your
gaze toward the nervous young man standing in your living room.
He's staring at her. You can almost see the drool forming. As a
father, you can only think, *Where's my crowbar?*

Your daughter has grown up before your very eyes. *I'm not ready
for this*, you think, and sweat forms on your brow.

Well, guess what? You haven't been raising a kid; you've been
rearing an adult. Tonight she's taken a big step in that direction.
No parent can quite be prepared for that moment. Today's kids
are growing up way too fast.

Life at Light Speed

Most parents of middle-schoolers today are in their 30s and 40s. But go back a generation to when I grew up, and you'll see how rapidly life has changed and moved into the fast lane.

When I was 10 years old, I had a shotgun. If I wanted to go pheasant hunting after school, I carried the gun through the neighborhood and checked it with the clerk at school. I simply asked him to hold on to it in the meanwhile, and he didn't bat an eye.

> You haven't been raising a kid; you've been rearing an adult.

At age 11, I walked half a mile to a bus stop with a friend, hopped a city bus for a five- to six-mile ride, played a baseball game in the next city, and returned on that same bus, carefree and happy. My parents didn't worry—even when I spontaneously decided to go from the bus down to the creek to fish, then hit the swimming hole after that. You see, back then, parents didn't worry where we were or what we were doing. And believe me, I was always up to a lot.

On the weekend, if it was a nice day, I was out the door by 8:00 a.m. and pounding on my buddy's door, yelling, "So what are we going to do today?" Together we boys created our day, whether it was making necessary repairs to our bikes or our parents' fences, or playing a friendly game of cops and robbers. Even on rainy or snowy days, we'd play hockey or some other game in one of our basements.

Contrast that to life today. Things have changed drastically, haven't they? But not necessarily for the better. Kids speed from activity to activity, their days planned from sunup to sundown. "Busy hands are happy hands" is today's mantra. Every parent wants their kid to be well liked by others and at the top of the success heap. But we often go too far in that direction, grasping at opportunities as if they are lifelines. In reality, many "opportunities" are distractions from getting the real work done—solidifying your family in these preteen years, before your teenager starts driving and going many places without you. For many families, managing a quick drive-thru dinner at Taco Bell is a miracle of arranging schedules.

No wonder today's kids, bombarded with additional responsibility at home and peer pressure at school, are growing up too fast. Some children in middle school are not only the ones to greet their younger siblings after school, but they also make them dinner, do their laundry, and help them with their homework—all before their parents get home from work. But the question is, are those kids ready for all that responsibility emotionally? Just because our world is moving at warp speed doesn't mean it's good for your kids . . . or for you.

There's a myth going around that "quality time" usurps "quantity time." However, without quantity time, you won't have quality time, because you won't get to know each other well enough. In our hurried world, it's no wonder families are becoming more fragmented.

When I was growing up, I never knew one kid I played with whose parents were divorced. A public school teacher I spoke with recently reported that, of the 27 kids in her classroom, only 3 come from first marriages, with both Mom and Dad in the home with the children. Obviously, the family is being shattered in many directions, and it is reaping a lot of problems relationally. Without a mom in the home, boys can't see firsthand how females like to be treated and how

> Every parent wants their kid to be well liked by others and at the top of the success heap.

couples who love each other unconditionally act. Without a dad in the home, girls can't see on a daily basis how males should

> There's a myth going around that "quality time" usurps "quantity time."

treat females, and they develop father hunger. They also don't have the opportunity to fine-tune their definition of love as enduring for all time and thinking of the other person's best first. The results are the same for children who have fathers and mothers who are physically present in the home but not emotionally and actively engaged. How can your child learn how to relate to others in a healthy manner if no one in the home is role modeling it for her?

We've also lost our sense of community, where neighbors looked out for each other. When I was a kid, living in a blue-collar New York area, we had an automatic neighborhood watch program, but nobody had to stick a metal sign into the turf to let people know. When I was 11, I got in trouble for smoking behind our garage because one of the neighbors spotted me and told my parents. How well do you know your neighbors? If you can name them all and give any personal details about them, your neighborhood is rare indeed. Back in my day, the neighbors helped raise your kids

---

What Middle-Schoolers Worry About

- "Embarrassing myself at school because I do something dumb."
- "If the group I hang out with would still like me if they knew the real me."
- "That my teacher will post my bad grade in front of everybody."
- "Getting teased at school because I'm different."
- "Being singled out and having kids stare at me."
- "My parents embarrassing me in front of my friends."

Notice that each statement has to do with how they appear in front of a peer. Wow, talk about peer *pressure*.

---

and didn't let them get away with anything. In my case, that was a very good thing.

But today parents outsource their kids to activities and programs, often with adults they don't know at the helm. That statement ought to scare you a bit. If it doesn't, check out some recent news headlines, where adults are caught in inappropriate situations with children.

Your middle-schooler fights battles all day long. She needs time in your home to rest, regroup, and know she's always safe there.

Out of the Starting Gate

I love to watch races like the famous Kentucky Derby, where 20 or so of the top horses compete against each other. The horses line up, quivering with energy, in the starting gate. When the gates are lifted and the race begins, the horses bolt out of there and start running. But there's a fine art to the racing that only a skilled jockey knows. If a horse starts as fast as it can out of the gate, it often runs out of energy in the most important stretch of the race. But if the jockey paces the horse, the horse is able to pour on the power right when it needs to. A horse might be hopelessly behind, yet with determination, talent, and a seasoned jockey, it can end up winning the biggest horse race in America.

> Parents often let kids run at a thoroughbred pace.

In a desperate attempt to keep up with the current culture and to please children at every turn, parents often let kids run at a thoroughbred pace outside the starting gate. In fact, many parents push the kids into the race at a very early age. After all, they fear, *If my child doesn't try as many things as possible and succeed at everything, he'll be left in the dust in life's race.* Parents who think that way put children on a collision track with trouble.

123

The smart jockey doesn't overrun or overcontrol the horse. He allows the horse to start well out of the gate and gives that horse freedom. But sometimes, for its welfare, that jockey pulls the horse back and paces it in order for it to run well, finish the race, and have the opportunity to win. Parents, that's what you need to do

What Worked for Us

My daughter, Adrian, developed fast. At 12 years old, she wore a 34C bra and was 5'7". At 13, she's a 36C, with looks guys notice. I was in the same place when I was 13, and that's why I'm worried. *But who are you to talk?* I always told myself. The choices I made at 13 led me to become a single mom at age 16. Even when I suggested she might want to get bigger or different shirts, Adrian rolled her eyes and continued to wear her clingy V-neck Ts. And those low-rise jeans? Don't even get me started.

Things changed when a friend said she'd seen my daughter at a nearby basketball court, flirting with high-school guys. After I calmed down, I realized I had two choices: either I could ground her until she went to college, or I could educate her about how boys think. I called my good friend Brett, who's been like a brother to me since high school, told him I needed his help, and invited him over for dinner.

I appreciated the way he jumped right into the topic. "Adrian, you've changed since I saw you last. Bet the boys are paying attention."

She eyed me and blushed. "I guess, yeah."

As we talked more, Brett naturally threw in some comments about how guys think—so differently from girls. Suddenly the lightbulb seemed to go on in Adrian's head.

The next day, I noticed she was still wearing one of her T-shirts, but she had a sweater on top of it. *So she got the message*, I thought and smiled.

Even better, Brett's message stuck. Six months later, Adrian bought a modest one-piece instead of her usual bikini to go to the pool.

I wish someone like Brett had been there for me, when I was a teenager, to tell me what guys thought.

Sienna, Texas

with your own little horse. Sometimes you need to pace her so she will run well and have a chance to succeed in life.

For the horse? There's some submission involved. The horse has to trust the jockey and take his commands seriously. When the jockey tells the horse, "Okay, this is it. We're nearing the finish line. You'll get extra oats—your payoff—in the next 200 yards," the horse listens and pours out a powerful stride.

The jockey? He's small. You wouldn't put a 250-pound guy on a horse and expect it to run as well as the horse next to him with the jockey who weighs 120 pounds. Some parents are like jockeys who weigh too much. They overburden their children with the unrealistic expectation of perfection, with no slack for failure and trial. Those children won't be able to run any race effectively.

Other parents, seeing how fast their kids are growing up, try to yank back on the reins and pull them to a stop. That only creates rebellion. Still other parents shrug and say, "Well, he's gonna run as fast as he wants to run, so why not let him?" and they sit back and watch the blur go by. But some parents take the time to consider the type of child and his areas of giftedness, fine-tune the long-term goal, and help that child get there by pacing him.

Trainers say there are four basic personalities of horses:

- The highly nervous, high-strung ones. One little thing will spook them. In fact, they might rear and hurt themselves unless calmed in a crisis.
- The relaxed, calm ones. These don't even break a sweat before the race. Some might consider them lazy, but they're far from it. They're observing everything around them.
- The combative ones. These horses are aggressive, already eying the competition before the race and ushering body-language warnings.
- The easily distracted ones. These horses need blinders to stay focused on the race and the finish line.

Which type of horse does your child resemble?

Trainers in the know say a great horse starts with a great breeder. What is the pedigree of the horse? What sire and dam did the horse come from? Once in a while horses will come out of nowhere and become great champions, commanding large stud fees. Yes, they need to have the natural talent for it, but at the core of their success is a trainer who worked hard with them to bring out the maximum potential.

Your child might have all the advantages in life—he might come from plenty of money, have lots of opportunities. Or she might have little, as far as other people are concerned. But people who have been written off in life can surprise you the most. I happen to be one of those people. Your kid can be too. Never, ever give up. What your kid is now can change greatly.

Rules without Relationship—It Never Works

You can set up all the rules you want for how your kids should behave, but without a relationship, they will all come to naught. Then the rules are only a big list of "don'ts." They're literally a waste of your breath.

> You can set up all the rules you want for how your kids should behave, but without a relationship, they will all come to naught.

The way you live your life and talk with your child, the kind of trust you have in her, the level of trust she has in you, the positive expectations you bestow upon her—these are all your best bet to guide her through Planet Middle School.

Be Proactive

A lot of meteors can come flying your way during the middle-school years. You can get so busy ducking their trajectories that you forget to get in front of the line of fire. Wise parents see those meteors coming, and they're proactive.

Let's say your cute 13-year-old likes boys—and now one particular boy. You could pull the "Young lady, you are not dating or even thinking of dating until you are 16. No way, no how!" But all that vehement statement will gain you is a defiant child who will be more than willing to go behind your back with an "I'll show you. You can't be the boss of me."

Instead, say, "Hey, why don't you invite him over to the house to have spaghetti with us?"

> Wouldn't you rather be on the front end of getting to know the boy who has your daughter in la-la land?

Afterward, if you can say so honestly, add, "I can see why you like that kid. He's respectful, polite, kind . . ." If the kid is a pain in the keister, either he won't agree to come in the first place, or he'll embarrass himself so much at your dinner table that he isn't likely to come around again. Either way, problem solved!

Some of you are saying, "But Dr. Leman, isn't that promoting early relationships? Pushing your kid into dating early?"

Well, isn't the relationship there already? And wouldn't you rather be on the front end of getting to know the boy who has your daughter in la-la land? Remember, in middle school, your child is away from you long enough that she can do anything she wants to do. It will only be her respect for herself, others, and you that stops her from doing just that. That's why the relationship you've built with your child already, and you continue to build, is so critical.

Realize the Only Person You Can Control Is Yourself

You can't control your child's actions, but you can control your own. Do you react to things or respond to them? When you react,

127

what your children see is your first impulse before rational think-ing can kick in. When you respond, you pause, take some time to think through the situation, and then speak logically after weigh-ing your options.

Reacting is easy. Simply open your mouth and blurt out whatever is on your mind. But later? Ouch. You have cleanup to do and a boatload of guilt to deal with.

Responding is much harder. It means swallowing anger, fear, or frustration. Some parents say they count to 10 before they open their mouths. That's a great idea. What's most important is that you don't add more solar energy to your child's flare-ups. Often saying, "I think we both need to take a step back and think through this. We can discuss it later tonight, when things have calmed down," is exactly what you should do.

> *Reacting* is easy. Simply open your mouth and blurt out whatever is on your mind. . . . *Responding* is much harder.

Above all, keep your goal in mind—a long-term relationship with your child where she will want to visit you when you're in a walker and you've got dentures.

Don't Treat Your Kid as a Pheasant under Glass

There's a wonderful, aromatic dish called pheasant under glass that gourmet restaurants still serve. If you like creating gourmet dishes yourself, perhaps you've made it. This dish is placed under a glass cover and presented to the guests, and then the cover is lifted. The tantalizing aroma is fanned toward the guests before they partake in the meal.

Pheasant under glass as a dish is delicious. But treating kids as if they are pheasants under glass as they grow up and then whisking the cover off of them when it's time for college can be detrimental.

As I've counseled families over the years, more parents than I want to count have told me, "We want to keep our kids from bad influences." Translated, that means, "We want to keep our kids away from the bad public school kids." So these parents send their kids to private or Christian schools, then sigh with relief because their kids are now safe. And the parents conclude that the school's teachings will satisfy their moral responsibility to instill good values. That gets the parents off the hook so they can get back to their own busy careers and interests.

Nothing could be further from the truth. If you want your kids to be taught in a way that adheres to specific teachings and values that are important to you, it's a great idea to send your kids to a Christian or private school. But if your purpose in doing so is to keep them safe, like a pheasant under glass, you're not doing them any long-term favors. Our world preys on the naïve and the innocent. Even young people of faith can fall into drugs, have sex, and become pregnant. You can do your best to guard your preteen's heart, mind, eyes, and mouth. But you can't control every minute of their day any longer. They will be outside your influence.

Matt was 11 when a friend offered him a sip of the can of beer he'd lifted from a convenience store. "No, thanks," Matt said. He stayed with his no even when the friend pressed. You know why? "Because I could hear Mom telling me, 'Don't ever drink. You don't want to get on that pathway.'" Matt's mom had grown up with an alcoholic father and had experienced both physical and verbal abuse as a result. "I didn't want to let her down," Matt said.

You see, it's all about the relationship. What happens in your home and the relationship you've formed will go with your child into places and situations you'd never imagine. In fact, it's probably better you don't know about some of them. You might pass out. But your voice in their head will be the steady reminder to choose to do what is right.

What Your Child Wants Most—the ABCs

Acceptance, belonging, and competence are three important pillars in a child's life. They have everything to do with how your child views herself—her true self-worth. Does your child think she is valuable? Lovable? Worthy? If so, she will be able to stand against peer pressure of any kind.

Acceptance

Every child craves unconditional love and acceptance, especially from the people most important to her—her mom and dad. Acceptance comes both from your words and through your actions. If you treat your child as the dumbest human being you've ever seen, your child will have low self-worth and feel like she can't accomplish anything. But if you say to your child, through your words and actions, "Yeah, life might be tough right now, but I believe in you. I know you can handle it. And you know what? I'm right behind you," then you've given your child a space shuttle to jettison to the moon and back.

Children who find unconditional acceptance at home want to talk to their parents about something that is bothering them. No, maybe not right at first, as they're processing. But they will feel

---

What Middle-Schoolers Want Most

Someone who . . .

- "Listens to me."
- "Likes me for me, not for what I can do for them."
- "Thinks I'm special and worth it."
- "Sees me even in the middle of a group."

---

free to ask later, "How would you handle this situation?" That's because the child knows he is accepted and won't be judged, no matter what he's struggling with.

> Acceptance comes both from your words and through your actions.

Kids who feel accepted on their home turf, who feel listened to and respected, struggle far less with peer pressure. They don't need to do anything to find acceptance in a peer group. They already have the acceptance they desire—at home.

Belonging

Your middle-schooler is like an astronaut floating in space, away from the mother ship. He's scanning the surface of the planet, looking for a place to land that's firm. If one of his peers says, "Hey, this is a good spot," your child might land there—especially if he's insecure and desperately wants to be part of that group. He'll wander around on that spot for a while and interact with that group. If they welcome him in, he might go ahead and enter the space station there . . . for good or bad.

However, if the mother ship is the place where he's grounded, where he feels safe and secure, he might take a look around that other space station and say, "This is not for me. I want to go back to the mother ship. That's where I belong."

Asa came to America from the Middle East. English was his second language. He struggled greatly in American middle school, but his family stood behind him. "You are a Menkel," his father told him. "You belong with us, and the Menkels always work hard. But when we work hard, we make a way where there is not one. That is what you are doing. At any

> Every child wants to belong someplace. What's critical is where they choose to belong.

time, you tell us what we can do to help you. We are one. We are a family." Because his family accepted him and he knew he belonged, Asa was able to go through middle school without the desperate need for attention and belonging in the peer group that he saw in so many of his classmates. Asa graduated fifth from the top of his eighth-grade class of 150 kids.

Every child wants to belong someplace. What's critical is where they choose to belong.

Yes, they may float in limbo from place to place for a while, trying out a few space stations that you'd really rather they not visit. But you always want them to come back to the mother ship. That's why it needs to be a comfortable place.

Competence

If you bring home a puppy, one of the first things you do is get him used to a leash. But the length of the leash is very important. You don't want it too long, or the puppy will hang himself if he jumps. But if it's too tight, the puppy will fight the restriction. So how much rope do you give him? You watch him carefully and figure out what length of leash is best for that particular puppy.

Translate that same principle to your kids. As they grow older, they'll need a longer leash in order to have room and freedom to explore. But they also still need to be on a leash in middle school.

What Your Kid Wants Most

- To be accepted
- To belong
- To be treated as competent

Will he get those from you or from his peers?

They need parameters to keep them safe. You want them to have freedom, but not too much. Choices, but not too many.

That's why it's important to empower your kids by giving them responsibility. When they take initiative to do

> It's important to empower your kids by giving them responsibility.

something without you pestering them, you say, "Great job. Bet that felt good inside to get it done, huh?"

Know what your child is thinking? *Hey, Mom and Dad noticed not only that I did it but that I did a good job. And it did feel good to do it by myself. Hmm, maybe I could do . . .*

See how it works? Parents who try to do things for their middle-schoolers that they should do for themselves don't help their children. They actually hinder their development of competence.

"But Dr. Leman, what if my child fails?" you may ask.

"So what if he fails?" I'll say. "He'll learn what to do differently next time. That's real life."

As responsibilities increase, your middle-schooler will grow in confidence in his ability to master the world. That's just as it should be. With today's kids growing up faster than ever before, that sense of competence will carry him a long way into the teenage world and then the adult world as a healthy, functioning member of society.

What your kids don't get from you, they'll seek in the peer group, where they will be pushed to grow up even faster. But if you accept and love your child unconditionally, emphasize his belonging to your family, and highlight and encourage his competence, you'll be amazed to see how he weathers the storms of middle school.

Finding the Balance

When do you hold your child close, and when do you let them go? Sometimes the answer is easy, other times it's hard, and still other times you have to get creative.

When Shelly's daughter asked if she could sleep over at her new friend's house on Friday, Shelly winced inwardly. She wanted to say no right off the bat. She'd never met Karen's mom and had barely seen Karen. Instead, she said, "Let me think about it, okay?"

That night she phoned Karen's mom and thanked her for the invitation. "We've always had a policy that she doesn't stay overnight at anyone's home other than ours and her grandma's," Shelly explained, "but I told her I'd call and talk with you about it."

She was pleasantly surprised when Karen's mom said she completely understood, and that she'd felt the same way about her own daughter. In fact, this was her daughter's first sleepover, and she was inviting only two girls. Together the moms strategized and then called the third mom. They all agreed it would be a great time to get to know each other since their girls were hanging out together, so they would have their own overnight at Karen's house while the girls had theirs. All brought food to share. The girls got their overnight, and sleeping downstairs in the family room gave them the independence and giggle girl time they wanted, while the moms got to know each other and find common ground upstairs.

> When do you hold your child close, and when do you let them go? Sometimes the answer is easy, other times it's hard, and still other times you have to get creative.

"When I left that sleepover," Shelly said, "I not only knew my daughter would always be safe there, but I'd gained two new friends who shared common concerns as moms and similar values."

Every child wants, at her core, to please her parents. That means parents' expectations should always be high. Notice I said "high" and not "unattainable." If you expect your child to behave appropriately, most of the time she will. But if you threaten her with what will happen if she doesn't, she'll test you just to see if you'll hold firm.

Kids are like that. And frankly, so are you. When someone tells you how something ought to be done, isn't there a part of you that thinks, *Oh yeah, well, I . . .*? Micromanaging will only turn her into a procrastinator and cause her to doubt her competence—that she can do anything on her own. She won't finish projects, because she knows she can't do them well enough to please you. Micromanaging diminishes independent thought and the desire to succeed and take risks in trying new things.

The art of parenting is in finding the balance in keeping kids close but allowing them to grow. With each kid in your family, it will be different, based on that unique child's personality and bent. But if your child feels accepted by you, belongs in your home, and has been reared to be competent, he'll blaze ahead, even in the growing-up-too-fast world. Even better, he'll be happy to live in the same stratosphere as you.

8

Becoming a (Gulp) Man/Woman

What you and your middle-schooler need to know about hormones and his or her changing body.

I'll never forget the dinner where my grandson, Conner, who was then 10 years old, pulled down his T-shirt sleeve so there was a five-inch gap under his armpit. After peering at the underside of his shirt for a few minutes, he looked at me with a strange expression. "Grandpa," he whispered, "I've got a big hair under my arm." And he showed it to me across the table.

"You know what I did when I was your age and got my first hair? I stared at it," I told him.

He grinned back and said, "Me too, Grandpa."

It was one of Conner's first forays into preadolescence, and I wanted him to know, "Hey, it's natural. Grandpa went through it too. Even more, it's going to be a fun ride."

Some kids seem to develop overnight. With others, it's little by little. But those changes are a-comin', and you need to be ready. Your middle-schooler is on his or her way to becoming a man or woman. Hormones really do talk, and they talk loudly. Good for you, if you've already broached the subject with your child of how their body is going to change, and how those changes affect how they think and how they feel about life and the opposite sex. If you haven't yet talked with your child beyond what they had in fifth- or sixth-grade health, it's time. Do you really expect your kid to be nonsexual until their wedding night, in the midst of intense peer pressure, without some real assistance from you?

Kids are maturing faster physically than ever before, researchers say.[1] But does that mean they are more mature in other ways—mentally, psychologically, relationally? In addition, they're exposed to many sexual experiences through television, movies, internet, and sexting—all of which can push them to think, *Okay, in order to be cool you have to dress sexy, talk sexy, have sex.* . . . Those who develop earlier than their peers can look older than they are and catch the eyes of older teens who are more sexually experienced. Those who develop slowly can feel like the odd kid out because they still look like little kids while their peers seem to grow up before their very eyes.

All kids are born with a puberty computer. The time when they'll develop is programmed into their genes. For some girls, their period might start as early as 9 or 10 years old. Girls definitely grow up more quickly than boys, both physically and emotionally. That's why sixth-grade girls won't usually give sixth-grade boys much of a look; they're busy scoping out the eighth-graders.

> All kids are born with a puberty computer. The time when they'll develop is programmed into their genes.

Hormones, Body Changes, and Sex Ed 101

When I talk with parents about hormones, body changes, and general sex education, I tell them, "Start at the top and work your way down." In fact, with a sex ed presenter and friend, Kathy Flores Bell, I did a whole book to assist parents in doing just that—talking with their kids about hormones, body changes, and the reproductive system. It's called *A Chicken's Guide to Talking Turkey with Your Kids about Sex,* and it has assisted hundreds of thousands of parents over the years in talking in a straightforward manner with their preadolescents.

Everybody seems to think that you have one "sex talk" with your kids about where babies come from, and then it's over. That's not true, and it shouldn't be true. Discussing hormones, body changes, and sexual information should be a continual process. How do you know when to say more? You delve into the topic with basic information. Your child will ask more questions if she wants more information. If she stops asking questions, she's satisfied enough for now . . . but may have more questions later.

> Everybody seems to think that you have one "sex talk" with your kids about where babies come from, and then it's over.

But you don't start by talking with your kids about sexual intercourse. You talk first about hormones and body changes they can expect and may already be experiencing.

In *A Chicken's Guide to Talking Turkey with Your Kids about Sex,* Kathy and I set up the discussions to cover first base, second base, third base, and fourth base. You start on first base and work gradually toward the big kahuna. In this chapter, I'll give you some highlights about first, second, and third base.

Where do you launch the discussion? One of the best places is when the two of you are in the car by yourselves. Then he's

> ## Four Tips for Talking to Your Kid about Sex
>
> 1. Be calm and straightforward.
> 2. Call the body parts their proper names.
> 3. Give information about the reproductive systems of both males and females. (If nothing else, curiosity about the opposite sex will keep your child listening through the "embarrassing" parts.)
> 4. Share how your values as a family match or don't match what they will see on television, in movies, and online and why you have those values.

trapped, and you can take as much time as you want on the way to your destination (until you run out of gas). Also, when discussing sensitive information, staring straight ahead instead of at each other can be a lot more comfortable.

But don't think you can handle the entire discussion in one sitting. There's a lot of ground to cover, and your child can only take in so much at once.

The Secret—Cross-Gender Communication

In talking about hormones and body changes, I suggest that moms talk to sons and fathers talk to daughters. I can already hear a pin drop in your living room as you read this. "Say what?" Your jaws are dropping.

"How on earth am I going to talk to my daughter about her period and pads?" you dads say. "No way. I'm not getting into that. I wouldn't even know where to start."

And you moms? "How am I supposed to explain erections and wet dreams to my son, when I've never had either of them and can only talk about them in theory?"

The simple answer is that you don't start with those things. You start with what you know about physical changes in their bodies

> No one knows better than you, Mom, how a woman likes to be treated by men. . . . And Dad, no one knows better than you what a young boy thinks when he looks at a girl.

and how hormones will affect them. You also convey what the opposite sex thinks and why respect is so important. If you, as a member of the opposite sex, can't address your child's physically developing body, he or she will see those physical changes as things to feel ashamed of and secretive about, rather than as a normal part of growing up.

No one knows better than you, Mom, how a woman likes to be treated by men—as treasured and unconditionally loved. You don't like to be pawed at, grabbed, or demeaned in any way. And Dad, no one knows better than you

✔ What Worked for Us

When my son turned 13, I saw a big shift in his personality. Aaron seemed a lot moodier, especially after school. Asking him anything seemed pointless, because he blew up and stomped to his room. He seemed jittery, always charged up. I caught him masturbating a couple times. I had no idea what to do. As a single mom who has never been married, I didn't have a spouse to go to for backup. So I talked to a couple I respect who has two boys in high school. They helped me come up with a great solution.

We live in a really old house, with a broken-down sunroom in the backyard that isn't attached to the house. It's been falling down for years and needs to be demolished, but I haven't had the time, physical strength, or money to handle the project.

As Aaron wolfed down dinner one night, I said, "Hey, I noticed you're developing some major muscles. I'm wondering if you might be able to help me out with something." I explained that I'd love his help in tearing down the sunroom, and that our friends had said he could borrow their tools.

what a young boy thinks when he looks at a girl—what physical responses are instinctively triggered by seeing the fine shape of a young lady's behind, the swivel of her hips, or the gentle curve of her breasts in a shirt.

First Base

When you talk with your child about body changes, you always address first the changes from the neck up—your child's face and hair. Start by saying, "Wow, it hit me how fast you're growing up. And with that come all sorts of physical changes."

There's a tremendous difference between boys and girls in middle school. A boy doesn't need long to get ready. He'll just put on a baseball cap and his clothes from yesterday and walk

---

Aaron perked up. "So you want me to smash it up and get rid of it?"

"Yeah," I said.

"All right!" There was a big glint in his eyes. "When can I start?"

"As soon as you want. We can get the tools after school tomorrow."

The next day Aaron started on the project as soon as we got home. I grinned to myself as I heard the smashing and crashing. Every day for two months Aaron came home from school and demolished more of that sunroom. His attitude improved, he didn't seem as stressed, and the physical workout toned his muscles.

The first week of summer, we rented a dumpster for a few days, and he and a couple of his friends hauled away the rubble. I was amazed. Now all we had left was the concrete foundation.

"I was thinking," Aaron said as we stared at it, "maybe this summer we could turn this into a patio. Lay some tiles on top of it so it's smooth or something. I could mow some lawns to make some money."

That's exactly what he did. He also rallied his friends to dig up the dirt around three sides of the foundation and surprised me by planting a flower border. Now when he's wound up after school, he digs up another portion of the yard and landscapes it. It's a win-win for everyone.

McKenna, South Carolina

out the door. A girl? She'll spend an hour staring at the mirror, rearranging her hair, trying out makeup, and experimenting with various outfits.

Open the communication with some hygiene basics—that hair gets oilier with preadolescence and, since the body produces more hormones, more frequent showers are needed to curb any potential BO. Talk about your first zit and how it sent you into a tailspin, and what you and your parents did to counteract the effects. This conversation sets firmly in your child's mind that, *Hey, Mom and Dad are willing to talk with me about anything. And they're not too weird about it either.*

> Open the communication with some hygiene basics.

What's important is for your child to understand that the changes happening are normal, as a result of his pituitary gland, which secretes hormones and then stimulates growth in his organs. This is basic information that will help your child be comfortable enough to say to you, "Uh, Mom, I'm having trouble with my zits. What can I do?" so you can take him on a trip to Walgreens or to a dermatologist.

With girls, explore some makeup—you can do it for free at a lot of stores. You also casually drop the comment that all those seemingly gorgeous models on magazine covers are airbrushed. The point regarding makeup and skin care is to make it simple so your child isn't weighed down, and neither is your budget. Focus on clear skin basics.

As for boys, some may have peach fuzz on their faces; others may be starting to get some bristles. No matter which is true, it's time to buy a razor and teach your son how to use it, even if it takes a while before his peach fuzz is thick enough to shave. Also, explain to boys that a little bit of shampoo and conditioner—a dime to a quarter size—goes a long way; they don't need a cupful.

Take your child to a hairstylist to find out a good cut and style to fit her face shape. It's also important to emphasize oral hygiene—brushing teeth, flossing, using mouthwash. Not only does it keep the dentist happy, but nothing can kill a middle-schooler's reputation faster than dragon breath. These small things will allow your child to put his best foot forward in middle school.

Second Base

Moving to second base means discussing the changes that are happening from the neck to the waist. All of these changes make a middle-schooler awkward. Changing hormones influence everything—fine and gross motor skills, hand-eye coordination, the ability to think through a situation logically, and how alert or tired a child may be. Is it any wonder, with hormones running rampant, that your kids sometimes feel or look off-kilter? And that they sleep in a lot on Saturday mornings or find it difficult to get up some weekdays? Most of them aren't lazy. They're genuinely tired from the whirl of changes happening both on the inside and on the outside. They'll be that way until the hormones settle down.

Think back a few years to your own middle-school years. Did you feel geeky? Think everybody was looking at you the instant you walked in the room? Your child feels that way too. Preadolescents are klutzy. They bump into things, drop things. All their body parts don't necessarily move together at the same time. When your daughter has her period, she wonders if everybody can see the bulge of her pad in her pants. If your son's voice is changing, he might be fairly mute until the squeaks settle down at least

> Preadolescents are klutzy. They bump into things, drop things. All their body parts don't necessarily move together at the same time.

to a consistent tenor. Yet both of those kids still try to walk as gracefully as they can into a room . . . until they fall over the chair they didn't see.

Also, because of these hormonal changes, your child will be more emotional. It only takes a heartbeat to move from the depths of despair to the highest of highs. Every little hurt turns into a big hurt. They begin to notice that the world around them isn't always fair, and sometimes that unfairness will be pointed at them.

This is also the age where deodorant becomes necessary. When the pituitary gland kicks in and sweat glands increase production, odors follow. Many boys still haven't adjusted to taking more frequent showers, and they can quickly smell like a locker room. So can girls. To prevent body odor that will embarrass them in front of their peers, preadolescents should shower daily, use deodorant, and wear clean clothes every day. Boys need reminders that taking a shower means using soap, and wearing clean clothes also means changing underwear. Do your kids a favor. Don't let them out the door without a sniff test. Yes, I know your kids hate that, but trust me, you're a lot more forgiving than their peers, who might catch one whiff of their BO and exile them for life.

> Do your kids a favor. Don't let them out the door without a sniff test.

When girls are in middle school, they become increasingly self-conscious about their body shape, size, and weight. They stack themselves up against models and come up lacking, even if you have told them those models are airbrushed. If you find your daughter groaning about how imperfect she is, take her to a place where there are a lot of normal-looking people, such as a shopping mall or a grocery store. Observe the people for a bit. How many look like Hollywood models? How many look like real people? You need to help your child identify her best features and learn how to accentuate them. Yes, makeup and flattering clothing can do a lot. But make sure you highlight the values that last—such as integrity, honesty, loyalty, and friendship.

Third Base

Just as children physically mature at different times, they're ready for information on sex and the sexual reproductive system at different times. That makes it hard when schools institute a standard sex ed class across the board for fifth-graders. Frankly, some kids are ready; others are not. It's very clear from a kid's response who is and who isn't ready.

For example, when Jason, who has no sisters, learned about girls having periods in his school's sex ed class, he used that information the next day to tease one of his female classmates. "Oh, so that's why you're crabby. You have your period," he loudly announced. Not only did he terribly embarrass her, but her friends rallied around her and let him have it as a group for a week. Jason may have understood some of the technical information in the presentation, but he completely missed the relational information because he wasn't mature enough to process it.

That's why, parents, it's critical you don't wait for the school to do the sex ed teaching. You should be the ones who prepare your children before they hear it elsewhere. Sure, you can keep your child home if you think she's not ready for that sex ed class at school. But don't be fooled—if she's not there, she'll still hear information about it from her classmates when she returns. And the information may be partly correct, majorly wrong, or downright ridiculous. Isn't it better for you to be in charge of what she knows up front?

> Don't wait for the school to do the sex ed teaching.

145

Especially for girls: Girls need to be informed about their miraculous bodies and how those bodies prepare to have a baby. Here are the basics they should know:

- Babies come from eggs, which are made and stored inside ovaries. All the eggs a girl will need for her entire life are already stored inside her ovaries when she's born. They come out once a month, during a time called a *period.*
- The eggs travel through thin tubes called fallopian tubes and into the uterus, where a baby grows.
- The uterus expands to fit a baby.
- When the baby is ready to come out, the baby passes through the cervix, which connects the uterus to the vagina.
- When an egg is not fertilized in the fallopian tube, it dies and disintegrates. The endometrium, the soft lining of blood and tissue on the outside of the uterus, is shed during a menstrual period. If a girl is pregnant, then the body keeps that lining, and it thickens and grows to protect the baby.
- A menstrual flow can be light, medium, or heavy, and can last anywhere from three to seven days. Every girl develops her own cycle, which is measured from the beginning of day one of a period to day one of the next period. But especially in the beginning, periods may not be regular.

Girls also need to know that they may need to change pads between classes, carry pads with them in their backpacks, and eat extra protein or other food during their period. If girls lose a lot of blood, they can become anemic and feel faint. Some girls experience nausea and cramps. Each girl needs to experiment with different types of pads to find out which ones work best for her. She also needs to know how to dispose of those pads properly. No girl wants to be mortified by having the family dog drag her pad out of the garbage can and around the kitchen in front of her brother's friends.

What do girls need most from you as they adjust to their cycles? Understanding, extra space, more time to rest, a little pampering, and some chocolate—it really is the feel-good drug for many girls and women.

Dad, let's be blunt between us guys, shall we? If you have a daughter, somewhere between now and the time she goes off to college, you *will* find yourself wandering down that special aisle in Walgreens. Might as well get used to it now so you can be the epitome of calm when your daughter is in the car and says, "Uh, Dad, can you . . . ?" The important thing is that you treat your girl's physical development and periods as normal and nothing to be embarrassed about. By treating hormonal changes that way, you're saying to your daughter, "You are unconditionally loved and accepted, and we can talk about anything."

Isn't that kind of communication with your daughter worth an uncomfortable moment or two in the initial discussion and all the Walgreens runs?

Especially for boys: When I start a discussion about hormone changes with middle-school boys, I ask them to give me some slang names for their penis. They have no trouble doing so. In fact, we have a rollicking session as they laugh and call out a multitude of descriptors. Then I ask them to come up with names for a girl's private parts, and they get squirmy. The room turns suddenly silent.

That reticence is a good clue that boys are, at their core, modest. They want to be gentlemen and to treat a lady like a lady. But often

> Dad, let's be blunt between us guys, shall we? If you have a daughter, somewhere between now and the time she goes off to college, you *will* find yourself wandering down that special aisle in Walgreens.

they don't know how. In addition to their lack of knowledge, boys experience strange stirrings inside and weird happenings, like getting an erection easily. All it takes is the sight of a girl's bra strap, the swing of her hips, or even a spring breeze, which has nothing to do with girls, blowing across the front of their jeans. That's because boys this age are in an ever-ready state. It doesn't mean they are weird or horny; it means that their developing bodies are in the midst of figuring out how many hormones to deliver and where. It's natural for Mr. Shmeengie to want to stand up and say hello, and he doesn't need a reason.

> Know how you can help your son the most? Prepare him for the inevitability of erections popping up at the most awkward of times.

Since this is a given, know how you can help your son the most? Prepare him for the inevitability of erections popping up at the most awkward of times. Buy him pants that aren't too tight. Suggest that he wear a shirt loose instead of tucking it into his pants. That way, if Mr. Shmeengie stands at attention right when the teacher calls your son to the front of the class, he's literally covered, and he doesn't have anything to worry about. When all else fails, give him the hint that a notebook held casually in just the right spot can cover *a lot*.

As your boy changes into a man, here are the basics he needs to know:

- Hormones send signals to the penis that fill it with blood, which is why the penis gets hard and erect and stands up at attention.
- The testes and scrotum, a boy's reproductive organs, are in a dangerous position—especially for those boys who play sports. For a guy, nothing hurts more than taking a fastball in the groin. But boys need to know why it's so sensitive—that it's the place where sperm is produced. During preadolescence each

testicle grows to be about the size of a walnut and produces about three hundred million sperm per day. Unused sperm are stored in the seminal vesicle or released during a nocturnal emission, better known as a wet dream. The scrotum, the pouch that holds the testicles, also responds by shrinking when cold and relaxing farther away from the body when hot—all designed to protect the health and longevity of the sperm.

- Once the sperm are made in the testes, they collect in a tube called the epididymis. From there, after they mature, they move into the vas deferens, long narrow tubes that start at the epididymis and wind over the bladder to the urethra.
- At the wide end of the vas deferens is the seminal vesicle, which produces fluid that helps the sperm get where they are going, protects them, and nourishes them. Sperm cells that aren't ejaculated are reabsorbed.

Just as dads need to learn about bras and pads, moms whose sons are in sports also need to learn about athletic cups and where they go (inside the underwear? outside the underwear?). So, moms, go with your sons to the store. Ask the clerk basic questions, such as, "We need an athletic cup. Do they come in specific sizes? What are they made of? How can you decide what kind is best?"

You see, Mom, when you go through this experience with your son, he knows he can ask you any question, and I mean *anything*, and you won't be embarrassed. You'll approach it the same frank way you did his athletic cup, or you might say, "Hmm, I don't know how that works. Let's do a little research."

Also, parents, your son will have a wet dream—every boy does—and he might as well be prepared for it. So you say, "Sooner or later, you're going to wake up from this amazing dream. . . . You dream of doing something sexual with a girl, and it feels really, really good. You may wonder what on earth happened. Well, that's very normal. It's your body's and mind's way of going through the process of growing up. There's nothing to feel guilty or ashamed about. It isn't something you can control. It will just happen. Your underwear will feel wet and sticky with semen, and sometimes your sheets will be like that too. So if you wake up and that has happened, just put your sheets and underwear in the washer. It's no big deal."

Think of it this way. Your daughter prepares for reproduction by having periods. Your son prepares for reproduction by having wet dreams. It's all natural, normal, and good.

> Your daughter prepares for reproduction by having periods. Your son prepares for reproduction by having wet dreams. It's all natural, normal, and good.

The M-word

Your children need to know that sex is not bad. In fact, it's an incredibly pleasurable experience created by God Almighty himself. But it has to be in the right context—of two people who are committed to each other for a lifetime. When it is, there is safety in those boundaries of love. Neither person is going to leave. However, what does a hormonally charged preadolescent, whose body is preparing for reproduction, do between the launch of those hormones and that day when he or she is blissfully wedded? Especially in a society where waiting for sex until marriage isn't seen by many as a viable or even wise solution?

For a lot of people, no matter what your stance on sex outside of marriage is, it's a long space from here to there. You cannot sidestep the reality that we are created as sexual beings. The way some preadolescents deal with the sexual tension in the meanwhile is through masturbation—fondling their own genitals until they reach a sexual climax. In all my work with preadolescent and adolescent boys, 90 percent of them will admit that they masturbate.

I think the other 10 percent are lying. For boys in particular, when sperm cannot be released, a physiological pressure builds up. That pressure turns into a wet dream, released unconsciously at night, or is released purposefully through masturbation. Girls too can discover that touching themselves can be pleasurable.

Many parents I've talked to panic if they think they see their children masturbating. However, it's fairly safe to assume that most boys, and very many girls, will occasionally masturbate to relieve sexual tension. The act of masturbation itself is not the problem. The troubling aspect develops if the masturbation is paired with sexually stimulating images, such as pornography or other fantasies. Then the act can become addictive and destroy the development of a healthy view of sex, marriage, and self-worth.

Children will experiment, but be careful that you don't jump to conclusions if you see a child touching that area. Just like every other body part, the penis and vagina can itch and need to be scratched. For girls, pads will need to be adjusted, or she may have a rash from a bubble bath. Boys may get jock itch, notice the sudden growth of pubic hair, or need to adjust their athletic cups.

If you spot your middle-schooler's hands down his pants, the best thing you can do is not flip out. But neither should you ignore the act. You should simply say casually, "Hey, I noticed you've got your hands in your pants—what's going on?"

If you have an open relationship with your child, and you've addressed sexual issues with straightforward honesty,

> You cannot sidestep the reality that we are created as sexual beings.

you'll have no trouble with the discussion that will follow. On any topic having to do with hormones, changing bodies, or sexuality, the most important thing is that you don't leave your child floundering. You don't want him to have to figure it out on his own.

9

Blue Chip or Penny Stocks?

Talking to your kids about sex—and respecting themselves and others.

When you got up this morning, there's one thing I know you didn't say: "Today's the day I get to talk to my son or daughter about sex. I just can't wait!"

Most of you saw the topic in this chapter, sighed, and thought, *Oh yeah, that. I guess I have to do that, huh? But didn't they sort of cover it in health in school? And I touched on it when I had that discussion about hormones and body parts changing. Maybe I can slide by. . . .*

If that's what you think, consider this. There's a game seventh- and eighth-grade boys and girls play called Rainbow. In this game, girls wear different colors of lipstick. Boys sit at a table and bare their male appendage, and girls sit under the table and administer oral sex on that appendage. The winner is the boy who has the most colors of lipstick on his penis.

Some of you are shocked. "But they are just 12- and 13-year-olds," you're saying. "That can't be."

But it is, and it happens every day at middle schools across the country. Sometimes even at cafeteria lunch tables.

What's even more shocking is that, if you asked these kids if they'd had sex, they'd say no. To them, oral sex isn't sex.

Bottom line, what's the game Rainbow about? It's about middle-school boys vying to be the alpha dog of the pack—flexing their nonexistent biceps and other muscles to not only fit in but rule. It's about girls positioning themselves to be popular, especially with boys. They'll do anything to be part of the in crowd, even administering oral sex on some boy's privates—a boy they don't even know and who won't care who they are after he wins the Rainbow game.

This, parents, is the world your child lives in. Don't think that, just because your kid goes to a small school, a private school, or a faith-based school, he won't be tempted by sexual games such as this. They don't happen only in public school.

So how do you prepare your child for this kind of peer pressure and give him a reason to say no? That's what this chapter is about.

The Sexual Revolution

I was recently talking with an 18-year-old from the Midwest who just got a sports scholarship to play at one of the big schools. He's handsome and well-built with six-pack abs, and girls routinely throw themselves at him. I watched it happen as I stood talking with him.

"I'm sick of it," he declared. "These girls . . . they're all bimbos. They expect to hook up on the first date. In fact, they'll do anything to hook up. I'm not going there. I don't want to get anything from anybody. And they're not the kind of girls I'd want to marry." So he steers clear even of dating.

The sad thing is, a lot of guys and girls are saying these days, "Why would I want a partner who is sexually inexperienced?" It's a far cry from the days where guys wanted to bring a virgin home to Mama.

We live in an era where, if you're an actress or a well-known sports personality and you get pregnant out of wedlock, you just call your publicist and announce, "I'm going to have a baby." Then the publicist gets busy and spreads the word on your Facebook and Twitter accounts.

What does this say to a 13-year-old girl who is sexually active? "It doesn't matter if I get pregnant. She did, and look at all the people who are supporting her on Twitter. So it's cool. Why should I worry?" But the disparity between a normal 13-year-old girl getting pregnant and not having the resources it takes to become a mom, and a wealthy public figure who can rally all sorts of nannies and other help, is sobering. Today it's no longer about the health and welfare of the baby. It's about what you want.

> We live in an era where, if you're an actress or a well-known sports personality and you get pregnant out of wedlock, you just call your publicist and announce, "I'm going to have a baby."

That same kind of thinking transfers to other areas of life. If you can have anything you want without consequences, there's no problem, of course, with living together before marriage. Society says, "You really don't need a husband or a wife. What you need is a willing partner, a place, and a time to make it happen and get it on."

Yes, we are sexual beings. That, in fact, is how each of us arrived on this earth. But if you said to your middle-schooler, "Well, you know, sex is how you got on this planet. Your mother and I . . . ," your middle-schooler would screech, "Ohhh, that is so gross!" That's because, to middle-schoolers, parents are as old as dirt, and they can't imagine you having a sexual experience. But does that dull the drive in them to explore? Of course not, because to preadolescents who are scoping out the opposite sex for the first time, the desire for physical intimacy is growing.

Sex is glamorized for kids at every possible turn of the head. Check out the billboard ad you pass every day that declares, "If you really love someone, you'll use Trojans."

> To middle-schoolers, parents are as old as dirt, and they can't imagine you having a sexual experience.

With the flooding of media and culture saying that casual sex is not only good but great and expected, children are drawn into sexual experiences at a younger and younger age. Preadolescents and adolescents are "hooking up"—their term for having oral sex or intercourse with people they may know but may not even date. Because of the hot sex they see in movies—with no consequences afterward—kids think that having sex is the greatest thing going. Even if their parents say, "Don't have sex, or you'll get pregnant, and you sure don't want a baby," that doesn't matter because the messages they get from peers and the media is that you have to hook up to be popular, cool, and liked by the opposite sex.

With such powerful peer pressure, inhibitions can go out the window. Many preadolescents see having sex as a rite of passage to show you're grown up. Today a lack of sexual experience is often seen as a negative, pushing preadolescents to have contests to see who can lose their virginity first. Being a virgin is no longer something you want to advertise, because it means you're a nerd and nobody wants you. That's why, to be liked, to gain acceptance in the peer group, some kids will go against everything they've been taught.

But the physical and emotional results of early sex are devastating. According to WebMD, "Most teens don't know much about STDs until they get one. And a lot of them *are* getting STDs. Half of all sexually active teens will catch chlamydia, herpes, or another STD by the time they turn 25."[1] That doesn't count the girls whose dreams are shattered when they become pregnant. Emotionally, kids are jerked from short relationship to short relationship when sex enters the picture and they don't learn how to form healthy, opposite-sex relationships. Their growth in self-worth and respect toward others is also short-circuited.

Times Are A-changin'

Take a two-minute walk down a middle-school hallway, and you'll see that times indeed are changing for the kids who were in elementary school a short while earlier. In fact, the open displays

---

✓ What Worked for Us

Our daughter, Missy, developed quickly. In sixth grade, she hung out with the older kids and, right before the school year ended, became enamored with a seventh-grade boy. He seemed to like her too. At first, my wife thought it was cute. Then, over the summer, Missy developed even more, and the seventh-grade boy became an eighth-grader "with a penis," as I told my wife.

My daughter liked the rush of someone liking her, but I didn't like the PDA I saw. When I came around the corner of my garage and saw that boy's hand up my daughter's shirt and her liking it, I decided enough was enough. I broke up the little party, sent the boy home, and then dealt with a tirade from my daughter for embarrassing her.

I talked with friends of ours, who had nine-month-old twins, and offered some free babysitting at our house on Saturday. I told my daughter we had surprise guests coming but didn't say who. The twins arrived, much to her surprise, and their mom started giving instructions to Missy about how to take care of them for the seven hours the parents would be gone. Missy's eyes got wider and wider, but we'd raised her to be polite, so she simply nodded.

---

of developing testosterone and estrogen can be comical. Take, for instance, the boy who eyes a girl, then slams his locker shut much more loudly than necessary when she smiles at another boy. His day is ruined. Then there's the girl who doodles her first name with the last name of a boy she likes, just to see what they look like together.

Especially for Boys

For as long as you can remember, your son hasn't thought girls were all that interesting. In fact, a couple short years ago, he ran from them, yelling, "Cooties!" Now, all of a sudden, he's walking down the hallway, checking out the tail of the girl in front of him as she walks to class.

When the parents left, I told Missy, "It's time for you to learn how to take care of babies, since you're heading in the direction of becoming sexually active. Your mother and I will be here in the house, but these kids are your responsibility until nine tonight, when their parents return for them."

She stared at me, shocked and angry. Then she lifted her chin and said, "Fine," with an "I'll show you" look in her eyes.

Three hours later, when she was trying to feed the two babies dinner, Missy looked a little ragged around the edges. By eight p.m. I could tell she was praying for the next hour to pass quickly. When she finally handed the babies back into their parents' arms and the door closed, she walked by me without saying a word and went straight to bed.

The next morning Missy was really tired. But she said, "Okay, Dad, I get it."

Funny thing, when that boy phoned later that day to get together, Missy said, "You know, I don't think this thing between us is working out."

Guess my daughter got the wake-up call she needed . . . before she had to plunge into motherhood for real.

Alan, Tennessee

Hmm, maybe I was wrong, he's thinking. *She is kinda cute.* He struts down the hallway, passes her, and does a little muscle flex, competing with the other boys for that girl's attention.

A short while later, he's in gym, and it's time for square dancing. That same girl puts her hand out and says, "Will you be my partner?"

He takes her hand and says to himself, *Crap. I'm holding a girl's hand . . . and it's kinda soft.*

It doesn't take long before they're dancing to the dance . . . in more ways than one. It's called *puppy love*, and it's the first explosion into exploring feelings about the opposite sex.

It's the time when a boy goes out of his way to do bra checks. He scopes out girls to see how they're developing and bumps into them, hoping he can tell whether or not she's wearing a bra. He has a sudden urge to carry his backpack or notebook in front of his waist because a certain part of his male anatomy wants to pop out and say hello. He experiences wet dreams at night and stuffs his sheets in the laundry before anybody in the family notices. But he won't forget the sexual images that swirl through his head. When the sexual pressure builds up too much, he might find himself masturbating . . . and worrying about the myth that it might make him go blind. Still, he can't stop doing it. Nor can he stop thinking about the information his older brother told him—about first base, second base, third base, and the ooh-la-la fourth base.

> What girls want most is cuddling and closeness, but that doesn't mean they want sex.

He dreams of being a knight in shining armor, rescuing the girl. He's just not quite sure how to make his entrance on that white steed.

What do boys this age need to know about girls? What girls want most is cuddling and closeness, but that doesn't mean they want sex. Girls don't want to be pushed, pinched, or hit. They don't relate in the same ways boys do to each other. In fact, if you slug them on the shoulder to show them you like them, they think exactly the opposite and, worse, may cry. But they do appreciate a little male bicep flexing every once in a while.

Girls want heroes—boys who will be kind to them, take care of them, and respect them.

Boys need to learn respect for the opposite sex. Two good questions for boys to ask are:

- Is this behavior something you would do with your sister or your mother? If not, don't do it.
- Would you want your future wife to tell you someone did this with her someday? If not, don't do it.

Especially for Girls

In middle school, girls change from thinking, *Boys are dumb*, to, *Ooh, isn't he cute?*

Girls comb each other's hair, sing into hair dryers, and dance around the room, wearing training bras even when they have nothing to train. Some already have their periods by now; others are still awaiting this rite of passage. If they're early bloomers, they might think they are ready for boys. After all, they've seen a lot of PG-13 movies by now and researched sex on the internet.

But most of them aren't dreaming of sex; they're dreaming of closeness—of some boy liking them enough to cuddle them, hold their hand, and tell them they're special. Some are even starting to imagine what their weddings will be like, how many kids they'll have, the house they'll live in. They're way down the track in their relational processing, blowing past the boys who can only think, *Oh, check it out. She's wearing a bra.*

I still remember the first time our oldest daughter, Holly, wore a bra. She had it on at the dinner table, and it was obviously uncomfortable. My wife and I tried hard to keep from laughing as Holly kept gyrating her shoulders, trying to adjust the thing so it would be more comfortable. She honestly had nothing yet to train in that training bra, but still, it was a significant milestone of growing up.

This is the time when parents need to pay particular attention to what their girls are wearing. Most girls have no idea how tantalizing their developing shape will be to boys, or how much they'll be ogled. But think of it this way—do you really want your daughter showing off her hardware? If not, you might want to suggest she change the shirt that's a little too tight, has a neckline that reveals too much curve, or is a bit too see-through.

I always told my girls that subtlety is far more sexy than showing it all. Males are drawn to mystery. If you show all you've got, there's nothing for a boy to look forward to! Yes, there are those boys who want all revealed, but seriously, are those really the boys you want your daughter hanging around?

> Subtlety is far more sexy than showing it all. Males are drawn to mystery.

In today's world where actresses show up on stage wearing basically nothing, *modesty* seems like an old-fashioned word. But God has built it into each of us, and if we listen to it, it'll protect us from trouble. Modesty is that little nudge that tells us when something is okay to do and when it's not. When kids fall into wearing sexy or revealing clothing, they can more easily become sexually active. That's because they depress the God-given nudge toward modesty and allow others to ogle them and then move too closely into their personal spaces—both physically and emotionally. Not only can that step reap lifelong physical repercussions, but once sexual innocence is shattered, the images planted by those experiences are difficult to remove.

What do girls need to know? They need to know how boys think. One peek at the vision of a cute feminine behind can make a boy salivate. A girl sitting in a boy's lap can make Mr. Happy more than happy. Because a boy is so visually stimulated, how a girl dresses greatly affects the way he perceives her.

Girls need to be encouraged to become friends with both sexes. Because girls are relational creatures, when they get boyfriends, they tend to become exclusive and miss developing other friendships with peers.

Girls also should be cautioned about giving away their secrets. Friends change fast in middle school, and betrayal happens even faster. Some will claim to be friends, but how many of those will stick close when the going gets tough?

And finally, girls need to know that we all have unique features, including body size, weight, and shape. Each girl is created to be uniquely her—valuable and worthy. She doesn't have to go on a diet, wear makeup, or look like somebody else to be important. What people think of as beautiful will come and go. In the Victorian era, chubby angels were in vogue. In other eras, stick-thin has been in vogue. Trends will change, but the person you are at your core is what is important.

Why Discuss Sex?

I talk to a lot of parents who tell me, "I've already told my daughter that she can't date until she's 16." I've got news for you. Today's kids don't date. They hang out or hook up. Dating is an archaic notion. Oral sex, fondling breasts or penises, or groping other body parts isn't considered sex either.

Parents who are chickens wait for the school to do "the talk" in health class. They also are the same parents who push their daughters to date early, because they live in fear that otherwise their kids will get lost in the shuffle. But silence about sex promotes shame. It tells a kid that sex is dirty and should be hidden, which only makes it more intriguing to figure out.

Annie grew up in a home where her parents insisted she be completely clothed at all times. She couldn't even walk down the hallway to the bathroom in just her pajamas. She had to wear her robe over them. The rules were the same for her brother, two years older. Sex and reproduction were taboo subjects. When Annie developed, her mother took her shopping to buy loose sweaters.

By the end of middle school, Annie was secretly promiscuous. She would go braless, wear an undershirt under her sweater, and then strip off that sweater or tie it around her waist as soon as she got to school. It wasn't long before her obvious shape attracted the attention of older boys. As for her brother? He started having sex in tenth grade, once he had his license, could drive, and therefore could come up with excuses for being late getting home.

When Annie, who is now in college, told me her story, I asked why she was so drawn to sexual experiences. "Anything having to do with the opposite sex was mysterious and hidden at home, so I had to find out what the secret was. I wanted to know what a penis looked like and how people had sex. The first time I hooked up was during spring break in eighth grade, when my mom was on a business trip. It was a painful experience. After that, I felt like I was used material, so what did it matter if I had sex again? I got attention from guys that made me feel good—at least temporarily." She shrugged. "It was more attention than I ever got from my father, who was hardly ever home and barely talked to me when he was."

> Today's kids don't date. They hang out or hook up. Dating is an archaic notion.

That first experience set off a pattern for Annie that continued into the rest of middle school, through high school, and into the summer before college, when she found out she was pregnant by a guy she barely knew. Three months later, she miscarried. The reality of that experience shook her up and changed her course. "I don't want any girl or guy to go through what I did. To this day, my parents have no idea how much I've experimented sexually. And I could never tell them."

How would Annie's experience have been different if that mother and father had set aside their own squeamishness and conservative backgrounds and talked straightforwardly about body changes, hormones, and the way sexual reproduction worked? And what if her father had been an actively engaged father instead of a distant man who provoked Annie's intense daddy hunger? Instead, by their refusal to address the topic of sex in their home, both parents set up their children for years of sexual experimentation, simply because they were curious. Sadly, Annie's brother is still pursuing that lifestyle and leaving a lot of devastated young women in his wake.

> Your middle-schooler will explore sexuality. Where would you rather he get his info? From you, or from his misinformed, over-the-top peers?

Some parents don't discuss sex because they grew up in conservative homes where you simply didn't talk about such issues. Others don't discuss it because they were sexually active themselves at a young age, so they don't feel they have a right to warn their kids. "After all," they say, "I did it." But that's the very reason they should talk to their kids about it.

However, sometimes parents fear a child will ask, "Mom, did you have sex in junior high?" It's always important to be honest, but that doesn't mean you give your middle-schooler a blow-by-blow of your sexual history. Simply say, "When I was in junior high, I had some experiences I would rather not have had. I don't want you to ever feel dirty or used, like I did. I want more for you."

Smart parents take control of their kids' sex education. Your middle-schooler will explore sexuality. Where would you rather he get his info? From you, or from his misinformed, over-the-top peers?

Talking about Sex

When I'm at middle schools, I often do a presentation called "Help! I've Got a Rocket in My Pocket." It's my way of addressing the hormones that kick in, body changes, and the sexual urges that can at times feel like an uncontrollable force about ready to explode into outer space.

How do you proceed when you notice your middle-schooler scoping out the opposite sex? "That's a natural thing to happen at your age," you mention casually. "So of course you'd pay attention. I did the same thing at your age. Girls/guys are fascinating creatures, aren't they?"

But where do you go from there? Here's what I suggest.

Share Your Perspective and Values

Now is a good time to solidify your family's worldview and values. "Sex is a good thing. In fact, a great thing. God Almighty created it. In the right context, it draws two people together in a powerful connection, and that's worth waiting for. Sex is not only a physical happening but an emotional, mental, and spiritual relationship in which you give pieces of yourself to another person. It's not just hooking up. The act itself is intimate and designed to cement two people for a deeper relationship—a lifetime marriage."

However, just giving your preadolescent that information isn't enough. For most of them, marriage is a long time off. They need more than values to stand against peer pressure.

Give Specific Reasons and Statistics

You need to honestly share with them the reasons not to get involved sexually. The consequences of sex outside of marriage are devastating:

- Venereal diseases, which are not only uncomfortable but can affect future fertility and even be life threatening.
- Pregnancy. "Four in 10 children are born to unwed mothers," says a recent study.[2]
- A broken heart, when the person you think loves you takes what he wants and then walks away scot-free, while you're left in a mess because you believed all his promises.
- The inability to form good, healthy relationships. You fear being dumped, so you can never trust anyone and gain that deeper relationship you long for at your core. And because sex has taken over your relationship, it short-circuits your ability to give and receive the connection of true, lasting love. You don't know how to have a relationship without the physical aspect of it.
- Pieces of your heart and body are scattered among people who use you, abuse you, and don't deserve your trust.

But all of those reasons, as good as they are, may still go over your child's head and not enter her heart. After all, what 13-year-old girl can imagine herself pregnant or with an STD? What 12-year-old in puppy love can imagine his girlfriend dumping him? Still, you would be remiss not to give your middle-schooler the information.

Too many girls do all the giving, and too many boys do all the taking. A relationship is never a win-win if it isn't for both parties. Outside of marriage, it's never a win-win for the girl. The girl is nearly always the pleaser, and the boy is nearly always the controller. And pleasers are almost always the ones who will hook up with the controlling male who takes advantage of her lack of self-worth. Give your middle-schooler every reason you can think of not to fall into that trap.

But it all starts with you and the relationship that middle-schooler has with you. Do you treat him or her as worthy and valuable? If you do, they'll have less reason to go looking for love in all the wrong places.

Emphasize That What Is Private Stays Private

Preadolescents need to know that no one touches their private parts. Here's an easy way to explain what private parts are: "If it's covered by a swimsuit, no one but you should be touching it." Kids also need to know that if anyone attempts to touch a private part, they should tell Mom or Dad immediately. "I promise you won't get in trouble for sharing that information with me. But I need to know if anything makes you uncomfortable. That includes pictures people might try to show you or things they might say to you. If someone asks you to keep a secret from your parents, that isn't acceptable either. If you are ever in a situation and have that 'uh-oh' feeling, you need to listen to it. There's something happening that shouldn't be happening, and I need to know so I can help."

Having such a conversation with your child is increasingly important because your preadolescent is outside your sphere of influence more as he grows older. However, the sad fact is that your child has a much higher probability of being abused by a family member, coach, or pastor/priest than of being raped or kidnapped by a complete stranger. There are a lot of perverted people in the world. They don't walk around with signs around their neck that say, "I'm a child molester." However, name just about any profession—including teachers, firefighters, police officers, and mail carriers—and you'll find a child molester among them. That's also why I am not a fan of sleepovers during the preadolescent years. They aren't as innocuous as you might think.

Sexual abuse is a sad fact in today's world. Because of its long-term effect on children, go out of your way to protect your child from it as much as humanly possible.

Clarify Your Terminology

There is a huge maturity level difference in middle-schoolers, and that influences not only what they know about sex but their understanding of the terms they use. For example, the terms *hot* or *hottie* can have a multitude of meanings—from sexy, to good-looking, to well-dressed. To 13-year-old Abby, the term *making out* meant just kissing. To her parents, the term meant a lot more than that. So imagine their shock when they discovered that Abby had texted a friend about her and Adam, an eighth-grade boy, "making out" behind the school.

> Golden Rule #1: Keep your pants zipped up.
> Golden Rule #2: Keep your hands to yourself.

When you use sexual terms, be straightforward about what you mean by them, since your definitions may not match what your child thinks. No, this isn't a comfortable subject, but neither would you want to discover that your 12-year-old son had gonorrhea or your 13-year-old daughter was pregnant because they didn't understand what "bases" were okay to touch and not touch.

There are two golden rules. Follow them and you'll never have to worry about STDs, pregnancy, or leaving pieces of yourself behind anywhere, physically or emotionally.

Golden Rule #1: Keep your pants zipped up.

Golden Rule #2: Keep your hands to yourself.

Simple and easy, isn't it? It's all about respect. If you respect yourself and others, you'll follow those golden rules.

Confirm Your Love of and Belief in Your Child

"Those are only some of the reasons," you conclude to your child, "but I hope I've given you a few things to think about. Most of all, I love you too much, honey, for any of those bad things to happen to you as a result of having sex. You are worthy of experiencing true love for a lifetime, and you deserve better. The person you're going to marry someday deserves better. I know this isn't a comfortable subject, but that's why I'm talking to you about it. You're heading into a time of life when not only will you be away from your family more, but peer pressure will intensify, and you might be tempted to do things you'd normally never do. I want you to have as many facts as possible to help you make wise decisions, because what you do in these middle-school years and beyond can greatly impact your future. And I know you. You're a smart kid, and I believe you will always choose to do the right thing, even when it's not easy."

> "I want you to have as many facts as possible to help you make wise decisions."

Blue Chip or Penny Stocks?

Who do you trust most in this world to teach your kid about sex?

I hope your answer is you. After all, who knows your kid better than you? Be careful who you trust to teach your kid about sex. It's not your kid's job to figure things out on his own. You have the opportunity to create either a home-grown kid, who shares your thoughts, ideas, and values, or a society-manufactured kid, where anything that culture says goes. I hope you choose the first option.

When I talked to my four daughters about sex, I used the analogy of stocks, since I had also talked with them about investing money. Here's a peek at what I said:

"We've talked a little bit about how you can make money through stocks. Well, there are some stocks called blue chip stocks—for example, stocks like Coca-Cola and Pepsi. Great stocks whose value will never go away. In fact, they'll pay great dividends over the years. People won't trade them flippantly or carelessly; they'll hold on to those stocks because they know they won't lose value. They'll only gain value.

"You, my girl, are like a blue chip stock. Among your peers, your stock value goes up if you're not like every other girl or guy. You know that I was a horrible student, always getting in trouble. But the parents of the girls in my class loved me because I had a reputation for not drinking and I could be trusted to treat a girl right. And that's because my mom taught me to treat girls like blue chip stocks, not penny stocks. Penny stocks are the kind you make a quick buck off of and then get rid of or trade in for something better. I saw girls as blue chip stocks. And that's how I see you."

Don't you think that made each of my daughters feel special? Loved by her daddy?

The truth is, parent, that many boys will find a girl who thinks of herself as a penny stock—a girl who doesn't feel good about herself, doesn't think she's worthy, and has a good degree of daddy hunger in her life. Those boys will pay attention to her in order to gain what they want—a sexual notch in their belt buckle that they can brag about in the locker room. And that girl will find herself doing things that, ten years later, she'll find disgusting. The same is true these days for young men who are the targets of sexually aggressive females.

But what if, instead of thinking of themselves as penny stocks, middle-schoolers treated themselves as who they really are—blue chip stocks? Stocks well worth waiting for? Stocks that will be even more valuable after they've matured? The kind that people want to invest in and keep for a lifetime?

Now that's the type of thinking that will encourage middle-schoolers to have respect for themselves and others and to gain the perspective that "wow" sex is worth waiting for.

10

Understanding Who Your Kid Really Is

. . . And how he or she got to be that way.

My grandson, Conner, is 11, beginning the middle-school years. He's always been a wonderful kid, truly compassionate and treating others with kindness. He's the kid who, a couple of years ago, stood at the dinner table and spontaneously told every person there a specific thing he appreciated about them. It brought tears to my eyes. I couldn't help but think, *Wow, Krissy and Dennis have done things right to have a kid like that.*

To this day Conner hasn't lost that sense of kindness and compassion, but I get a kick out of the emerging signs of adolescence. When he was 10, he ripped off his shirt, threw it on the floor, adopted a Tarzan-like stance, and pounded his chest, roaring, "In your face, Grandpa!" Then he flexed his bicep . . . well, what would someday be a bicep. He had no muscle, so he put his other hand behind the muscle to push it up so it looked like he had something there. I had to chuckle. The testosterone was already starting to take over.

Let's be honest. Some days middle-schoolers are completely goofy, and other days they can be stupid or mean. On those days you wonder, *Did they really grow up in a home with parents?* Then again, are *you* always on your best behavior? Don't you have bad moments—er, days—too? And on those bad days, don't you want others to extend grace to you and then not continually bring up your bad behavior later? Your middle-schooler wants the same thing.

Personality 101

The kid you see in front of you now wasn't jammed into a space capsule, jettisoned from Cape Canaveral into space, and then *bam*, dropped into your living room. He's been there all along. In fact, by the age of six or seven, he already had formed his personality and cut his path in life. Don't believe me? Take a careful look at your children. Whatever personality your child had in his earlier years will be magnified in the middle-school years.

> Whatever personality your child had in his earlier years will be magnified in the middle-school years.

Was your son an introvert? Did he love to play by himself? Then is it any surprise now that, when he gets home from school, where he's been bombarded by noise and people, he withdraws to his room and you rarely see the critter?

Was your daughter bubbly? Making friends with everyone? An extrovert? Is it any surprise now that she has a group of girls gathered around her, talking 24/7?

When my granddaughter, Adeline, was eight years old, she hand-delivered a letter to me. (She and her family live a mile away.) I laughed out loud when I read it, because of what it revealed about her personality.

Dear Grandma and Grandpa,
For my birthday, I would like a Fin Fun mermaid tail.
My size is medium. The color I would like is petunia pink.
Finfunmermaid.com is the spot where you will find it. Don't
forget to . . . [She went on to describe specific directions about what we were to click on, how we were to view the options, which ones she wanted and didn't want, and how to order.]
Thank you for thinking about this.

Love, Adeline

At age eight, Adeline's worldview and personality were already set. No one is going to run over that strong-minded and precise little girl now or in the future. She already has a mastery of the internet that amazes me.

In contrast, at age eight, I was catching pollywogs. My world was small—the swamp close to my home and the creek half a mile away captured my leisure time.

Kids today live in a whirlwind, high-tech, warp speed, ever-changing world. That culture is imprinting more on them than we think. It influences who they are and what they aspire to be.

What Worldview Are You Reinforcing?

Everything in media and culture is telling today's kids, "You are the most important being on the planet." Many parents have already reinforced that worldview in their homes by putting kids' needs first, even before their spouse's. But that can only lead to a destructive path—kids who are "all about me."

But, as I said in my book *Have a Happy Family by Friday*, the core person of who you really are will determine, more than any other factor, if you will have a happy family or not. So the core person your son or daughter is now will also determine their future happiness.

What do kids need to learn about life during Planet Middle School?

- To consider others' feelings
- To be thoughtful and understanding
- To be gracious and kind
- To be a giver without expecting to receive

Do you have a middle-schooler like that?

Some of you are nodding. Others are shifting nervously. Some of you are leaping out of your comfy chair to push the panic button. But panicking won't help. Neither will blaming your spouse for the genes he or she brought into the mix.

What Kind of Parent Are You?

Before you can fix things you don't like about your kids, it's helpful to take a look at your own parenting style first. Take a minute to complete the quick "What Sounds Like You?" inventory on the next page. Go ahead, I'll wait.

Okay, did you finish the inventory? And were you honest? No peeking ahead? You tell your kids never to cheat, so don't do it yourself.

If you wrote down 1, 3, 6, or 9 (or any combination of those), you are an *authoritarian* parent. You like to call the shots, you run the show, and it's your way or the highway. In this time of middle school, where your child is straining toward independence, you're set for a head-to-head, nasty battle. And you've got a lot more to lose than your child does. He knows exactly what buttons to push to drive you completely insane and what will embarrass you in front of your colleagues.

If you wrote down 2, 4, or 7 (or any combination of those), you're a *permissive* parent. You bend over backwards to do everything for your child and make sure she is happy, happy, happy. You want to smooth her highways in life. But doing everything for your

What Sounds Like You?

Which of these are you most likely to say to your middle-schooler?

1. "I told you to get it done. I shouldn't have to tell you again."
2. "Sure, honey, whatever you want. Sounds good to me."
3. "I'm the adult here. You're the kid. I don't need to explain myself to you."
4. "I guess I could leave work now to take you to your friend's. But couldn't you wait until I get home?"
5. "I know you want those shoes, but we can't afford them right now. Let's discuss some options. Maybe you could save up your allowance."
6. "I said no, and I mean no! What, are your ears clogged?"
7. "Wait until your father leaves for the office. Then we'll figure it out. We don't have to tell him. It'll be our little secret."
8. "Sounds like you've got a boatload of homework tonight. I know you'll not only get it all done, but you'll get it done right and on time. I have faith in you."
9. "I expect you to be on your best behavior at the store. If you aren't, I won't buy you what we talked about."
10. "I noticed you were sitting by the new girl after school today. That made me smile, because it showed me a lot about your heart and who you are."

Write down all the numbers that sound most like you.

child when she is trying to separate herself from you won't gain her friendship (something permissive parents strive to have with their kids). It'll make her think she can run over you, use you, and say anything to you, and you'll still do her bidding. But you're not put on this earth so your child can wipe her shoes on you.

> Too much control and not enough control are disconcerting for children who need guidelines and boundaries in order to feel safe.

Both of these parenting styles—authoritarian and permissive—will backfire on you during the middle-school years. Either extreme creates chaos in your home. Too much control and not enough control are disconcerting for children who need guidelines and boundaries in order to feel safe.

If you wrote down 5, 8, or 10 (or any combination of those), you're an *authoritative* parent. You always listen to what your kids say, but you don't cave in and always do what they want. You treat your children as equals, but you each play differing roles—you are the parent, and they are the children. In situations you let reality be the teacher. You know that if kids save for and work hard for an item, they will own it themselves and take care of it. You're always looking for the best in your kids and encouraging their acts of kindness.

> Your kids are still kids. They need you more than they'll ever admit.

Parenting styles greatly influence your child's response to you and to life in general. Your kids aren't planning to make your life miserable. They're simply responding in the way they've been trained to respond. What's most important is that you realize what a unique time middle school is. Your kids are still kids. They need you more than they'll ever admit. And at this juncture, you can still have a great influence on the trajectory of their life.

What Kind of Child Do You Have Right Now?

What kind of child do you want? What kind of adult do you want that child to become? *Planet Middle School* will help you get there. But first you have to understand who your child really is and how she got to be that way.

The Thrill Seeker

These kids are Ms. and Mr. Excitement, and they have the need to be right in the middle of everything. She's the queen of Dramaville, where every small occurrence becomes a crisis. He flashes from one extreme to another in a matter of seconds. These kids are often loud and charismatic, having the natural people skills to be able to gain a following. But what they're best at is drawing attention to themselves. They're entertaining and good at basic things like having fun. However, they're also very insecure, which is why they crave being in the limelight.

What kind of home are the thrill seekers from? They grow up in an environment where people are very competitive. Mom and Dad compete in marriage; the kids compete for Dad's and Mom's attention. This family worships material things and success. After all, success makes you a beautiful, well-liked person. The things you have and acquire, especially trendy things, put you at the top of the ladder. They make you feel better about yourself and your position in life.

The Wallflower

These middle-schoolers hang on the fringes of the crowd. They don't volunteer for anything. In fact, they hope no one will notice them because getting attention is never a positive thing. If anyone says anything critical, they melt into a puddle on the floor and can't recover. Fear runs their lives. Because they fear new situations and new relationships, they don't engage in either. They stay to themselves in order to retain some semblance of control. They're always on the outside of life looking in, but frankly, that's fine with them. That means never risking being criticized and put down. His solace might be in getting good grades or perhaps working independently on an Eagle Scout badge. She reads thick novels and researches unique music groups on the internet . . . all within the safe confines of her bedroom.

What kind of home are the wallflowers from? They grow up in a house where things are pretty laid out for all the kids in terms of expectations. Perfection reigns, and expectations are off-the-charts high. Making any mistake is fatal. They are not allowed to bring home bad grades. When they get to middle school, where they have a bit more freedom, they don't know what to do with that

What Worked for Us

We have three kids—an 11-year-old son, an 8-year-old daughter, and a 6-year-old son.

Mitch, our firstborn, has always been a handful, but when he started sixth grade, his attitude got worse. The teachers said he made sarcastic comments about other classmates, and at home he constantly picked on his sister and made her cry. We had no idea what to do. So we tried a new system. We told Mitch that if he could be nice to his sister for a whole month, we'd get him an iPod. It worked for three days. A week later, Mitch had his iPod.

"Where did you get that?" I asked him.

He shrugged. "Mom got it for me."

Suddenly it hit me. Mitch was a pain in the backside because he was playing my wife and me against each other. Worse, he was getting away with it. My wife and I had a long talk. She cried. I felt bad. But I knew things had to change. We were headed downhill fast with our son.

freedom. Their lives have been prescribed for them. Wallflowers are like trains that stay firmly within the rails laid out for them, never changing tracks . . . out of fear.

The "It's All about Me" Prince or Princess

Life is easy when everything is all about you—at least for a while. These kids are self-centered and think the world revolves around them. They act like it too. They can't be in a group without turning the focus to themselves. They're always asking, "What's in this for me?" They reign supreme among their siblings and treat others as if they are servants, meant to make their lives better and easier. This technique is temporary, until a more powerful prince or princess comes along and knocks them right off their pedestal. Then they might find themselves shockingly friendless.

At last we agreed that Mitch's life was going to be "streamlined" (that was the way we decided to put it) while we worked on his attitude. That meant his iPod went back in the box, we no longer paid for his extra internet minutes on his cell phone so he could game, and he didn't get to play with his friends after school and on Saturdays anymore.

He majorly tested us, especially my wife. She started to break down once, then realized what she was doing and simply walked out of the room, away from the temptation. Later he tried to play me against her.

It took five weeks of streamlining, but Mitch finally saw we meant business. He walked around like a zombie for a while, not knowing what to do with himself since he couldn't do his regular activities.

Then one day I walked in the kitchen and stopped, shocked. Mitch was sitting at the table, helping his sister with her math homework. He'd even gotten milk out of the fridge for our 6-year-old. Well, wonders never cease. That was the day things changed in our home . . . for the good.

Mark, Illinois

What kind of home are the "it's all about me" princes or princesses from? Sometimes a single-child home, where they are used to the sole attention of two doting parents. Children from wealthy families and firstborn sons also can be used to more attention than they should receive. These pampered darlings are very easy to pick out, because nobody can put up with them for long. Honestly, they irritate the heck out of everyone who comes in contact with them, except for their adoring mama and papa.

The Middle-of-the-Road Charlie/Charlotte

Whichever way the wind blows, these kids waffle back and forth with it. They exhibit very few leadership qualities. They'd much rather go with the flow of what everybody else does. When asked what they think, they'll hedge. "Oh, you know, I agree with you." These middle-schoolers will do things that are completely out of character, not matching the values they grew up with, merely to be "one of the group." They'll laugh at jokes they don't understand. They'll say yes to things they're not even sure they're saying yes to. Their motto? Peace at any price.

> I can guarantee that child #2 won't be like child #1.

What kind of home are the middle-of-the-road Charlies/Charlottes from? Most likely they have one parent who is a pleaser, and usually it's the mom. She doesn't have enough backbone to stand up for herself and say no to anyone, including her kids and her husband. She finds acceptance by going along with what others think and say. If she goes to a restaurant, she asks the server, "What do you think is good?" Honestly, how would the server know what an individual he's never met likes? She lacks self-worth, and that pleaser mentality has transferred to her child.

However, the rub comes when there are two or more kids in the family, because I can guarantee that child #2 won't be like child

#1. If one's a pleaser, the other is definitely not. He'll see what's up with his pleaser brother or sister and go completely the opposite direction. So the parents end up with one limp noodle and another that refuses to get in the pot to be cooked.

The Antiestablishment Rebel

These are the middle-schoolers who are against anything you say, no matter what it is. If you ask them to do anything, they're "not gonna do it." They are critical of everything and everybody, most particularly authority figures. Nobody but them knows anything. Keep in mind that they're only 11 to 13 years old, but they think they have the answers to life already in their back pocket. Rebellion is written all over them. Many of these kids have also taken a good look at the adults around them and seen their phoniness. The ones from faith-based families may balk at going to church because of the hypocrisy they see there.

Basically, these kids have an axe to grind. With their hairstyles, clothing tastes, and attitudes, they're saying loudly, "I'm not going to be you, and I'm not going to be what you think I ought to be. You're certainly not who you ought to be. So who are you to tell me what to do?"

What kind of home are the antiestablishment rebels from? Take one peek, and you'll see a dysfunctional home with little stability. The relational signals people give each other change daily or even from hour to hour. There's little or no training and, as such, not much moral development for the child. There's a basic lack of understanding or caring about other people's feelings and ideas. Everyone does what they feel like doing, and they don't give in to anyone else. What's important is winning—winning a fight or making your point.

The antiestablishment rebel is often conflicted, caught in the middle between the parents (if there are two parents in the home) who give him opposite signals. He might feel like a wishbone—pulled both ways, with different expectations from each parent, and about to snap. Perhaps a parent favors one child over another or disregards the individuality in their kids. A competitive spirit has always paid off. Usually at least one parent is overprescriptive and granite-like in believing there is only one right way to do everything—his way.

> Extremes always cause rebellion.

Simply stated, extremes always cause rebellion. Rebellious, antiestablishment kids can come either from authoritarian parents, who never gave them their own choice about anything, or from laissez-faire, anything-goes parents, who didn't stand up for anything. Or they may have had one parent of each type.

The Missionary

These are the kids who are almost too good to be true. They're on target, the future movers and shakers of the world. They're always on a mission; that's why I call them the missionaries. They have a strong sense of responsibility and an unshakable sense of what is right and what is wrong. Their value system is highly developed. They're not satisfied with giving less than 100 percent of themselves. They also have high expectations for others, which can sometimes run them into trouble with group members who aren't as committed to the cause. Dedicated, diligent, hardworking, and confident, they have positive self-worth. They tend to see the big picture and are ready to work to make it happen.

What kind of home are the missionaries from? They come from homes where creativity, independent thinking, and forward action are all encouraged. Parents are supportive of their children's efforts. They show up at their concerts and games and allow their kids to grow in the bent they seem to be turned in or directed toward. The parents are authoritative—they are in authority over their children but treat them with respect, unconditional love, and acceptance. They provide a strong sense of belonging to the family and major on responsibility and accountability so their children feel competent in today's world. As a result, these children are extremely successful in life. They are leaders. They are also few and far between, and we desperately need more of them. We need the kinds of homes where balance and good judgment reign, not volatile emotions.

Of all the middle-schoolers described, which one most closely resembles yours? Do you now have a better idea of why she is the way she is? If not, reread the kind of home she's from. Some of you will pat yourselves on the back. Others will say, "Hey, I've got some work to do . . . and I think I might need to start on myself first." And you might be right.

In the meanwhile, what behaviors do you let go, and what do you not let go?

Reinventing: Part of Growing Up

I saw an ad once that featured a preadolescent boy who walked into the living room at his house. He was wearing black lipstick, white makeup, and all black clothing. He turned to his parents and gave them a weird look.

The wife whispered to her husband, "There's something wrong with him."

The husband whispered back, "I hope it's just a stage."

Middle school is a time of exploration—or, in truth, "reinventing yourself." When I was in middle school, some friends and I bleached our hair at one of the guys' houses. Mine came out semi-orange. Thankfully, it was gone in a couple of days. My mother, wisely, said nothing.

For years, you've probably shopped for your child's clothing—with or without your child. Now your child is developing his own taste, and suddenly Mama's won't do.

There are some kids who are way out there in the stratosphere with their appearance. They seem to be saying by their hairstyle and clothing, "Notice me." They're also saying, "I'm going to be who I want to be. . . . Well, I guess I don't know what or who I want to be, but I'm working on it."

> Changing clothes and hairstyles is a statement of emerging individuality.

Either way, changing clothes and hairstyles is a statement of emerging individuality.

When I was an assistant dean of students at the University of Arizona, I saw a fascinating pattern. Young adults from wealthy, traditional towns—such as Wilmette, North Bluff, and Shaker Heights—would come out with their parents to visit the school. Those students would wear preppy, classy, traditional clothing. Yet within a month of them actually being at the school, I could hardly recognize some of those same kids. They didn't wear clothes; they wore costumes. In fact, they spent an inordinate amount of time trying to look cooler than cool.

Funny thing is, by the time most of them graduated, they were back to the traditional look to do their job interviews. The nose rings and other piercings had mysteriously gone missing. What were these kids doing? Simply reinventing themselves, away from Mom and Dad's eagle eye. But when they graduated, they reverted back to many of the same values and the look they'd grown up with.

There are commonalities between a kid going into middle school and a young adult going off to college. Both are times of huge transition, when lots of independence comes their way, as well as a lot of stresses and strains. Either they make it on their own or they don't. What you see on the surface isn't always what you get. Middle-schoolers are all auditioning for the parts they want in life, and sometimes what they come up with as a costume is laughable . . . or maddening.

For a lot of middle-schoolers, abnormal dress and behavior are simply just a stage. Some try on different personalities the way they try on clothes. If your child decides she has to put a blue streak in her hair for a while, is it really the end of the world? Even if you do have to explain it to a very confused grandpa, who wonders if she fell in the paint while you painted your front porch. No, eventually it will fade, and she'll be on to something else . . . like a neon-pink streak. What's important is that you pay attention to your child's heart more than what is on the outside. What's outside will morph as she reinvents herself.

However, if your middle-schooler wants to be tattooed or pierced all over, would you let that go?

Some parents acquiesce too easily. "I guess it's what kids do these days." But when the choice has to do with permanent body markings or piercings, the wise parent of a middle-schooler isn't afraid to be the parent and say no. "I know you want that, and I hear you loud and clear. But it's not going to happen now or in the immediate future. Your body is too beautiful and precious to have permanent markings like that cluttering it up. I know you won't believe this now, but someday you'd wish you hadn't done that. And since you can't get a tattoo under the age of 18 without my permission, you're out of luck."

> Do you really want your kid to be like everybody else?

Yes, there are those times you need to stand up and be a parent.

Is your kid going to like you for taking that stand? No, especially if he wants something that everybody else has. But do you really want your kid to be like everybody else? Take a look around at other middle-schoolers. Hopefully, the answer is no.

And here's another practical reason. Relationships and tastes change at lightning speed in middle school. If your 13-year-old son gets his girlfriend's initials tattooed on his bicep, will he really still want them there a month later when they've broken up?

You will have to make judgment calls all throughout your child's growing up. Tattoos and piercings are things you have to decide for yourself. But there are two issues you should never acquiesce on. One is drugs, the scourge of our nation. The other is sex. The girl who gets pregnant in middle school has a much lower chance than other young women her age for a good life, and the baby who is a product of that pregnancy has an even lower chance for a good life, unless the middle-schooler allows the baby to be adopted. The risk for venereal disease is high and can cause infertility later. Also, the concept of sex is way overdone. It's simply an excuse for horny boys who are beginning to peak in sexual interest to use girls.

Telling kids, "Sex out of wedlock is wrong," won't change anything, though. Instead, the emphasis has to be on the middle-schooler. "You are a special person. I don't want you to become a statistic, used by anybody. You deserve more than that."

The summer my daughter Hannah finished middle school, I gave her a *Dos Pesos*—a little gold coin—that was minted in 1945. On the note that went with it, I had written, "You're growing up, my precious Hannah. This gold coin signifies your worth in my eyes and in God's eyes." The coin had a loop on it so she could put it on a chain. But I didn't give the chain to her. And I didn't tell her, "Okay, we'll go shopping and I'll buy you a chain." No, I wanted her to decide what she would do with the coin. I wanted her to go to the trouble of finding a special chain herself.

She could have said, "Thanks, Dad," hugged me, and stored the gold coin in her jewelry box.

Instead, she took money that she'd earned, searched for a chain she loved, and bought it herself. Tears formed in my eyes when I saw the chain with the gold coin on it around her neck. From that moment on, whenever she needed a reminder of my love, God's love, and her worth, that necklace was there.

Even when I couldn't physically be there with her.

11

How to Talk So They'll Listen

. . . And how to know when to shut up.

Do any of these conversations sound familiar?

Parent: "Where have you been?"
Kid: "Out."

Parent: "How was your day?"
Kid: (Grunts and turns head toward the car window.)

Parent: "So what did you learn today?"
Kid: "Nothin'."

What would you give for your child to come home, tuck her cell phone into her backpack and plop it on the floor, and say to you, "I can't wait to tell you what happened today"? For most parents of middle-schoolers, that's a far-off dream.

But it doesn't have to be. If you want to change the dialogue of your conversation with your middle-schooler, you can.

Are You Talking—or Communicating?

Before we go any further, take the Communication 101 quiz below. Don't worry. You can easily complete it in less than a couple minutes. I'll wait right here.

Mmm, the majority of us can use some work in our communication skills, huh?

I asked a middle-schooler last week how he felt when his parents talked to him.

He looked at me blankly. "Talk *to* me? Nuh-uh, they talk *at* me—in my general direction—when they want me to do something."

Are you talking *to* your kids or *at* your kids? They're smart enough to know the difference.

Let's say you're online in the morning, reading a blog you love. You take a sip of coffee and say to your child, who's in the kitchen with you, "Your lunch is in the fridge. Remember to put it in your

Communication 101

Take this quick quiz to see how you and your kids are doing on communication basics. Answer yes or no to each statement.

- You say you're going to do something, and you do it.
- You ask your kids to help only once, and you trust them to follow through with your request.
- Your kids are respectful of your time and your conversations with others.
- You don't have to nag to get things done around the house.
- Your kids take directions from you well.
- Your kids feel free to ask you what you think about an issue or to ask for help.
- You listen respectfully to each other, and nobody has to get the last word.

backpack." That's talking *at* your kid. You're throwing at him factual information that you don't really need to say. After all, you've been packing his lunch and leaving it in the fridge for him to pick up since he's been in kindergarten. Not only that, you're treating him like he's still in kindergarten, reminding him to put it in his backpack. At his advanced age, he doesn't appreciate that.

Is it any wonder you get a double scowl and no thanks for your service?

> Are you talking *to* your kids or *at* your kids? They're smart enough to know the difference.

Contrast that with this scenario. You're online in the morning, reading a blog you love and sipping your coffee to wake yourself up. Your son enters the kitchen. You look up, catch his eye, and smile. "Hey, check this out. Only 20 percent of people who say they eat cereals like Wheaties in the morning actually eat Wheaties. Many of them eat Pop-Tarts." You laugh. "No wonder I don't like Wheaties. Want some of my brew?"

He nods, still his usual silent self, and you pour him some brew. "I put a surprise in your lunch," you say casually.

Your son perks up. "Really?" He yanks open the fridge and can't resist a peek in the bag. His face splits into a grin. "Mom, this is awesome. You made those homemade cinnamon donuts?"

"Yeah," you say. "And check the sack on the left of the fridge. Thought the guys might like some too."

By now your dragging-in-the-morning son looks like he just drank an espresso. You even get an awkward hug with a "Thanks, Mom!" as he races out the door, backpack and sack of donuts in hand, with one donut already in his mouth.

You grin after the door slams shut and think, *Well, that communication trick worked pretty nicely.*

What did you do? First, you stopped what you were doing to engage your child (as much as he was capable of engaging since he's not a morning person). Second, you made a general comment

190

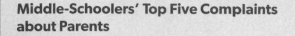

Middle-Schoolers' Top Five Complaints about Parents

1. "They don't understand me or the world I live in every day."
2. "They never listen."
3. "All they care about is whether I do my chores on time and keep my room clean."
4. "Dad's never around."
5. "Mom's too busy to talk."

about something you were reading to open the communication line, and it wasn't a comment he had to respond to. Third, you tempted him with coffee and then a surprise. Fourth, since you know how important peer acceptance is to him, you sweetened the deal and supplied a bag for his friends.

Now that's a very wise parent who wants to communicate to capture her son's heart.

Four Major Don'ts in Communicating with Your Middle-Schooler

If you want a two-way stream of conversation with your middle-schooler—without sparking a solar flare-up in your direction—here are four things you don't do.

#1: Don't Ask for Trouble When There Isn't Any

Arguing is a middle-schooler's middle name. Even the kid who has been fairly mellow all his life may turn a little combative. "Oh," you say to make conversation, "look at the sky. It's so blue!"

He blows out a breath. "No, it's aqua."

That's the beginning of those little feathers popping out on his baby bird wings. So expect that as a given, and don't let it fluff your feathers.

But you shouldn't let your child walk all over you either. When you need to, wave the parental flag to call a halt. Just make sure the flag isn't red.

If you want to stay out of an argument with your child, follow these simple rules:

- Say what you need to say once, and then walk away.
- Don't pour gasoline on the fire. Saying with an edge, "Well, aqua is a *shade* of blue . . . or didn't you know that?" only ups the ante on him wanting to win in combat.
- Don't feel you must have the last word. If you let him have it, chances are, later he might think, *Wow, that was a really dumb thing to say. What was wrong with me anyway?* You didn't even have to do the chiding. Sometimes I call this "defanging the werewolf."

If there is trouble and you have to confront it, present facts simply, without emotion connected to them. If you know your child stole something—you actually saw it happen—state the facts. Don't ask if she did it. State, "Kelsey, I saw you take money out of my purse this morning." Be straightforward. It doesn't leave any wiggle room for her to back out of the truth. Instead of an argument, the "I'm in trouble" mentality kicks in, and you'll likely have a meeker child to deal with.

Remember that not everything in life needs to be negotiated. Let your yes be yes and your no, no. Your child has to know you mean business when you say, "No, we're not going there," and that pleading, cajoling, or screaming won't change your mind. If you don't hold firm in this category, you'll end up with a DA in your home who will make it her business to best you at every argument.

#2: Don't Fall for the "Silence Is Golden" Philosophy

Many parents have taught their kids that silence is golden—and that if you do what Mom or Dad says, you might get a reward.

Just yesterday I was in the grocery store and heard a mom say to her younger child, "Mommy's talking now. If you're quiet, I'll get you a treat." The mom went on to yak with a friend on her cell phone.

Kids are often taught, "You do as you're told. You sit and listen. You obey all adults, no matter what." This is the authoritarian, barking-out-orders style of parenting that may work temporarily, when children are younger and you're a lot bigger, but it never, ever works in the preteen years. It creates rebellion and an "I'll show you" attitude. Take a look, parent. How big is your son now? In a year or two he might outweigh and outmuscle you. Can you really force him to do anything?

If that's been your modus operandi, it's time for a big change. Saying, "Do it because I said so, and I'm an adult," is not helpful. It's harmful. One of the things I always taught my kids was, "Deep inside you there's a barometer that tells you, *Hey, something's not right. There's danger here. I better be careful.* It's that little 'uh-oh' that goes off inside you. Always pay attention. If you listen to that barometer, you'll get yourself out of many situations before they become situations that could be harmful to you or others." If your child has been taught to obey adults no matter what and an adult approaches her inappropriately, how will your child respond? She'll likely go along with what the adult asks. See how dangerous that is in today's world?

> Saying, "Do it because I said so, and I'm an adult," is not helpful. It's harmful.

Stop and take the time to explain why you've asked your middle-schooler to do something or not to do something. Reveal consequences that might come. Affirm your trust in your child and that you know she'll do the right thing when the time comes. Silence might be good for a while, but it hurts in the long run. What you want most of all is a preteen who will dialogue with you on any subject that's important to her or to you.

#3: Don't Continue to Do What Doesn't Work

Have you ever walked through a cornfield that's set up like a maze, using bales of hay and cornstalks? If that maze is set up well, you might wander in and out of dead ends for quite a while before you finally figure out the direction to go. In the meanwhile, you feel like you're getting somewhere, only to turn a corner and find out it's another dead end.

If you keep doing what doesn't work in parenting, it's like walking through one of those mazes. You think you're getting somewhere, but then you run into another dead end. So if you're in the middle of a conflict with your child, ask yourself, *What's this argument really about?*

Often it's the same argument, except that the dialogue takes a slightly different form. If you are ever going to move ahead, past the conflict, you need to identify the fundamental disagreement. Sweeping the topic under the rug only creates an even bigger problem.

> Ask yourself, *What's this argument really about?*

When Patrick and Lucy married, Patrick became the instant father of three boys: 12, 11, and 6. The oldest boy and Patrick constantly butted heads. Finally, Patrick called a time-out and addressed what he'd figured out was the real issue. Jacob felt replaced as the head "man" of the house and was always competing with Patrick for his mom's attention. Once Patrick assured Jacob of his respect, said that he wasn't trying to take Jacob's place, and encouraged him to be a role model for his little brothers, the tension in the house dissipated greatly.

If you have tension in your home, take care of it now. Don't go to sleep without addressing the situation. For your family to move forward, you may have to tread lightly on some rocky ground, as Patrick did. But it will be worth it.

How do you start such a conversation?

- "I could be wrong . . ."
- "I might be out in left field on this . . ."
- "I don't have all the facts yet, but let's talk . . ."
- "I'd like to hear what you think, or your opinion on this . . ."

These are words that tell your child, "Hey, I'm not perfect, and I could be wrong. But I care what you think. Let's talk, and I'll listen."

When your child does talk, don't be Dr. Phil. Let your child say what's on his mind. Don't interrupt, overanalyze, or overinterpret. Take his words at face value. Think of your child right now as an overinflated balloon. If you don't allow some air to escape, he'll blow.

> Let your child say what's on his mind. Don't interrupt, overanalyze, or overinterpret. Take his words at face value.

The point of conversation—talking and listening—is to find common ground.

#4: Don't Blow Smoke at Them

Permissive parents fall easily into this category of "don'ts." "Oh, Johnny, you're just the best baseball player ever. Everybody saw you make the pitch that won the game. I bet you'll easily get on the high school baseball team this summer."

If Johnny has any brains in his head, he'll be thinking, *Uh, no, I'm not. That was a lucky pitch, the best one I've made all season, and I can name four guys on my team right now who can pitch better than me. And I don't even know if I want to play baseball next summer.* Your child knows when you're blowing smoke his way, and your praise doesn't feel good because it's false.

What Worked for Us

My daughter Lisa, 13, really wanted a tattoo. She'd googled them and found some designs she liked. But I know some things about my daughter. She doesn't like pain. Her tastes change fast. Real tattoos are permanent ink, unless you go through the painful process of having them removed. We also live in a conservative area, where tattoos are looked at as rebellious.

I tried all the typical parent tactics of "here's why you don't want a tattoo." It only made her dig in further.

Finally, I got help from my dad, who's retired and always up for some fun, and an artist friend. They found one of Lisa's favorite tattoos online, and our artist friend drew a rendition on my dad's chest and down his arm with ink that could wash off but looked real.

My dad showed up for dinner. He winked at me, then said, "I'm kinda hot. Want to ratchet up the AC in here?" He rolled up his right sleeve, unbuttoned a few buttons of his shirt, and fanned himself, revealing the tattoo.

My daughter's eyes about popped out of her head. "Grandpa, you got a *tattoo*?"

"Yup," he said. "Wanna see the whole thing?" He took off his shirt to display the tattoo in all its glory. "Pretty cool, huh? Sags a bit here and there, though," he added, accentuating where the wrinkles in his skin had wrinkled the tattoo.

"Uh, yeah . . . I guess," Lisa said.

Funny thing, she never mentioned a tattoo again after that.

You're right, Dr. Leman. Keeping your head and your sense of humor can end a lot of battles that don't need to be fought.

Frank, Ohio

What does feel good is your honest encouragement. "Wow, Johnny, that last pitch you made has to feel good. I know being part of the team means a lot to you."

Your daughter is grumpy and overwhelmed after school. It's not hard to tell. She's slamming her books around and muttering. Finally, she spouts like a teakettle, "Mom, I have so much homework. I'm never going to get it all done tonight."

What would the blowing-smoke parent say? "Oh, you poor thing. You have a project due tomorrow in science, and a paper in English? Both on one night? No wonder you're feeling stressed. Say, maybe I could . . ."

What would the authoritative parent who wants to encourage her child, yet teach her about life's reality and hard work, say? "Wow, sounds like you've got your plate full tonight. Knowing you, you'll not only get it done, but you'll do it well and on time." What is that parent really saying? "I believe in you. You're competent, and you'll get your tasks done." That speaks volumes to your child about who you think she is.

Five Ways to Keep Communication Open

There are times when your child won't want to talk, and that's okay. But even in those quiet times, your attitude toward her makes all the difference in her willingness to talk with you when she's ready. How can you keep your communication lifeline open?

#1: See Life through Your Child's Eyes

You walk into the living room, and your middle-schooler is watching a television show you think is ridiculous. Worse, your son is saying, "Awesome!" What do you do?

Drop your jaw and say, "What on earth? That's the stupidest thing I've ever seen!"

Or do you say, "Oh, really? Tell me what just happened on the show. I missed it."

Parent, some of the best conversation starters you can have are "Really?" and "Tell me more about that."

When your son tells you what happened, you'll be acutely aware of something fascinating—what the world looks like to your son. He often sees life completely differently from you. What you think is hip and cool isn't to him. And what he thinks is hip and cool will probably raise your eyebrows. But if you want your kids to be able to talk to you about anything, then get used to talking about anything.

That means you talk about things of interest to your child. If it's his music, you say, "Oh, hey, can you turn that up louder? I can't catch the words." If it's a funky hairstyle in a magazine, you say, "Oh, purple on one side. Cool. I just don't know if your mother would look good like that, but it's sure fun and different."

As soon as you start making judgment calls on things your kids like, they'll shut you off. Get good at seeing life from behind their eyes.

Anna stomped home from school because a girlfriend didn't take her side in an argument she had. Her mom, Kate, watched her demeanor as she whisked through the door. "You seem upset," Kate said quietly. "If there's anything you want to talk about, honey, I'm here. If not, I understand." She didn't push for more information; she just made herself available.

At this prompting, Anna angrily blurted out what had happened and then burst into tears.

Kate listened without interrupting to the entire story, with all the blow-by-blows preadolescent girls love to give, then gently said, "I've always marveled at your common sense and your ability to make friends with a lot of different people. As you do that, you'll run into a lot of views that may be different from yours. I could be totally off base here, but maybe you want to hear your friend out on her opinion. She might be right; she might be wrong. Or she might be some combination of the two. I know you'll figure it out. You always do. What I appreciate the most is that, in this argument, you stuck up for a kid who others were talking about in a not very kind way, and you did that in front of your friends. Wow, when you have the courage to do something like that, sometimes others won't be happy. But inside, you know you did what you had to do."

> Your middle-schooler doesn't need you to solve her dilemma. She merely needs you to be there.

Kate didn't take sides. She was the neutral voice of reason and the encourager of the way her daughter was handling the situation. Your middle-schooler doesn't need you to solve her dilemma. She merely needs you to be there.

#2: Allow Your Child Time to Process

A heartbroken mom walked up to me recently after I had finished speaking and shared her story. "My oldest son doesn't talk to me anymore. He's pulling away from me in everything. Driving him to school is excruciating, because he won't talk. All he does is shrug and give me a quick 'No' or 'Don't care.' I jump from topic to topic, trying to get him to talk, but he won't. I'm losing him." She started to sob.

You know what that kid is saying through his behavior and body language? "Back off, Mom, would you? I'm at a very important developmental stage of my life. I'm trying to sort out where I belong in this crazy, mixed-up world. Soon I'm going to go into high school. Then I'll have to grow up and get a job. I have no clue what I want that to be. I don't even like raking leaves in the backyard, so how am I going to work for the rest of my life? Can I go to college? Are my grades good enough? If I do, will I get paid enough to live somewhere other than home? Ooh, I think I'm getting a zit. . . . Gosh, I wish she'd leave me alone. She's so annoying."

You see what a jumble it is inside your kid's head? If you had all that going on, you might be a little cranky yourself.

After I explained that to the heartbroken woman, she said, "Okay, so what am I supposed to do when I drive him to school?"

"Nothing," I said, "other than drive him to school. If you want to tell him you love him and to have a great day when he gets out of the car, that's fine. But don't expect a response."

You see, sooner or later, that mute son will start talking. In fact, within a few short years, he might be talking more than you might want to hear. Kids change greatly at this age, and they have a lot of changes to adjust to. Sometimes any extra "noise" from you is a barrier in their processing of all that's going on.

> "Getting out of the egg is something the chick has to do by itself."

The other day I heard a guest on a radio show talk about the time her grandma took her to a farm in Minnesota as a little kid so she could watch baby chicks hatch. Seeing how hard one chick was struggling, the little girl reached to help break the egg open.

"Oh, honey, don't do that," her grandma told her. "If you do, the chick won't emerge strong. Helping it will only make it weak. Getting out of the egg is something the chick has to do by itself."

Sometimes that's exactly what your child needs to do—get out of the egg by herself.

#3: Be a Great Listener

When your middle-schooler asks you for advice, it's your lucky day. Until then, learn to fine-tune the art of listening and keeping your judgments to yourself. Your child is learning to navigate the meteor field of social relationships on Planet Middle School and to dodge the meteors that come whizzing his way as a result. He needs someone to listen. The best person is you, because you care about his long-term welfare.

But if you want your kid to talk, you have to keep your mouth shut and listen first. When you do talk, parrot back whatever you think you heard him say. That helps him fine-tune his own thinking, which is what you want him to do as he heads toward adulthood. You can't be beside him, making every decision and holding his hand, like you did when he was little. Think how silly you'd both look doing that in a high-school classroom.

> When your middle-schooler asks you for advice, it's your lucky day. Until then, learn to fine-tune the art of listening and keeping your judgments to yourself.

Peers are the only ones who can get away with talking over each other. Watch a group of middle-school girls talk sometime. I did recently, and if it had been a television show, I would have changed the channel. Everyone was shouting over everyone else. It was physically impossible to hear one clear sentence. If *you* did that, your kid would shut you off. But is it any wonder she's nearly deaf to your words by the time she gets home?

Listening isn't an easy occupation. In fact, when most people are listening, they're actually mulling over in their mind how they're going to respond. That means they're no longer listening to what the other person is saying. If you are the kind of parent who does that and then pronounces your opinion on your child, good luck to you. Your child will wall himself off and become intimate friends with his bedroom. He'll go on the internet with his buddies and oust you right from his life.

I know it's hard when you, with your greater experience, spot fallacies in your child's processing. You might have already gone down that road, and you wish to spare your child the pain. But this is your child's first rodeo, and he needs to find out some things for himself. Sometimes kids will come up with majorly stupid schemes. That's why God gave them parents, to take the edge off many of those schemes.

> Sometimes kids will come up with majorly stupid schemes. That's why God gave them parents.

In my book *The Way of the Shepherd*, I compare good leaders to shepherds. As a parent, you're supposed to guide your sheep, not throw a leash around them and drag them through the fields of life. When you listen, you show your child that you care about what she thinks and that you value her as an individual.

#4: Be Consistent with Your Own Life

Take a look in the mirror. I know the love handles are there, but look beyond that. We've all gained a few pounds since our own preteen years. Look inward to that little voice that tells you who you are every day. Is it a positive recording or a negative one?

All of us have tapes running through our minds. For many people, it's a constant reminder, *You're not good enough. No matter what you do, you fall short. You're not worth it.* Anyone who grew up with a critical parent has those tapes running through her head.

Others may hear, *You only count if you're the center of attention and people notice you.* If that's true for you, your child's preteen years will be really tough. She's already a drama queen. If you try to put yourself in the spotlight instead of her, you can expect some major solar flares.

The point is, you need to identify what tapes are running in your own head. Until you do, you can never be consistent in your actions toward your child. You can either believe the lies in your head or believe the truth that your life has tremendous potential if you're brave enough to face who you are. Otherwise you will be projecting your unfulfilled dreams, wishes, and desires on your child. And you know what? Your kid's not you. He has his own dreams, wishes, and desires. You'll constantly clash if you don't accept that reality.

Think of it this way. When you're on an airplane, the flight attendant goes through the safety features. If you're traveling with children, you're told to secure your own mask first and *then* put on your child's. If you're passed out, you certainly can't help your kid, can you? It's the same in parenting. Sometimes you have to fix yourself first before you can see the result you want in your child. If so, you'll find my book *Have a New You by Friday* helpful.

If there was a lot of dysfunction in your family growing up, you have quite a hill to climb. You've absorbed a lot of negative teaching. You told yourself you'd never do or say to your kid what your parents did to you, but you find yourself doing and saying the same things. Either you can feel defeated or you can figure out, *Why do I do that? And how can I change my thinking so I change my actions?*

> Look inward to that little voice that tells you who you are every day. Is it a positive recording or a negative one?

A lot of it goes back to who you believe you really are. Are you a person who believes that amino acids gathered in space billions of years ago, and from that, donkeys, giraffes, goldfish, polar bears, and human beings suddenly—*poof!*—came into being? If so, quite frankly, you need more help than I can give in this book. But if you believe that you were created by almighty God, then there's hope. You can become who you want to be. I truly do believe that with all my heart. Yes, you are imprinted by your own parents, and that imprint will remain with you throughout your life. It can be a negative

---

Eight Ways to Get Your Kid to Talk

1. Don't ask questions.
2. Engage with their world. (A couch potato isn't interesting.)
3. Be their advocate, but don't rescue them or make decisions for them.
4. Be open for business 24/7.
5. Shut your mouth unless asked for advice.
6. Never act surprised by anything they say. Memorize the words "Tell me more about that," and use them often.
7. Catch them doing something right.
8. Listen, listen, listen.

---

imprint, a positive imprint, or a combination of the two. But if you realize what that internal voice is saying, you don't have to be controlled by it.

It's time to clear the slate. Start from where you are now. Your kids deserve the best you. And so do you.

#5: Be Like Denny's—Open 24/7

Denny's restaurant is open 24/7. It never closes.

The parenting job is like that. There are times when your middle-schooler suddenly wants to talk to you at 11 p.m. just because some boy likes her or she got an ugly email or she's not sure what to wear tomorrow. All you can think is, *Oh, she should be sleeping, watching sugar plums dancing in her head. And so should I.*

But this is not the military. It isn't boot camp, with a strict schedule. You need to be available for life to play out. When the kid who was happy and bouncy 12 hours earlier is now distraught, you might as well give up your place on that comfy pillow and listen.

There are only two choices: either you're open and available, or you're closed and dogmatic. For middle-schoolers, there is no in between. If you say you care, you're available. The more your actions line up with your words, the more attention your children will pay to your words. If you're authentic, if you really do care, you'll take the time to have productive conversations with your kid that will help him navigate Planet Middle School. When you do, you become your child's hero, even if he won't admit it publicly.

So, parent, never sell yourself short. Learn to talk so your kids will really listen . . . and know when to shut up. Then when you do choose to speak, your words will make a greater difference than you can ever imagine.

12

Expect the Best, Get the Best

Why training your kids, believing in them, and having positive expectations are power plays in the game of parental poker.

Have you ever heard the phrase "What you think is what you'll get"? Well, in parenting, it's nearly always true. Many parents project not only their unfulfilled dreams and wishes on their kids but also their fears.

Shawna worried that her daughter wouldn't be accepted at school. In fact, she worried so much that it became a litany of conversation. "You have to be friendly to make a friend," she would tell Jennifer. "You can't just sit in the corner like you're probably doing. Who did you sit with at lunch today? What did you say to her?"

As the grilling commenced, Jennifer's mouth soon resembled a tightly shut clam shell. No way was she going to open up. Honestly, would you?

Shawna would urge her to have a friend over. Jennifer would roll her eyes, retreat to her room, and play computer games. Everything

Shawna did merely pushed her daughter more in the opposite direction.

Why was it so important to Shawna for her daughter to be accepted at school and have friends? Because Shawna had struggled with loneliness when she was in middle school, and she didn't want her daughter to go through the same things she did. But since she expected her daughter not to do well in the area of friends, she got what she expected—Jennifer became a loner.

Imagine if Shawna would have said this instead: "Wow, you're going into middle school. New people to get to know, a new place, new classes. A lot of changes all at once. It might seem kind of scary sometimes. It was for me when I walked into middle school. I didn't really know how to reach out and make friends. But you? You've got a great start already. Just think how many kids you know in the neighborhood who'll go to that school this fall—like the girl who fell off her bike. I bet it felt good to help her when she really needed it. In the process you made a friend too. Going into middle school will be like that. A chance to make new friends and to help others, like you're already doing in the neighborhood. I believe in you, and it'll be fun to see what happens together!"

> What you think often ends up being what you get.

Such a comment would empower Jennifer to think, *Cool. Mom saw me help that girl. And she thinks I'll do great at the new school. She believes in me.* Off to school she'd go with a positive attitude toward the new situation because of her mom's encouraging words and positive expectations.

See how it works? What you think often ends up being what you get. So what do you think about your middle-schooler? Are your thoughts full of good expectations for who she is, what she'll do in the future, and where she'll go? Have you trained her well so you can trust her to fly? If so, you've already helped her set her best foot forward in middle school. If not, why not? What can you do to help your child get there? It all starts with you.

What Kind of Parent Are You?

Are you present with your kids and engaged? Or are you so busy running your own life that there's no way you can keep up with your kids or connect with them? The atmosphere in your home has everything to do with you. Is it a tension-free zone, a place that fosters positive relationships and belonging? That has everything to do with your parenting style. We've discussed these briefly in the book before, but which one of these three styles fits you best?

Authoritarian

- Are you quick to criticize? Pick at flaws?
- Do you meet a putdown with another putdown?
- Do you compare one kid to another?
- Are you a different person at home than you are in business situations with your colleagues or social situations with your friends?
- Does a B on a report card make you see red?
- Do you remember your father or mother saying, "I told you . . ."?
- Do you say rash things you regret later?

In this parenting style, one or both parents rule. No egalitarian environment here. Your kids have nothing to say. Nobody trumps the parents. You are the pilot of your rocket ship, and nobody is going anywhere without you. But look out. Somewhere along your journey into space, you're going to end up with mutiny from your crew. Pronouncing on and ordering children around will only lead to rebellion. You can say anything you want to your children, but your actions of lording it over them are speaking so loudly, they can't hear what you're saying.

Authoritarian parents often are different at home than they are in public. One father I know is touted as "honest, honorable, trustworthy, and charming" in the business world. In the home realm, his kids overhear him lying to a colleague about where he is or what he's doing. He says he'll show up for his son's games but never comes. And he spends the rest of his time harping on his kids for the projects they haven't finished or for getting caught in a lie.

If you're an authoritarian, you likely grew up in an authoritarian-ruled home. So you naturally relate to your kids the same way your parents related to you. But think back. How did the way your parents related to you make you feel about yourself in your middle-school years? If you could change anything about their parenting style, what would it be?

> You naturally relate to your kids the same way your parents related to you.

Why not change the same things in yourself as you relate to your children? I know it's easier said than done, but nothing that's worthwhile doing is easy. Yet it's so important in the long run.

Ted said he'd always had a good relationship with his son—until Luke hit middle school. Then they hit a lot of rough patches and went head-to-head multiple times a week. Enough that, in Luke's eighth-grade year, Ted finally admitted to me that his wife had begged him to contact me and get some help and ideas.

"How does a normal conversation start out between you and your son now?" I asked him.

"Well, I usually don't see him until right before dinner. He's buried in his room whenever I get home from work, and he doesn't come out until it's time to eat."

That was a big clue right there.

He went on. "Over dinner, I ask him to tell me how his day went, and he just gives me a one-word answer like 'Fine.' When I can't get an answer about that, I move on to other things."

"Like what?" I prompted.

"I ask him how his homework is coming or if he's doing better in math, or I tell him what I need him to get done on the weekend. That kind of stuff."

Now I had the picture.

Ted was acting as dictator over his son instead of having a real relationship with him. That kid didn't want to be interrogated or told what to do. Their dialogue had "worked" when Luke was younger, because Luke did what his father told him to do with no questions asked. There was no argument, because it was easier for Luke than fighting a battle he knew he couldn't win. His dad's word was the law. Nobody went against it.

But when Luke started developing what his dad called "an independent streak" (normal development for a middle-schooler), the real problem was revealed. Ted had never taken the time to really get to know his son. He hadn't shared with his son that he believed in him.

> Ted was acting as dictator over his son instead of having a real relationship with him.

Ted and Luke's relationship needed a lot of work because, frankly, there wasn't one. But it had to start with good ol' Dad first.

The first thing Ted had to do was figure out why he was parenting the way he was, and that meant looking back on how his parents did things. He realized that his dad had been "the old-fashioned kind, mainly silent unless he was barking out orders. We kids saw him when we were supposed to do stuff. He provided for us, but I can't remember him ever telling me he was proud of me, loved me, or believed in me."

His mom tried to pick up the slack and went overboard in the permissive department, quietly trying to make the kids feel good. "I often felt jerked from one to the other," Ted said. "Dad would bark out an order for us kids to follow. Then, as soon as he walked out the door, my mom would say, 'Okay, I'll help you so we can get it done before your father gets home. I won't tell if you won't.' I guess that has made me more watchful of my own wife and kids, to make sure my kids are doing what I tell them to and that my wife isn't doing it for them."

The atmosphere he had created in his own home was understandably tense.

After working through his own growing-up years and seeing how what his parents did affected his own style of parenting, Ted agreed he needed to make a major change. I helped him think out some plans in advance, but he was the one who needed to carry them out and then stick to them.

The next time the family had dinner, Luke was quiet as usual.

Ted said, "You know, the garage really needs to be cleaned." He eyed Luke, who stiffened, expecting the usual lecture about not doing what he'd been asked to do. But Ted did something surprising instead. He laughed. "Who likes to clean a garage anyway? Not much fun there, unless you make it that way and there's a purpose. I was thinking about Grandpa's old car that's under that dustcover. I know it doesn't run now, but I have a few favors to call in with a mechanic friend. If we can get the car unburied, he said he'd come over and take a look."

Luke raised his head.

Ted zeroed in for the kill. "Sooner than we know it, you're going to be getting your driver's permit, and I know Grandpa would smile down from heaven to watch you driving his car."

Now he really had his son's full attention.

"Uh, Dad," the usually mute Luke said, "I could clean the garage this weekend."

What Your Child Wants from You

- "Allow me to grow and change."
- "Believe in me. That means everything."
- "Trust me and I won't let you down."
- "Encourage me instead of criticizing."
- "Step in when I ask, but not until I ask."
- "Set an example."

"Hey, let's do it together."

The shock on his son's face was priceless.

Old habits die hard, and Ted and Luke still went a lot of rounds, but that week and the weekend following were the start of a real relationship between father and son.

The same thing can happen with you and your middle-schooler. It's not too late to change—to turn the types of conversations you have with your kids into positive expectations that grow your relationship. But for them to change, you need to make the changes in your own life first.

Kids can spot a faker—someone whose words and actions don't match—from 50 paces away.

Permissive

- Do you bribe your children to do what you ask?
- Do you side with one child (the one who flatters you or makes you feel good about yourself), favoring him over the others?
- Do your kids take advantage of you? Are you a pushover and easy to manipulate?
- Do you give your kids too many things?

- Do you ask your child to do something and then end up doing it yourself?
- Do you make excuses for your kids? Easily allow them off the hook?
- Do you find yourself doing their science projects?
- Have you written notes for your kids to take to school that have at least one white lie in them?
- Is your value dependent on what others think of you?
- Do you make a quick decision and then cave in later after your kids harass you, beg, or whine?
- Do you sometimes feel like running away because you never have time for yourself?

I'll be blunt. Your child doesn't need you to be his friend; he needs you to be his parent. Trying to please a kid, going overboard with praising him and raving about how special he is, makes him feel anything but. *Wow, she's majorly blue-smokin' me. I know that's not true*, is what your kid is really thinking. The lack of boundaries in permissive parenting creates fear, insecurity, and rebellion. After all, if the parameters continually move and anything goes at any time, your middle-schooler will never feel safe. You don't have his back. You're by his side instead, trying to hold his hand. And no middle-schooler in his right mind—especially a boy—wants that.

> Your child doesn't need you to be his friend; he needs you to be his parent.

Permissive parents glamorize what their kids do. Too much is said about too little effort. Not only does it create an "all about me" kid, but it doesn't set up a good work ethic for them in the future either.

If you're a permissive parent, you were likely raised in a home with a permissive parent. You watched one of your parents (usually your mother, since a higher percentage of women have a pleaser mentality) bend over backwards to please her spouse and her kids, and you've adapted that behavior as your parenting mantra. But was it really good for your mother in the long run? Or did you see her "sacrifice" wearing her out as she took on more work than should have been hers? Did she adopt a martyr personality that worked with her girlfriends, so they gave her the sympathy she needed to recharge her emotionally to keep going?

What are you doing for your child right now that she should be doing for herself? Are you short-circuiting her development socially, emotionally, or physically by trying to snowplow her road for her? If so, how might you change your conversation?

Every time Amy's daughter, Stephanie, had a fight with one of her friends, Amy would tell her, "Oh, I'm so sorry. It wasn't your fault. People can sometimes be so mean. The only ones you can really trust are your family. I'll always be here for you, even when life isn't fair."

> Misplaced empathy doesn't help kids grow; it holds back their emotional and social development.

Amy thought she was being helpful to her 12-year-old. But I pointed out to her that misplaced empathy doesn't help kids grow; it holds back their emotional and social development. There are two sides to any conversation, and to have a fight, at least two people have to contribute. Often things are said on both sides that shouldn't be said. Amy should be encouraging her daughter to think about and own what she did to lead to the situation—whether that was small or large. Even more, I said, the attempt to console Stephanie and point out that only family can be trusted was based on Amy's fear that her daughter was growing away from her. She wanted to keep Stephanie close and be her best friend.

At first Amy looked startled at my words. Then realization dawned in her eyes. She got it.

A few weeks later I received an email from Amy. The next time her daughter had a fight at school, Amy decided to simply listen as she processed. When Stephanie finished, Amy said, "Mmm, sounds like you had a rough day, and you have a lot to think about—what you said, what she said, and why the situation happened in the first place. But I believe in you. I know you'll figure it out. When you do, I'd love to hear all about it, if you decide you want to share it with me." Then she walked away.

Her daughter was silent a minute, then called out, "Uh, Mom, you feeling okay?"

"Yup," Amy replied, "feeling fine. In fact, better than fine." She grinned to herself because she'd done what we'd talked about:

- acknowledged her child had a rough day;
- was available and listened to the story;
- affirmed her belief in her child's ability to work things out;
- shared her positive expectations that her child would work it out with her friend; and
- opened the door for future conversation.

Way to go, Amy. Parent, you can do it too.

A Combo of Authoritarian and Permissive

Some parents are a combination of authoritarian and permissive. Their first response might be to bark out orders at their kids, say no, or tell them, "Because I said so!" But afterward, guilt pours over them. Those bad feelings make them swing the other direction, toward the permissive parent. "Oh, honey, how about we go shopping and get you that computer game you said you wanted." They go overboard trying to make up for what they did a short while earlier.

Kids who deal with combination parents get majorly confused. They don't know which type of parent to expect at what time. And they also learn to play the game—to induce guilt so they get what they want when they want.

Authoritative

- Do you do what you say you'll do when you say you'll do it?
- Do you teach and model respect for everyone in the family?
- Do you hold your kids accountable for their actions?
- Do you treat them as responsible members of the family whose contributions are important?
- Do you listen when your kids talk and let them come to their own conclusions?
- Do you let reality do the teaching instead of telling them what to do?
- Do you model giving to others?

The parents act as parents, and the children act as children—each playing their own particular roles. All are respected and treated equally. Everybody counts and works together, and every family member's feelings are taken into consideration. All get input on family decisions. The authoritative parent welcomes thoughts and ideas and isn't threatened if others don't agree with him. He himself models the values that are important to the family: responsibility, accountability, respect, positive self-worth, and giving to others. He sees the family as a lasting relationship and takes time to nurture it, even when life isn't easy.

When a home is authoritative, the kids will be more respectful. Since they have a say in the home, they take pride in ownership. They care more whether their home looks good. These are the kids who will bend down and pick up dog plops from the yard instead of assuming someone else will get them. You don't have to force them to replace toilet paper rolls and help with general maintenance. Those flow naturally, because kids from authoritative homes like to give back to their family.

If your home is an authoritative one, congratulations! Things are probably humming along pretty well for you. But if you need to work toward authoritative parenting, you'll appreciate and find help in what Marcy did.

Marcy had always been a pushover with her daughter, who tended to rule the roost at home. But a couple of days after she attended a seminar of mine about being an authoritative parent, she had her first opportunity to put what she'd learned into play.

She and her daughter, Sandi, were at a store, shopping for school supplies and working within a budget. When Sandi threw in a comment about needing to get a specific item that wasn't on the list, because all her friends had it, Marcy said, "No, we can't get that on this trip."

"But Mom . . . ," Sandi started to argue.

> Kids from authoritative homes like to give back to their family.

"I already said no," she said quietly and moved to the next item on the list.

When Sandi rolled her eyes and flounced off with an attitude, Marcy stashed the three items they'd already found back on the shelves and headed for the store exit.

Confused, Sandi followed. "Mom, we have to get my stuff."

"Not today," Marcy said and walked out the door.

Now Sandi was running to catch up with her mom. Once at the car, she jumped in and slammed the passenger door to show how irritated she was. "Mom, we have to get my stuff."

"I heard you the first time you said that," Marcy replied calmly. She started the engine and drove toward home.

"But school starts tomorrow," Sandi yelled. "If I don't have my stuff . . ."

"Then I guess you won't have it."

When Marcy didn't respond to her daughter's yelling, Sandi tried pleading, then crying. "But everybody else will have it."

It was a mom's testing moment. No mom likes to see her girl cry. But this mom knew how important the stakes were. She couldn't and didn't give in.

Finally, Sandi asked, "Mom, why are you doing this?"

Now was the teachable moment Marcy had waited for. "Because I don't appreciate what just went on at the store."

Sandi was silent the rest of the way home.

> No mom likes to see her girl cry. But this mom knew how important the stakes were. She couldn't and didn't give in.

The next day, the first day of school, Sandi went to school with a backpack full of used supplies from previous years. Mom didn't rescue her. Neither did Dad, who backed what Mom was doing.

Sandi got the message and gained a new respect for her mother, who had turned a new leaf in becoming an authoritative parent—for the welfare of the entire family.

Training a Child Up

If you take time for training your kids, you'll never regret it. But in order to train your kids, you have to first stand up and be the parent you were created to be. Passive or overbearing parenting ensures failure and rebellious kids. As the parents in the above situations figured out, they were not put on this world to be used or abused, dissed, or taken for granted by their kids. Authoritative parenting allows parent and child to work from within their roles, with boundaries and guidelines that are respectful of both parties.

The method of training is simple. Simple, but not easy.

- If you want a child who is respectful, teach and model respect.
- If you want a child who gives to others, teach and model giving.
- If you want a child who is accountable, teach and model accountability.
- If you want a child who has positive self-worth, teach and model positive self-worth.

It's all about the power of positive expectations. Expect the best, teach the best, model the best, and you'll get the best.

Your child has an eagle eye on you—the way you respond to life's stresses, the patterns of relationships you've developed, even the way you treat yourself. Do you see yourself as a person of value? If not, how can you see your kid as a person of value and pass that on to him?

If you wrestle with your own worth, you'll find help in my book *Have a New You by Friday*. You might even want to pause in this book and read some chapters in that one before moving on. If so, great! I love working with people who are motivated to build lasting change into their lives that benefits both them and their families. Bravo for you!

The ABCs of Parenting

In order for your middle-schooler to feel worthy and have positive self-worth, he needs to see himself as worth loving, not as the scum off someone's shoe. He needs to be confident in his actions, not easily taken advantage of. Remember the ABCs of parenting from chapter 7? They're so important that here's a quick little refresher:

- I *accept* you. That means right now, as you are. Unconditionally. No changes are needed for you to be a valued member of this family.

- I *believe* in you. You are created as one of a kind, with gifts and talents, and I am confident you will use them for your own and others' benefit.

- I know you are *competent*. You can handle this. You can face anything. You won't crumple. There's no doubt in my mind about that.

What Worked for Us

My daughter and I get together every year with a group of kids who are, like her, adopted from Russia. The kids communicate with each other a bit during the school year, but then we gather in one place for a big outing in the summer. When the kids were younger, it was easier. We'd just provide games and crafts, and they'd play together and giggle. Now that they're all in middle school, they're too "cool" to do that, so things get awkward.

Last year some of the girls were sitting on the stairs, and I sat down to talk with them and tried to get some conversation going. I asked the usual stuff, like their favorite subject in school, what they had done this summer, those kinds of things. They answered me and finally started to talk.

I walked away thinking, *Okay, whew, got things rolling.*

My daughter was quiet when we drove home. Finally she said, "Mom, don't *ever* do that again."

"Do what?" I asked.

"Try to get me and my friends to talk. We'll figure it out on our own. Just trust that we'll do it ourselves."

I got the message loud and clear. I'd pulled a parental faux pas. But I learned my lesson. It wasn't my place to step into the middle of her relationships with her peers.

This year I'm going to let them be awkward all by themselves, and I'll hang out with the other parents. Just as it should be.

Who says old dogs can't learn new tricks?

Julia, Texas

If you train your kids, believe in them, and share your positive expectations, then, to quote one of my favorite Dr. Seuss books, "Oh, the places they'll go!"

There's another thing your kids can also use a lot of: encouragement. I call it Vitamin E.

Let's say your 13-year-old daughter is sitting at the kitchen table, working on her math homework, when you walk in the back door. You put your arm around that girl and say, "Honey, I'm so impressed with the way you keep everything together. Life is so busy for you this year. Especially with adding yearbook to your schedule. I marvel at how you keep it all together. My head would be spinning some days. But look at you. You know you've got a concert tonight, so you're hitting your homework early. Wow."

What have you done? Slipped your daughter a commercial announcement that's loaded with Vitamin E. You've said through your words, "You really are on the right track. I notice all you're doing and approve of it, and we appreciate you, your attitude, and your hard work."

When your daughter feels inadequate, when her peers pick on her and she feels isolated, don't you think she'll remember this moment in the kitchen when you gave her Vitamin E? Encouraging your child is like walking alongside her when she's learning how to ride a bike. She knows you'll cheer her on when she does well but you'll also be there when she topples over and needs someone to help her get back up.

When You Expect the Best but Get the Worst

If you believe in your child and have positive expectations, she won't have any urge to go in some aberrant direction, to do something that is destructive. She won't have a psychological axe to grind.

I said in *Have a New Husband by Friday* that if a husband feels wanted, needed, and respected by his wife, he is not going to stray. If your child has those three needs met, she's not going to stray either. At least not for long and not very far.

However, nobody is perfect. You're not, and neither is your child. So here are some ways you can deal with both your and your child's worst moments.

When Your Child Is Upset with You

It's a Friday night. Your daughter wants you to drop her off to see a movie with her friends. You say, "Normally that wouldn't be a problem, but tonight it won't work out. We need to be somewhere else."

Your daughter gets huffy because her last-minute plans are completely ruined. She tells you in a heated tone, "You make me so mad." Then she declares with a defiant, lifted chin, "Maybe I'll just run away."

Go back a step. "Let's clarify that. You decided to get angry because you feel like this is terribly unfair. But the reality is, your mother and I have to go out tonight for my company dinner, so the answer is no. We can't take you to that function, nor can we pick you up from it. We realize that you're unhappy and that you'd like to UPS us to Somalia for the evening. We know you'd like to spend time with your friends, but it's important for our livelihood as a family for your mother and me to attend this dinner. It means we won't be living in a tent or on the street, but in this nice three-bedroom home instead. One of the reasons we have this luxury is because both your mother and I work while you kids are in school."

Some of you are saying, "Well, isn't that a bit harsh? You could get a friend or neighbor to run her to and from the movie."

And what exactly is that teaching the child? That everything will always go her way? That she as an individual is more important than the whole of the family? The reality is, there's something you have to go to, and thus she won't be able to go to an event she'd love to go to. It's called *sacrifice*. There are plenty of times you sacrifice for your kid. Why shouldn't she sacrifice sometimes for you?

If your kids don't experience and work through some disappointment with life now, how will they be able to deal with it later? Rearing kids is all about training, and saying no is part of the process. It's real life.

> There are plenty of times you sacrifice for your kid. Why shouldn't she sacrifice sometimes for you?

Also, are you really going to fall for that "Maybe I'll just run away" statement? Little Ms. "I'm Having a Pity Party" is in full swing, and she's trying to use that comment to guilt you into giving in. Do you honestly think she's going to leave behind three square meals a day, a comfy bedroom with all her favorite stuff, and her cell phone and iPod, and walk away?

Not likely. And if she does, try what some friends of ours did when their daughter declared she was done with home.

"Well," the mom said calmly when the girl started to pack, "I guess you'll need some clean underwear. I'll get it from the dryer. And maybe a sweater, since it gets cold at night now."

The daughter was stunned that her mother was helping her pack.

Other friends of ours followed their son, with his backpack in hand, and watched him from their car for six hours as he texted and played games until his cell phone died. Then he decided to hightail it for home and his phone charger.

Parent, you hold all the cards in the game of parental poker. Without you, that child wouldn't even have clean underwear or that cell phone. Your job is to play your cards calmly and at the right time, and you'll let reality do the talking instead of you.

When Your Child Makes a Mistake

Your kids won't always like you. Frankly, you won't always like them. But at their core, your kids want to please you. They don't like it when you're upset with them. When you reveal to your child in a calm way that you're disappointed with a decision he made, that statement never feels good to him. He knows he's let you down. He may at first be defensive, but in his heart, he's struggling to find a way to make peace with you.

The hardest thing for anyone to say is, "I'm sorry. I shouldn't have done that."

It's hard for your kid too. So when he says, "I'm sorry. I blew it," what should you do?

Embrace that child, say, "I forgive you," and love him anyway, and life goes on.

We've all heard about kids raised in incredible homes, trained well by loving parents, who have derailed somewhere along the way. But we've also heard about the return of some of those prodigals to the values and arms of their loving parents. The significant part of those stories is that the parents loved those children unconditionally, expected the best of them in the long haul, even as they strayed, and welcomed them home with open arms.

The Power of Positive Expectations

When my kids were growing up, I'd always say as they went out the door, "Remember you're a Leman."

One of my daughters once fired back, "Okay, but what does it mean?"

I smiled. "I don't know what it means to you, but you do."

And off that child went.

The very fact my daughter first said, "Okay," meant that she had already identified herself with the group called the Lemans.

But I also accepted her, believed in her, and knew she was competent enough to figure out what I meant. Saying "you're a Leman" showed my kids that I had positive expectations they would conduct themselves well. That was an important concept in the Leman house, and one that Sande and I always worked to master.

Even when our kids started driving, we never had curfews and rules. We expressed positive expectations and confidence in our kids. If we trusted them to take the car out and be responsible for a vehicle that could kill themselves and others, why wouldn't we trust them to come home at "a reasonable hour," as we'd say?

One of my kids said, "Well, what time is that?"

I just repeated, "At a reasonable hour."

It was all about trust. We had trained our kids, believed in them, and shared our positive expectations. The rest was up to them. Never once did our kids come back at an ungodly hour. Most of the time they were home before 10:00, and they'd tell us all about their events.

The power of positive expectations changes your conversation with your kids.

It's no longer, "Did you rake the leaves? Mow the lawn yet? Well, I told you it had to be done by . . . ."

Instead, it becomes, "I know you probably haven't raked the leaves or mowed the lawn yet, but I want to thank you in advance for doing the extra work that needs to be done this week. With the Johnsons coming into town and spending five days with us, it's more work for everyone, but most especially your mom. I know she and I both appreciate your help."

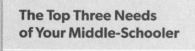

The Top Three Needs of Your Middle-Schooler

1. To be wanted.
2. To be needed.
3. To be respected.

Isn't thanking your child in advance better

than the harping you catch yourself doing when the work isn't done? Bet your child's jaw will drop when you change your tactics. Try it, and shoot me a note on Facebook to let me know how it goes.

> The power of positive expectations changes your conversation with your kids.

You know why the power of positive expectations works so well? Because what your kids want most in life is a relationship . . . with you. If you expect the best, you'll often get the best. And when you don't, let their guilt do the talking rather than you. Guilt can be a powerful motivator toward positive change . . . and you don't even have to worry about a spike in your blood pressure.

13

Raising a "Home" Boy/Girl

Your kids will belong somewhere. Why not make it your home?

When I was growing up, there was no such thing as a playdate. You just played with your friends in the neighborhood until it was dinnertime, and their parents would shoo you out the door to go home for your own dinner. Then you'd walk home.

My best friend, Moonhead, and I lived probably 500 yards apart. One game we'd play was imagining that a monster named Huggy Hairy was after us. When we'd leave each other's homes, the last thing we'd say was, "Don't let Huggy Hairy get you." We were boys, after all. And we would never, ever admit in any form that we might be afraid, because that would be a sign of weakness.

But to this day, I still remember the feeling of standing on the front step outside Moonhead's house. We lived in western New

---

✓ What Worked for Us

I got the best compliment from my son Aaron yesterday. He was sitting with his friends at lunch, and one of them said, "Wow, you always have the best lunches. You think your mom would make one for me?"

Aaron thought that was pretty cool. He even admitted it was the first time he'd really noticed that I made special homemade stuff for his lunches, while the other guys had prepackaged food from the grocery store or got fast food dropped off. "Thanks, Mom, for making me feel special," Aaron said and gave me a hug.

It was the first hug my seventh-grader had given me freely in months, and boy, it felt good. I can't wait to see the look on his face when he comes down the stairs and sees two packed lunches today—one for his friend.

Maybe I'll start a side business catering lunches. Ha.

Vicky, New Mexico

York, and with the eastern time zone, it gets dark early, by 5:30 in the winter. As soon as his door closed, it would take me only about three giant steps to make those 500 yards back to my own front door. Shadows from the streetlights and branches loomed, looking larger than usual on the snow. Huggy Hairy was an imaginary monster, but he was real to us. And every time I left Moonhead's door, Huggy Hairy was after me.

But home? Now that was safe ground, and my mom was there to meet me. No way would Huggy Hairy do battle with Mama Bear. He would just fade away into the shadows.

Is your home safe ground for your children? A place where they are welcomed?

I'm amazed at Sande, my wife. She's a relational genius. I watch her when kids come over to our house. She always greets them with a smile, a hug, an "it's great to see you," and food. Believe me, if you have food, kids will come, especially if it's homemade. Then she backs off and lets the kids do their own thing. When in middle school, nobody wants Mom in the middle of their conversations.

I get a kick out of watching my grown daughters morph into their mother in their own homes—especially now that one of them has a middle-schooler herself.

The other day our daughter Krissy called to say, "Oh my goodness, I just asked Dennis [her husband] if we could take a ride someplace. I hated rides as a kid. But Mom, I'm becoming like you." Sande and I had a good laugh. You see, when kids feel love and encouragement in your home, they internalize your values if you live them out. Sande always loved rides because it gathered our big family into one car and allowed for a lot of fun, as well as deep conversation. Nothing intruded on us—no phones, no emails, no people from outside the family. It was just us.

See how your personality, values, and home atmosphere rub off?

If you have a "homey"—a child who likes being home and bringing his friends home—that's the best news of all. You want

10 Ways to Keep Your Kids Close

1. Encourage their dreams.
2. Prepare meals together.
3. Plan special, one-on-one events.
4. Learn a new skill together.
5. Eat dinner together.
6. Make house maintenance a shared and fun activity, with a reward afterward.
7. Put on a family talent show.
8. Experiment in the kitchen. (It may not be edible, but you'll have fun.)
9. Take a walk or go for a drive.
10. Allow them ownership. (It's their room, their music, their decisions.)

your child to identify with his home, be a participant in his home, and be a giver in his home. You want him to take pride and ownership. When he starts to break away in middle school and establish his own identity, you want him to always be drawn back to the acceptance, comfort, and encouragement waiting for him at home.

Our five kids are now grown up and out on their own, but they're all still homeys who don't even need an excuse to come home. They show up as much as they can.

How to Raise a Homey

As your middle-schooler's universe expands, she will spend a lot more hours outside your influence. Hours during school and in after-school activities. More time with peers. More time with internet videos, games, movies, music, and googling the lives of the stars she admires. Culture rules, so yes, you do lose some influence over what happens outside your home. That scares a lot of parents, and rightfully it should. But gathering all your child's electronic devices and storing them in a safe isn't the answer either. The electronic age is here to stay, and it's the new method of communication for today's generation. To today's middle-schoolers, texting and googling are like breathing.

> What you do inside the home and the kind of environment you establish has everything to do with what your children do outside the home. In fact, it trumps it.

Although your child lives on Planet Middle School, and it looks very different from the one you lived on, you still do retain some control over his crazy world. You can control the kind of life your child has within the home. Is your home a place where your child wants to be? Where she feels like she belongs? Where he knows he can talk to you about anything, or not talk when he needs to process? Where she can bring her friends without you turning into an attorney, interrogating them? Where he feels like he has a unique, important role and he matters to your family? What you do inside the home and the kind of environment you establish has everything to do with what your children do outside the home. In fact, it trumps it. If a daughter has her daddy's love, she won't need to be a boy's sexual toy just to experience what she thinks is love. If a son respects his mom and his sister and understands what women really want—affection and gentleness—he'll treat his dates as if they were his mom or sister. If your home is founded on the principles of hard work, where everybody in the family works together, you won't have to check up on your children's homework . . . or see if the cat got fed either. See how it works?

Keep It Simple

I'll give the Leman family five stars for this one. We never over-indulged our kids in anything growing up. Just because I brought home a surprise for one child, because I saw something he or she would love, didn't mean I scrambled to find presents to bring home to each of the kids so everything could be even and fair. Is life always fair? Do you get a new car just because your neighbor does? No? Then, if life doesn't work that way, why would you always try to make things even and fair for your kids? That's setting up false expectations for them about what life outside your nest will be like.

Also, we looked at events and decided each of our schedules was subject to perusal and comment by the entire family. When there was too much on the schedule and the kids asked about another activity, we kindly said no. We

> Do you get a new car just because your neighbor does? No? Then . . . why would you always try to make things even and fair for your kids?

231

also had a family rule: one activity per semester per child. With five kids, our lives were more than full, and we wanted to focus on nurturing our kids at home.

Find Common Ground and Share Your Experiences

When Amy came home on the first day of school and cried because she was terrified of her history teacher, who seemed very grouchy, her mom, Angela, told her, "Wow. I remember feeling the same way about my sixth-grade math teacher, Mr. Lavey. He had thick, dark eyebrows, and he scowled at us the whole first class. I was terrified of him. When I went home and told my mom, she smiled and said, 'Well, there's an easy fix for that. At the end of the next class, walk up to him and ask him a question. Show him that you're interested in the subject matter.' It worked like a charm. Got me over the fear of that teacher, and wonder of wonders, he even said, 'Thanks for coming up to ask that question.'"

Amy pondered that answer, then brightened. "Hey, Mom, would you look at my history homework with me and help me brainstorm a couple good questions?"

A seed was planted. The next day Amy came home smiling and gave her mom a thumbs-up. "It worked! Thanks, Mom!"

> Sharing your experience not only helps ease your child's fears but can provide practical solutions.

Sharing your experience not only helps ease your child's fears but can provide practical solutions. Even more, it solidifies for your child the knowledge that you are in the trenches with her and that you care what happens to her when she's away from you.

What Amy didn't say to her mom but was thinking was, *I appreciate so much our ability to talk and understand each other. That means more than you'll ever know. I know I'm a little goofy*

232

and act scared sometimes, but the stories you share about your life make me feel better about myself and what we're going through.

Monitor Your Child's Workload at Home

Adults who have success in the workplace share a common denominator: they learned how to work hard when they were young. Why do we have kids work around the house? To make our work as parents easier? No. In fact, sometimes assigning our kids tasks makes our own work harder and longer. It's often less time-consuming to do a task ourselves than to coach or nag a kid through doing it. But why should kids take ownership of their room and help with maintenance around the house? Because, to be healthy adults, everyone needs to learn to carry out tasks that have to be done, be part of a group, and serve others . . . whether they feel like it at the moment or not.

However, we also need to be smart about what we expect and when. Your middle-schooler doesn't have the same life experience or personality you do. You might be a neatnik freak; he might be a messy. So you'll need to come to a happy medium that both of you can live with; that's part of being in a family.

If you're a firstborn perfectionist, lighten up on your kid and monitor his workload at home, making adjustments when needed. Sure, it's important that your child's room doesn't smell like a garbage can, but if it's a lot messier than usual for the first few weeks of school, will that kill either of you? Cut your kid some slack. He expends a lot of physical, emotional, and relational energy at school. He's tired when he gets home, and in the morning his brain is working to prepare for his day, especially socially.

> Cut your kid some slack. He expends a lot of physical, emotional, and relational energy at school.

Before school starts, try this. Tell your child, "You know, I've been thinking. You've got a lot of things going on before school in the morning, including walking the dog. I know middle school will be tougher, and you'll have a lot more to organize in the morning. So how about if we split up the dog walking for the first month? I'll walk the dog Monday and Wednesday mornings before I go to work, and you can take Tuesdays and Thursdays. We can switch off on Fridays, and then you can take over on the weekends again."

Anytime you can come up with practical solutions and show you're willing to go the second mile for your kid, it will cement in his mind that you're in his court.

Provide a Cooling-Off, Friendly Atmosphere after School

There's nothing that says "Welcome home" to middle-schoolers more than having food ready when they walk in the door. Any kind of snack will do. Providing food meets an immediate physical need—they're *starving*, because they're growing like crazy—and makes a gentle connection. All you need to do is smile and offer the food, and some kids will open up and talk. Others may grab the food and retreat, but don't let them fool you. Your simple "Welcome home" and offer of food has sunk into their hearts. They'll know exactly where to go when they're ready to talk. And since you didn't pump them for information, sharing is on their own terms, and you're likely to hear a lot more about how their day really went.

> Providing food meets an immediate physical need—they're *starving*, because they're growing like crazy—and makes a gentle connection.

I know this suggestion is tough for many of you who are working parents. You might not get home until 6:15, and you consider yourself lucky if you have time to take Lunchables out of the fridge or warm up a can of SpaghettiOs for dinner. But if you want to connect with kids, you need to both find and be a conduit of friendliness.

Carmen, a working-outside-the-home mom with two middle-schoolers and a high schooler, is one of the busiest moms I know. She gets her three kids off to school in the morning, dashes off to work, and isn't home until 5:00, an hour and a half after they are. But she also wants her kids to be homeys, so one of the ways she's helped to accomplish that is by becoming a whiz with the Crock-Pot. The minute those kids enter the house after school, they're greeted with a cooking smell. Sometimes it's a taco bake, other times chicken and rice, but it's "real food," as her kids say.

Nothing says a mother's love like aromas when you come in the door. You might not be a cook or a baker, but honestly, how much work does it take to plug an appliance in and throw something raw in the Crock-Pot?

> Nothing says a mother's love like aromas when you come in the door.

Carmen says, "I throw whatever I have in the fridge or freezer in the Crock-Pot—sometimes even whole, if I don't have time to chop it up—while the coffee is brewing in the morning and I'm making lunches simultaneously. Within 20 minutes, all those jobs are done, and I get my kids and myself out the door." She grins. "Best of all, when I'm tired at night, I can walk in the door and be greeted by those warm aromas myself, with no additional work. The kids are all fed, they've had time to think through their school days, and they're ready to talk. When my husband gets home around 6:30, we have dessert together and talk around the table. He doesn't mind eating his dinner backwards—dessert, then Crock-Pot food. It's the best way we've found as a family to connect."

See how creative that is? It's a win-win for everyone. Her kids have even gotten into the action. When they make cookies, they make an extra batch of dough, roll it into balls, and stash the cookie balls in a freezer bag. Half an hour before their dad gets home, they thaw a few and bake them. They're tasty and homemade in a flash, plus the house smells great. Having dinners and desserts at home is easier on their budget, which means neither Carmen nor her husband has to take on additional work in the evenings, and it's better for everyone's health, because no one is tempted with quick drive-thrus when there's a Crock-Pot feast and yummy cookies awaiting them at the best place of all—home.

There's another bonus too. Kids who eat dinner together as a family are more likely to get better grades in school; are less likely to become involved with smoking, drinking alcohol, and using marijuana; and have stronger family ties, better communication, and stronger family identity.[1] Talk about some additional powerful reasons to gather your family at the dinner table!

Use the middle-school years as ones to build a lot of great stories that will keep you all entertained, even years from now, over the family dinner table.

Control What You Can and Let the Rest Go

This statement is true for all parents, but particularly for single parents who need to take this reality a step further: you can't control your ex, but you can control yourself.

Many kids come from divorced families, and one parent might now be living with someone.

Tessa was told as she grew up that sex was meant for marriage only. Then her parents split up. Her dad moved a mile down the street, and soon a girlfriend showed up. Tessa passed her dad's house as she rode the bus on her way to school, and she noticed that his girlfriend's car was in his driveway at 7:15 every morning. Do you think Tessa was getting a mixed message from her own parents? You bet.

If you're a single parent, I've got news for you. You have no control over your ex, your ex's girlfriend, where they live, or your ex's sex life. What you can control is who you are and what happens in your home. You can model doing the right thing. Skip the cheap shots toward your ex or his girlfriend. Your kids may come home all fritzed out on sugar and sassy-mouthed because things are run differently at your ex's, but in spite of that, you remain consistent. Realize that what you're seeing is the result of the difference in environment. The way your ex and his new partner treat each other, plus the tension your kids feel going back and forth between you, will be evident. It's even harder if the kids are pulled back and forth in a tug-of-war each week.

So don't expect Mr. Whatever to walk in the door on Sunday night with a happy face after spending the weekend with your ex. Chances are, he'll sport an attitude. But do you react to it, getting on your high horse with your quirt in hand? No, you lay low. You don't ask questions about what happened at the other house. You allow your kid to make the adjustment. And then, if he wants to tell you, trust me, he will.

> You have no control over your ex, your ex's girlfriend, where they live, or your ex's sex life. What you can control is who you are and what happens in your home.

Yes, you're hurt. Especially if you were a faithful partner who got dumped for a bimbo. But at this point, it's water over the dam. What happened in the past won't change, but you can change the present. You can make your home an oasis, a place where your kid and his friends can come, be refreshed, and find lots of Vitamin E. That might mean that when he enters the door, all you do is hug him and say, "I'm so glad you're home. I missed you. And good news—we're getting pizza tonight. In fact, I'll order it right now!"

No judgment, ever. No questions. No putting your kid on the defensive.

Simply a welcome home, with his favorite food to boot.

Follow Your Child's Lead When Friends Are Around

It's important for you to know the kids your child is hanging out with—and their parents too. Your daughter might be on a volleyball or soccer team. If so, make sure you go to those games and hang out with those moms, because they and their families are part of your child's social network.

But let me caution you. You never, ever put yourself as the center of attention when your middle-schooler is with her friends. In general, most kids want you to be a distant backdrop. They are painfully aware of your presence when their peers are around. So maintain a low profile. Look welcoming, but speak only when you're spoken to. Don't hold your breath waiting either. You might turn blue. Some middle-schoolers, frankly, won't even acknowledge you exist.

> Never, ever put yourself as the center of attention when your middle-schooler is with her friends.

Don't ever embarrass them by fixing their collar, picking lint off their shirt, or telling them anything about how they look—positive or negative—in front of their friends.

But you also have to have a nose like a bird dog. A bird dog can detect the scent of a bird from a long distance away. We parents need the ability to do the same—to detect the scent of the situation before we wade into it. Different situations call for different judgment, maturity, and action. No one knows your child better than you do.

Don't Forget the Fun

The Leman family has always majored in fun—rollicking, goofy, silly fun. Sande and I want our home to be the most fun, awesome place for our kids to be. That's why our kids, who now live all over the United States, don't even need a nudge to come home for even the smallest celebration. We still make a big deal out of birthdays.

One year, when our children were young, we decided to invite some friends of ours over for dinner. We wanted to give our daughters and son the opportunity to learn how to serve others too. So we decided to combine those concepts into a crazy holiday dinner. We allowed our kids to decorate the place however they wished. Together we brainstormed and offered a surprising menu. What made it even more fun is that, when our guests ordered from the menu, they had no idea what they were getting:

- Frankincense (a hot dog and two cents, the "frank" and "cense")
- Santa's little elf drops (chocolate chips)
- Dried timber (toothpicks)
- Santa's moustache (coconut strands)

Of course, the house smelled great because there was a roast in the oven. (That was the real dinner, but the *before* dinner was the best part, even though Sande's roast dinner is not to be missed.) The kids dressed up to be the servers. It was a riot. Our kids still talk about that dinner, and so do our friends.

Whenever we'd have friends over for a cookout, our kids wouldn't disappear into the house to do their own thing. They'd hang out with us old people. They liked being around us and our friends because we were fun and made life fun.

Kids love to have fun. That's why Disney makes millions upon millions of dollars. People go to Disney theme parks over and over again. They know exactly what they'll see and experience, but they go there again because it's fun.

If your house isn't fun, your middle-schooler will find someplace else that is.

So raise a homey. You'll be glad you did. Trust me, before you know it, they'll be out the door for college, a career, and/or

---

What You Don't Do to a Middle-Schooler

- Pretend to be hip.
- Smother-mother them.
- Try to dress like them.
- Use their slang.
- Mimic their demeanor.
- Cheer loudly at their games.
- Hug or kiss them in public.
- Tease them about anything.
- Criticize or chastise them in front of their peers.

---

marriage. You'll live in Seattle, and he'll be in an apartment in New Jersey. What's important is developing the kind of relationship of mutual respect, trust, and keeping the heart close.

Now's the time to ask yourself:

- What values do I want my kids to have?
- Am I living my own life in such a way that my kids will naturally absorb those values?
- How do I conduct the family business?
- Do I teach and model for my kids that others matter by including my kids in family conversations, showing empathy for others, and helping others outside my family?

Relationships will trump rules anytime. So allow your home to be the fun place where you laugh uproariously together. But also make it the safe ground where kids have freedom to fail, learn from mistakes, and realize that, even when they're not perfect, life can go on. Not only that, but they are still accepted and loved unconditionally . . . by you.

No wonder it's called "home, sweet home."

14

Life-Mapping

It's never too early to plan your child's future, but you shouldn't be the one in the driver's seat.

Multiple generations since the late 1960s have found themselves fascinated by the voyages of the starship *Enterprise*. If you are one of those individuals captivated by either the original *Star Trek* with James T. Kirk or *Star Trek: The Next Generation* with Captain Jean-Luc Picard, or you've discovered the series through new movies such as *Star Trek Into Darkness*, you can probably mouth its mission: "To explore strange new worlds. To seek out new life and new civilizations. To boldly go where no one has gone before."[1]

Sounds a little like Planet Middle School, doesn't it? For both you and your child. But in the midst of the strange new world that sometimes has you both floundering, you can't forget the long-term mission—to rear children who can step forward with boldness into the future.

That's what this life-mapping chapter is about—helping your child identify his bent and pursue his interests in ways that make sense to his personality and gifts, and preparing him with the basics he needs to live on his own someday.

Toilet-Paper Wisdom

My friend Kathy Flores Bell, with whom I wrote *A Chicken's Guide to Talking Turkey with Your Kids about Sex*, has a unique way of highlighting exactly the window of time that a child has at home with his parents. When she does her presentation, she starts with a strip of 18 squares of toilet paper. The 18 squares represent the 18 years you have with your child as he is growing up. As Kathy talks, she starts ripping them off one by one and tossing them onto the floor.

By the time your child has reached Planet Middle School, parent, at least 11 of those 18 squares are already lying on the floor. And by the time he's reached eighth grade, you're left holding only 5 squares. What will you do with the squares that remain? How will you make the best of that time—for both you and your child?

> Time is short, and together you need to make it count.

I suggest you use Kathy's idea and do your own demonstration with 18 squares of toilet paper. It's a powerful visual to convey the concept that time is short, and together you need to make it count.

"Hey, honey," you call to your child, "I'd like to talk to you for a minute."

If you have a typical middle-schooler, you'll get the inevitable, "Mom, I'm busy."

"Okay, but when you're done being busy, I need a few minutes of your time."

Your child grudgingly and hesitantly approaches, then stares at the toilet paper in your hand. "All right, Mom, what do you want?" "Have a seat," you say. "I was thinking about something. You're 13 years old."

"Duh. What else is this meeting about?"

You rip one square of toilet paper off and toss it on the floor, then another, then another, until 13 squares are lying on the floor. By now, your child is stupefied and thinks you've lost your mind.

"I was thinking that of the 18 years you have in this house, under our roof, 13 of them are already gone. You only have 5 left. It struck me the other day that I don't really have a solid plan for those remaining years. I don't think we'll move across the country in that amount of time. I have steady work. But I'm wondering, is there some kind of a plan that you have? You're getting into that stage now where you're playing for keeps. As you go into high school, you'll be building grades that will count and make a difference in what you do next, for college or your job. Five years from now you'll be moving on and doing something—working at a specific job, attending community college or a university, or maybe joining the military. You may even live away from us, out of state. I'd love to hear your thoughts on that. Where do you see yourself five years from now? Ten years from now? Twenty years from now?"

As your child's eyes widen, you add, "I know it's a lot to be thinking about, but it's time to do so."

You then have an opportunity to share some of your own thoughts from when you were in middle school. "When I was your age, I wanted to be a dentist. A dentist. Can you imagine? I'd be the worst dentist in the world. I'd take out the wrong teeth! It's a good thing I ended up in sales, since I love people and engaging with them. It took me a while to figure out I didn't have the personality or the attention to detail to be a dentist. But I could sell a product to anybody. Now it's your turn to figure out what types of careers you might be interested in. Maybe you've shared some of them with me in the past and I've heard them but dismissed them. If so, I ought to be better clued in than that. I'm all ears now, and I'd love to hear your thoughts."

> "I'm all ears now, and I'd love to hear your thoughts."

A very appropriate time to do life-mapping like this is in eighth grade, since once the freshman year of high school hits, the practice games are over. Grades will now be part of your child's permanent record and will count for or against any school your child wants to get into.

As you talk with your child, share your own thoughts and fears. It wasn't until the spring of my senior year in high school that I realized everybody seemed to have a plan for life beyond graduation . . . except for me. I wondered, *What the heck am I going to do with my life? No college will take me. What kind of job should I get? Can I support myself?*

Don't let that happen with your child.

Middle school is when the cement of your child's foundation begins to harden. How your child sees life, what he thinks of himself and others, settles in and firms. Now is the time to get behind your child's eyes to view life as he sees it. The reality is, the little boy he was early on in life is still the person he is in middle school, and it will be the person he is at age 41, when he has three kids.

My life mantra growing up was, *I only count when I'm entertaining people and I'm the center of attention.* As an adult, I still have that bent to entertain people. However, it's been fine-tuned not only through years of practice but for a significant purpose. Now I use my natural gift for entertaining to get across critical concepts to families that change the way they dialogue with and treat each other. It's my calling and my passion.

Every Child Needs a Passion

You may have in mind where you want to see your little pumpkin
go and what you want her to be three years from now, but that's
not necessarily where your child is going
to go and what she is going to be. Children will cut the path that's right for
them. They need a guide, not a prison
guard. But if you've done your job right
in raising a homey, they will submit to
your authority and values without even
knowing it. That's because they catch
those values from you. It all goes back
to relationships. How well do you know your child? What is she
good at? What makes him break into a wide grin?

> Children will cut the path
> that's right for them.
> They need a guide,
> not a prison guard.

When I was an assistant dean of students for 10 years at the
University of Arizona, a lot of students would come in and ask,
"Dr. Leman, I have no idea what I should major in."

My stock answer? "What do you have a passion for?"

"Well . . ." One kid hedged, looking uncomfortable. "Tell you
the truth, I love horses."

"Uh-huh. I see you're in a civil engineering program," I said.
"That seems a far removed place from horses. However, if you
could ever use your bent for civil engineering and combine that
with your passion for horses, then wow, you'd fly!"

The important thing is to help your child find his bent, follow his
passion, and then ride that pony all the way out into the sunset. Many
people going to work today don't even like that work. Don't let that
happen to your child. Assist him in finding something he'll love to do.

Watch for Emerging Personality Traits and Interests

Let me tell you something shocking. I have never, ever treated
my kids the same. That's because, plainly, they are not the same.

Each of my five kids has had a different bent or inclination in life ever since they came out of the womb. And those interests emerged early.

Holly: Our firstborn was determined from day one. When she was three and a half years old, she saw a circus on television and heard the pitch: "Be one of the lucky kids to ride on the train that goes around the auditorium floor." The marketing staff finished their sales pitch with flashing a picture of happy children on the train.

Holly turned to me and said with a glint in her eye, "I'm going to be on that train."

I did my best to tell her, "Honey, they show that in order to get kids to come to the circus. But they probably already have the kids selected who will ride on the train. They might even be friends of people who work at the circus." I didn't want to throw cold water on my daughter's dreams, but I also wanted to prepare her for what I was certain would be a letdown.

Sure enough, we got to the circus, and the kids had already been handpicked. They were sitting on the train, but it hadn't moved yet. I was thinking, *Oh boy, what is Holly going to do?* She was known for making her opinion *loudly* clear.

Holly looked over the situation and figured out she wasn't going to be on that train . . . even though I had purchased good tickets to get us as close as possible.

But right before the train took off, one of the kids started screaming, "Let me off! Let me off!"

An attendant plucked the kid off the train. Guess where that child was sitting? Right in front of where we were. The attendant looked up at Holly and asked, "Would you like to go on the train?"

Holly leaped out of the stands and into the attendant's arms. Then, once she was on the train, she looked up at us with "the look." It said, "Oh, ye of little faith."

To this day, Holly still gives that "you don't get it, but I'm going to win" look.

That same determined nature later got her into a college that was difficult to get into, and she's excelled at everything she's done. Holly is competent with a capital C, but thankfully she also has my wife's gracious spirit. It's a winning combination that has taken her far in life.

> Once she was on the train, she looked up at us with "the look." It said, "Oh, ye of little faith."

Krissy: Our secondborn is easygoing yet shows her emotions on her sleeve. She's a go-with-the-flow person. The first day of kindergarten, Sande put Krissy on the bus. But when she waited at the bus stop at the end of the day, there was no Krissy.

Sande called the school.

"We know she got on the bus," they reported.

By then, Sande was frantic, wondering where her four-year-old was.

The answer came in a phone call five minutes later. "Hi, Mom! I'm at my best friend's house," Krissy reported.

Best friend? Sande was stumped. This was only the first day of kindergarten, and Krissy didn't know anyone. "Whose house are you at?" Sande queried.

She heard a clunk when Krissy put down the phone and ran to ask, "What's your name?"

That was Krissy.

Today she's not only a wonderful, creative teacher for young children, but she has two children of her own.

Kevin II: Our thirdborn child had an artistic bent early in life. He was continually drawing all over everything—even things we didn't necessarily want him to draw on, such as the walls, the tables, and, once, even his male appendage (yes, he really did . . .

with a purple permanent marker). When he was in eighth grade, he came to Sande and me and asked, "Can I paint my room?"

"Sure," we said. After all, it was his room, and in our family if it's your room, you can feel free to decorate it in any way you wish. We didn't even ask what he had in mind.

So he painted the room. And not only painted it, but painted huge Aladdins (the Disney character) all over it. They're eight feet tall—from floor to ceiling. We still call it "the Aladdin Room."

> In our family if it's your room, you can feel free to decorate it in any way you wish.

You see, it was important to Kevin to express who he was artistically, and we allowed him to do it.

When Kevin was nine and a half years old, his little sister Hannah was born. When Hannah was five years old and in love with Tinker Bell, big brother Kevin created a Tinker Bell on a string that sailed back and forth across the room. To this day, I still don't know how he did that. But I remember Hannah's squeals of delight as Tinker Bell danced across her room.

Later Kevin attended Ringling College of Art and Design in Sarasota, Florida—one of the top art schools in the country.

Hannah: Our fourthborn wasn't like either of her sisters Holly or Krissy. When Hannah went to school, I watched her cross the campus and chuckled. More things were falling out of her backpack than staying in it. Yet Hannah was very gifted with creativity, with a unique way of looking at things, and with forming relationships. She passionately helped those in need and was sensitive toward those who were hurting.

Hannah has also boldly gone where others have feared to tread. She's been involved in social issues, including fighting human trafficking, assisting the victims of that horrific crime, and helping the poor in other countries through ministry organizations. She also has been a creative director and is a tremendous photographer with a gift for seeing unusual angles. Now she's establishing a name for herself shooting weddings.

Lauren: Sande and I were in a conference with a middle-school teacher when she commented, "Lauren is a natural leader."

"Why do you say that?" I asked, curious.

"Because I watch her in the lunchroom. When Lauren gets up to leave, everybody else also gets up to leave and follows her."

So Lauren did get something from good ol' Dad. When I was in middle school, I was a leader too. I could take over a classroom with my antics and make everybody laugh. But my leadership was a far different kind than Lauren's. It wasn't until April of my senior year in high school that a teacher first told me, "Kevin, you've got skills. Did you ever think you could use these skills you have for something positive?" It came at that same time when I was looking at colleges and realizing, *Nobody wants me. What am I going to do?* That was when things started to change in my life.

> Nobody knows your child better than you. . . . What personality traits and interests are emerging?

Lauren's bent for leadership was obvious enough. She, like her brother Kevin and her sister Hannah, also had an artistic bent, but it was completely different from theirs. She loved to create presents for each family member, and she'd spend hours and days making intricate creations. While in college in California, she interned for some high-level companies and fine-tuned her creative and marketing skills.

All of our cubs came out of the same den, yet each has a unique bent and personality.

Parent, nobody knows your child better than you. So you tell me what you see in your daughter or son. What personality traits and interests are emerging?

Realize That Just Because You Like Something Doesn't Mean You're Good at It

When Holly was growing up, she shared a common interest with her mother. They both love music and love to sing. Unfortunately, neither can sing. It just goes to show that the things you enjoy aren't always what you're good at. When Sande sings, she hears Celine Dion, but we hear her, and trust me, there's a world of difference between the two. Ditto with Holly.

As a competitive firstborn, Holly always wanted to have singing contests with Krissy. They would be in the backseat of the car "singing" along (Holly was wailing) to whatever music we were listening to. I was supposed to be the judge of who won the contest.

Now, as a parent, what would you do? Holly was, to put it bluntly, hard to listen to. Clearly, Krissy would win every one, because she could sing. So would you go for honesty and declare Krissy the winner every time, or change it up and declare Holly a winner every once in a while?

I switched off—Krissy, 3; Holly, 1. I wanted Holly to win every once in a while if for no other reason than to bring the contest to an abrupt halt for my own sanity. To this day, I can remember glancing in the rearview mirror and catching a glimpse of Krissy's face when I'd announce, "Holly won that one." Krissy was saying by her expression, "Say what? Dad, you need to get your ears checked."

To this day, Sande and Holly still can't sing, but they continue to try. Thankfully, neither has pursued a musical career.

Let Them Cut Their Own Path

If you asked any of our five kids, "Did your parents ever push you into doing anything?" they'd all say a definitive no. We had the mentality in our family that each of our kids would cut their own path in life, like a stream that finds its own direction for where it's going to flow. And they did.

Every kid is different, and each has unique talents. Whatever direction the firstborn goes, the secondborn is likely to go the opposite. Holly and Krissy spent a lot of time going head-to-head as they grew up, competing with each other and for our attention. It was only natural—two girls, 18 months apart. But here's the funny thing. Though they are so different in personality, they now are both in education. Holly, once an English teacher, is now a school principal. Krissy has taught kindergarten and second grade as well as developed curriculum for an elementary school. Both sisters place a high value on educating today's kids so they become individuals who are committed to giving their best to society. Where do you think they got those shared values? They're Lemans, and we always emphasized education as the road to a bright future.

> Every kid is different, and each has unique talents. Whatever direction the firstborn goes, the secondborn is likely to go the opposite.

If your firstborn is a whiz at math, your secondborn Mollykins is likely to struggle in math but perhaps excel in sports. What's most important is that each child finds her own bent. Is it art? Music? A certain sport? Threads of who your child is will continue to emerge early. One child may be very mechanical or show streaks of perfectionism. His Skylanders are lined up perfectly. Your other child's favorite position may be sprawled on his stomach, surrounded by messy paints and broken crayons. But both are happy in their own worlds. So take a look at your child's natural-born tendencies and interests, whether that's leadership, athletics, art, language, music, or whatever.

Let's say your seventh-grade son seems to have an interest in math. Try fine-tuning his interest this way:

"Honey, I've been thinking about you all week. I can't get you out of my mind. I don't know if this would be of interest to you,

251

but I made a little chart. It's not very good, but it might give you something interesting to think about. You seem to have a real affinity for math. I can't remember a math paper you brought home that didn't have an A on it, can you?"

Your child perks up because you've noticed something about him, and some discussion is generated.

Then you say, "I was thinking about people who do well in math and also in science, like you do, and wondering what kind of occupation they might end up with."

Let the child throw out some ideas . . . and the seed will be planted.

If your kid has a business mind and had a lemonade stand when he was five years old (it was his idea and he did all the work, as

✓ What Worked for Us

I'm a hands-on guy who works construction. My wife and I have four kids, all between the ages of 9 and 15. When my oldest was about to enter eighth grade, we wanted him to get an idea of different careers. So we asked him to make a list of jobs he might like to pursue. My wife and I asked friends who were in those occupations if they'd be willing to consider taking our son for a day and letting him see what they did in their "real" job. They happily agreed, and our Career Day was born. That summer my son was able to visit an architectural firm, a building site, and a factory where they built computers. He said those days were the highlights of his summer.

When we talked about it with our friends who also had kids, we decided to form a network of people who would be willing to do a Career Day for middle-school and high-school kids. Now, three years later, our three older kids are part of that Career Day program and loving it. Our 9-year-old can't wait until it's her turn. There's a perk for me too. I get the joy of introducing other middle-schoolers to what I love to do—construct beautiful and safe buildings.

Sean, Illinois

well as the counting of the shekels afterward), now might be a good time to show him how to buy some stock with the money he has saved. Even better if you can find an article about the CEO of a company who started out buying stock in middle school and now makes $55.7 million a year. That would really set your child's business mind whirling with ideas.

Encourage your child to get involved with the activities that make his eyes light up. But a caveat first: agree to only one activity per semester. You want a homey, not a gerbil that runs around on a little wheel 24/7.

Allow Them to Explore Careers and Ask Questions

Middle school is a natural change point where interests can vastly switch direction or be fine-tuned. It's a perfect time to encourage your child to learn more about his interests. In my book *The Way of the Wise*, which is about simple truths for living life well, I emphasize the fact that Proverbs 3:6 uses "paths" plural: "And he will make your paths straight." When I was in seventh grade, I wanted to be a forest ranger or game warden because I loved the outdoors, hunting, and fishing. Contrast that with what I'm doing now—speaking internationally to help families. Your child has many paths, not just one. Why not help him explore the wide range of possibilities?

Let's say your eighth-grade son has an interest in aviation. You discover that a local high school has a weekend program where they bring in a pilot and also airplane mechanics to talk about their jobs. So what do you do? You call that school's office and say, "I have a son who is in eighth grade, but I'd love to bring him to your weekend program. Is that all right with you?"

Or perhaps your daughter has always loved caring for animals. She's patient, kind, and interested in becoming a vet. Why not talk to a local vet and ask if your daughter could come to his work for a couple of hours on a Saturday, watch what he does, and even help out with cleaning animal habitats?

Maybe your daughter wants to be an attorney. Do you know an attorney who might be willing to take your kid to work for a day so she can see what he does?

When you allow your child to explore, he discovers things such as, *Mmm, the guy who is a manager at Walgreens works year-round, but the guy who teaches English at the high school has summers off. Having summers off is important to me so I can spend time doing other things I love.*

You never push an interest, though. You don't map out life for your child. "Well, Johnny, I see that you are interested in medicine, so here's what we'll do. We'll make sure you take chemistry, physics, biology, all the high-level science classes in high school, and . . ." That's a huge no-no. Kids who feel like their life is mapped out for them can become lethargic, depressed, even suicidal. *What's the use?* they wonder. *It doesn't matter what I say. I don't have a choice anyway.*

In the movie *A Cinderella Story* with Hilary Duff and Chad Michael Murray, the character Austin Ames, a popular football star, wants to go into the field of English, but all his father can see and talk about is his son's sports scholarship. When Austin walks off the field when a football scout is watching him, Austin's father races after him and says, "You're throwing away your dream!"

"No, Dad," Austin replies, "I'm throwing away yours."[2]

Are you allowing your child to pursue his dreams, or are you pushing your own agenda?

Keep the tennis ball on your child's side of the court. Let him make the choice regarding pursuing his interests. You assist in opening the doors he spots. Then when you see an interest grow, go out of your way to support it. Is your child good with people? Data oriented? Mechanically minded? Who knows how far that bent and a particular interest could take your child?

For example, you ask your son what he enjoys doing and he says, "Trading baseball cards." Your first response might be to roll your eyes, but I've got news for you: a lot of successful businesspeople started off trading baseball cards.

Our daughter Lauren always had craft projects scattered across her room. She loved making presents for people.

> Are you allowing your child to pursue his dreams, or are you pushing your own agenda?

Today she's turned her present making into a business called MiniatureLiterature, creating one-of-a-kind treasures on Etsy.com. All careers and entrepreneurial surprises start with a dream. That dream then turns into a desire and a plan to build something from the ground up. Amazon, Apple, Disney, and Google all started out of a garage.[3] Bill Gates left Harvard to launch a career in computers; later he completed a few degrees through online courses.[4]

Choose a School That Fits Your Child

Years ago, life was simple. Where you lived defined where you went to school, and you walked however many blocks to the local public school. Today there is open enrollment. If a school is 18 miles away and you want to be there for one reason or another, you can apply. There are all sorts of schools—public, private, charter, college prep, classical, homeschool . . . you name it.

What kind of school best suits your child? Take a good look at his personality, interests, and relational skills. Ask yourself these questions, for starters, to find the environment and learning style that best suits your child:

- Is my child fast-paced, slow-paced, or somewhere in between?
- Does he love social interaction, or is he quieter and more withdrawn?

- How does my child hold up against peer pressure?
- Would he benefit from sports, music, or theater as part of the school program?
- What uniquely gifted areas does my child have? Are they a match for what the school offers?

Also consider your own comfortability:

- How important is it to me that I know exactly what my child is learning?
- How important is it to me that the instructors share my family's morals and values? That I am able to interact with those instructors personally?
- How important is it to me that my child has the possibility of having like-minded friends?
- How important is a classical or faith-based education to me?
- What can I afford?
- How long is the drive, if it's to a private or charter school?
- Am I educated, trained, and of the personality that would foster a healthy homeschool environment?

Every parent needs to carefully consider these questions not only for the family as a whole but for each child uniquely.

Diane and Mike have three children at three different schools. Their oldest son is homeschooled but attends a trade high school part-time because of his interest in mechanical engineering. He has his eye on finishing high school early and then enrolling in DeVry Technical Institute so he can get more hands-on training in his area of passion.

Their secondborn son is in seventh grade at a public middle school and excels in sports—football in the fall and soccer in the spring. The kid lives and breathes sports and dreams of a sports scholarship at the University of Arizona.

Their sixth-grade daughter is a social creature who jumps at helping anyone, especially younger kids. Her Christian middle school has a special program where select students go to a nearby church and spend time after school with the children of immigrant families. Kari is a natural. The younger children flock to her like fledglings to a mama bird.

As Diane said, "We made completely different schooling choices for each of our kids, based on their personalities and interests. But it wasn't us making the choices. We talked as a family about all the options and then asked each of the kids to carefully consider what they thought. We asked them to put the pros in one column and the cons in another column. A couple weeks later, we met again as a family to discuss what they thought."

Dream On!

Say to your middle-schooler, "Pretend you're 10 years older." Then ask:

- "Where would you live?"
- "What job would you have?"
- "How much money would you make every week?"
- "What would you do on your time off from work?"
- "How much vacation would you get a year?"
- "Would you like to travel? If so, where would you travel for fun?"
- "What kind of car would you own? Or would you skip car ownership and take the bus or train?"

Now's a great time for your child to start an idea/dream notebook or computer file. Even better if the two of you can research specifics about the cost of a car, housing, a salary she might make, what flights and hotels cost for her vacation, etc. If you're planning your own vacation as a family, let your middle-schooler help out by doing some of the research.

"We were amazed," Mike added. "Each of the kids took our request seriously. One even had five pages of pros and cons!"

I laughed. "I can guess which child that was—the firstborn."

Because those children respected their parents and had their respect, they were able to make wise decisions as a family. The results are clear in the fact that each of the kids is pursuing a unique passion and each is at the right school for him or her. None of the siblings are competing with each other. They're free to fly . . . and to cheer each other on at their activities.

Life Prep 101

There are certain basics we all need to know to survive on our own. The sooner your middle-schooler learns them, the better. Within a few short years, your child will be driving a vehicle. Two years after that, he'll be 18 and a legal adult. With all the furor of Planet Middle School swirling around him right now, though, he needs your assistance to realize he has a future . . . and it's coming faster than either of you could possibly imagine. Anything you can do to prepare him with life skills will keep his head above the wolf pack.

Teach 'Em the Basics

There are some basic things middle-schoolers should learn how to do if they don't know how to already:

- Clean and organize their room (and bathroom, if they have their own).
- Do laundry (what colors go together, how much soap to use, what can't go in the dryer, why clothes shouldn't be left in the dryer for a week).
- Make a couple of basic meals (even if that means reading the directions off a box of macaroni and cheese).

- Know north, south, east, and west, and be able to read a map to get from one location to another.
- Make a grocery list and shop for the items on the list.
- Manage money. That means setting aside a portion of their allowance and earnings in a savings account and keeping track of expenses, small and large. Even better if you can buy a few shares of stocks. Show your child how even tiny investments can pay off in dividends down the road.
- Say thank you when others do something for them, and write thank-you notes when gifts are received.

Those are just for starters. I'm certain you can add other things to the list. Some parents teach kids how to thread a needle, fix a rip in a seam, and sew on a button that has fallen off. It's a lot more economical to spend five minutes fixing a shirt than to toss it in the trash because it's no longer wearable and you have to buy a new one. Other parents teach kids how to use a hammer properly. The sky's the limit in what you'd like to teach.

Remember the most important end goal of all: that you develop a long-term relationship of unconditional love, acceptance, and trust with your child. After all, what your child wants most in life is a relationship with you. Anything you do together—working, playing, learning—means more time with you.

Think Green Power

People today are thinking green—recycling, conserving energy— and that's great. But what about some green power for your kid? How do you teach your child that money doesn't grow on trees?

When I was young, my dad used to yell, "Hey, who left the front door open? What are we doing—heating the neighborhood?" And, "Who left the light on? What, you think the squirrels need to see it from outside the window?" Today when I walk around my house, if I see a light on with no one in the room, I turn the light off. Just like my dad did. And we live in Arizona, where water is as costly as liquid silver. You don't waste it by letting a faucet run unnecessarily.

I've got one daughter who uses a coupon for everything on this earth. She's always saving money on anything she needs to buy. But many of us don't use our money well. We spend what we make,

---

✓ What Worked for Us

We have twins—a boy and a girl. When my mother was in the hospital for two weeks, I realized how much our 12-year-olds didn't know about life basics. I'd get texts from them, asking me where this or that was, if a certain shirt was clean or dirty, if I could pick up a certain food item from the store, what they should have for dinner. Their lack of knowledge made a very intense time even harder.

I decided spring break was the perfect time to launch my plan. Every morning we spent an hour learning a basic skill—preparing a meal, doing laundry, shopping for groceries, cleaning, etc. At the end of the week, they planned a meal themselves, shopped for the groceries, and made the meal. They called it a "fancy dinner." It was a casserole that had meat, potatoes, and green beans in it, and they served it on our best plates, with a plastic flower in a vase for decoration. The food tasted great, and my husband and I appreciated the beautiful décor and their creativity in thinking of it. My kids were pretty proud of their accomplishments.

The night before school started, I overheard my daughter talking to one of her friends on the phone. "What did we do over spring break? Oh, we worked. But it was kinda cool. Like one of those cooking shows. . . ."

I was amazed how much our kids could learn quickly, once we set our minds to it. Funny thing: my daughter's friend's mom just called to ask me how I did it. She wants to try it too. Maybe I've launched a new spring break trend.

Rachelle, Ohio

---

then wait for the next paycheck. Prudent parents teach their kids how to monitor and save money. For example, if your child saved $5 a week from his lawn-mowing money, by the end of the year he'd have $260 plus some interest. He can buy a lot more with that than the $5 he'd spend on candy or trinkets that would be eaten or useless by the end of that year.

In most states a person can't have their own checking account until they're 16. However, you can still start a separate checking account in your name that will become your child's. Take him with you each week to make the $5 deposit, and show him online how the money adds up.

There's another more immediate way to show your child green power. Set aside the specific amount of cash you would normally spend on her clothing, shoes, etc., for the school year. Then give that amount of money to your child in cash. Allow her to spend it any way she wishes, but with a caveat: "This is the amount of money we have to spend. We've gone over the list and your wardrobe, and you know what you need. It's up to you to spend the money however you like. Just know that whatever you get has to last you until the end of the school year."

> Prudent parents teach their kids how to monitor and save money.

Your daughter is going to take one look at that big stash of money and think, *Wow, I've just struck it rich.* Her spending spree might be a little wild the first time. But don't say, "If you buy that, you won't have enough for . . ." Let reality do the teaching.

Chances are, she'll learn a few swift lessons when she arrives home with a high-end pair of jeans that will make her peers jealous and several T-shirts that you think are outrageously priced. But as she's looking over her purchases, suddenly it hits her: *Uh, none of these are gym shoes or a winter coat.*

She goes running to you. "Mom, we've got to go back and check out the gym shoes and coats. I didn't get those yet."

Now is the time for some reality therapy to sink in. "Okay, honey," you say. "How much money do you have left?"

She deflates. "Well, $24."

You nod. "Do a little research about where you can get a coat and gym shoes for that amount of money, and I'd be happy to take you."

You already know what's going to happen. She will declare it's impossible to find those items for that amount of money and will tell you she has to have more money. But you're going to hold firm and say no. You know the only places she can find gym shoes and a coat for that amount of money are at resale shops. Which is exactly where you end up—after you say no, she sulks for a while, and reality does the talking.

The next time you place money in her hand, do you think she'll spend it differently? You bet! You'll do your kids a big favor if you teach wise money management at this critical stage, as they're gaining some independence.

If your child says he hates school and doesn't want to go to college, but he expects to make a couple grand a week working at the local gas station or mini-mart, he needs a wake-up call. Do some research together to find out how much gas station employees make per hour, then multiply that by 40 hours a week for a full-time job. Deduct at least 40 percent (to cover income tax for federal and state, as well as FICA and all the other assorted line items deducted from a paycheck) to see what he's left with. Research how much the monthly rent is for apartments in your area, and deduct 25 percent of that for what rent would cost per week. Take the rest of the money out of the bank in cash (if there's any left!). Fill up the car with gas, using the cash. Make a list of the groceries he'd need for the week, and go shopping with the cash. Very quickly your child will figure out it would be pretty tough to live on that wage when he is able to purchase only a couple grocery items on the list.

Sometimes such reality checks are exactly what kids need for them to grasp why school is important and they need to take it seriously.

Make Important Life Topics Part of Your Regular Conversation

A lot of parents don't prepare their kids for life basics until they're ready to go out the door for college. Then, all of a sudden, your son scrambles to learn how to do laundry, and he learns the hard way that a red shirt and white shorts together in the wash make for pink shorts that could embarrass him if he's trying to look macho in front of the girl the next washer over. And your daughter texts you as she stands at the gas pump: *Uh, how exactly do I fill the car up with gas? Where's the thingy that I unscrew?*

Make life skills a part of your regular conversation. When your son brings you his laundry and starts to dump it on the floor, say, "Oh, sorting is easy," and have him do exactly that, put in the proper amount of detergent, and start the load. He might not take the clothes out of the dryer because he's running to a sports practice, but you at least have a start on the first half of the process.

Dad, if you're riding with your middle-school daughter, she can get out of the car with you and watch what you do with your credit card and how you pump gas, even if she's not old enough to pump it legally.

Other discussions are fair game at dinner and as you drive in the car.

"I remember when I met your mother. We were both in seventh grade. She was interesting to me because . . . ," and you go on to say what attracted you that still attracts you to this day and made you say, "I want to marry that woman."

You might even share, "But back then, I was kinda dumb. I thought love was all about these tingly feelings, and I was drooling over this cheerleader. Even went out with her once to an eighth-grade dance, and it was majorly uncomfortable. Neither of us knew what to say. That's when it dawned on me that I could talk easily with your mother, and we shared a lot in common. I wished she was there instead of that cheerleader."

You laugh. "But I was still clueless. Even though we kept up with each other via phone and email, it took me until mid-college, when we were both home on spring break, to finally ask her out."

> Sharing stories of what you did right and the mistakes you made are better than a sermon every time. And they have long-lasting effects.

You pause, then deliver the punch line. "Real love needs time to develop. When I asked your mother out, I already knew she was the woman for me, and she knew it too. We had been good friends for a long time. Now here we are, three kids later. I still feel the same way about your mother that I did the first time I asked her out and she said yes. Like she's the most special woman on earth, perfectly suited to me, and whoa, am I a lucky fella to have her."

You don't think that will make a hormone-laden middle-schooler evaluate his own crushes in the light of real love?

Sharing stories of what you did right and the mistakes you made are better than a sermon every time. And they have long-lasting effects. They'll come back to your kids when they least expect it and assist them in making positive choices.

To Boldly Go Where No One Has Gone Before

If you ask a kindergartner, "Where do you want to live when you grow up?" the inevitable answer will be, "With you, Mom/Dad!"

Ask your middle-schooler that same question, and many will say, "As far from you as possible." Just be grateful if you get the response, "I'd like to live in the same town as you do."

On Planet Middle School life zips by at warp speed, and it's hard for parents to keep up. But it's also critical that you do. Can you believe your onetime kindergartner is now a middle-schooler? You have anywhere from five to seven squares of toilet paper left with your child as of this moment. How are you going to best take advantage of them? Why not put your all into striving for a relationship that's so filled with trust and respect that when you suggest something, not only do they follow your wisdom, but they pass the suggestion along to their friends?

That only happens when your child feels valued by you. Then he will boldly go anywhere, even places no one has gone before, and know he is still always welcome in the place he loves most—home.

> Life zips by at warp speed, and it's hard for parents to keep up. But it's also critical that you do.

Your job as a parent is not to entertain kids; it's to rear adults. When they leave your home, they need enough armor to win the battles that they will face by themselves on the big planet—whether at college, in the job market, with social relationships, or in the military. So teach them the basic skills they need to survive in that adult world. But most of all, help them fine-tune their bents and find their passions.

15

Creating an Attitude of Gratitude

Why modeling and teaching this single character quality within the home is so critical.

When my five kids went to college, every one of them came home saying, "Wow, I assumed every family was like ours. But some of my friends come from totally dysfunctional homes. I guess I thought families always laughed and had fun together. That they worked together. That they supported each other. Now I know that's far from true." That knowledge notched up my kids' gratitude for the way they had grown up. They had often expressed their gratitude for things we'd done for them as parents, for things their siblings had done for them. But now they realized how our home environment had shaped them to be grateful for the small things of life and, as a result, to give freely and generously to others.

Take a look around. Do you see an attitude of gratitude in most middle-schoolers? Or do you see a sense of entitlement? "You owe me, and if you don't pay up and give me what I want when I want it, I'm going to make you pay every day of your life."

The other day, when I was at a middle school, I saw an altercation between a preadolescent boy and his mother. He gave her the what for, took his lunch out of his backpack and threw it at her, then stomped off toward the door. She picked up the lunch from the ground and slinked away like a beaten puppy. What could possibly be so wrong with a bagged lunch that it would result in such behavior?

I came to the swift conclusion it couldn't be the lunch. The problem lay with the child, who probably would have treated a dog better than his mother. Do you think he will treat his peers any better down the road? Or his girlfriend? His wife? His colleagues?

But the problem also lay with his mother. The beaten puppy posture told me similar scenarios had happened time and time again between them, and she had allowed him to get away with treating her like that. What in her background caused her to think such treatment was all right?

Why Be Grateful?

All of us could use some work on our attitude of gratitude. If you look at most of us, our basic needs—shelter, food, water, a restroom—are covered. That gives us plenty of room for our wants. But when those wants turn into demands, we've got a problem. We become people who demand to be treated a certain way and who view reward as our right for anything and everything we do. Life becomes all about what's in it for me and getting applause and reward.

Steering your child in the direction of learning gratitude takes time, but

> All of us could use some work on our attitude of gratitude.

trust me, you don't want an adult 10 years from now who hasn't learned that lesson.

After I spoke to a group in the Midwest, a woman walked up to me with tears in her eyes. "Dr. Leman, I heard what you said, and I believe it's true. We do need to develop gratefulness in our kids. But I'm a single mom. I have a very uncooperative ex—a real creep who just took off—and I don't have the money to drag him into court to help pay for child support. I understand what you're suggesting. But I have very little energy or resources. When I get home from my double shift, all I want to do is sit. I have enough trouble just getting up for work every day."

"I understand," I said. "Being a single mom is tough. But it's all the more reason to pay attention to what I'm telling you. You do a lot of things routinely at home, like cooking, laundry, and paying bills, right? Things that keep you up late at night and fill up your weekends?"

She nodded.

"Think of how the pressure and time of doing those things might be lessened if you get your 12-year-old off his heinie in that comfy chair and out of his Xbox world to help. And if your daughter texted an hour less a night and pitched in to do some of those tasks."

"But I've tried that, and all I get is hassle from them." She hung her head. "Honestly, it's easier to do it alone."

"I get that too. But unless you try it and stick with it, you'll never get anywhere. How about you assign each of them a task and ask them to have it done before you get home? For example, you could tell your daughter, 'I'd like you to clean up your science project in the kitchen so I have room to make dinner when I get home tonight.' You arrive home, and it's not done. So you tell her, 'I can see the kitchen isn't ready for me to prepare dinner. So I'll be back in an hour.' You leave and go eat fast food if you can afford it. Or you eat the other half of the tuna sandwich you made for lunch that you didn't have time to eat. The point is, you don't make any dinner because she didn't do her part to prepare for you to do your part."

Chances are, if that mom follows through, she'll arrive home to a clean kitchen and two kids who will have gotten hungry enough to start spelunking in the kitchen to find dinner for themselves. What's important is that your child sees your cooperation. "Hey, I'm willing to meet you halfway—I'll prepare dinner if you get your mess cleaned up in the kitchen—but I need you to step up to the plate."

Yes, it does take time and energy. But unless you make a plan and stick with it, you'll never see the results. And honestly, do you really want to be a slave dog to your kids for the rest of the years you have with them until they walk out the door? If you cave in, what are you teaching them? Believe me, your son-in-law or daughter-in-law will thank you someday for sticking to your guns. So don't be a martyr. Don't sacrifice everything for your kids. You're not doing them any favors. Let them see when you're unhappy with them. They won't like it, because under that noncaring exterior, they really do care and are bothered if Mom or Dad is unhappy with them.

> Don't be a martyr. Don't sacrifice everything for your kids. You're not doing them any favors.

If you allow opportunities for your child to help, you will develop in them an attitude of gratitude for what they have and the hard work it takes to maintain it. As a result, they'll take better care of your stuff and theirs, have a better handle on life basics and what things cost for when they're out on their own, and be more disciplined in the way they choose to live.

You might have been a martyr in the past. You might have been a pleaser and given too much to your kids. Let go of the guilt for the too many things you've done for your kids. Let today be the day when things change. If your kid doesn't experience responsibility, accountability, and giving to his own family with no expectation of getting back—just because he's a part of the group—he'll become a person who has his hand out at every turn, saying, "Gimme, gimme, gimme."

How to Counteract the Gimmes

Walk into any public place, and you'll see the prevalent "gimme" attitude—from the kids shopping with their moms at the mall who demand purchases rather than asking for them, to the players telling their coaches off because they don't get to play enough, to spouses who decide, "You haven't done enough for me lately," to the workers who demand higher salaries for less work. Where did these attitudes come from? They all started during the growing-up years, with how those people were treated by their families and the worldview they developed as a result.

What does your middle-schooler need to learn?

What Worked for Us

My dad traveled a lot for 10 of my growing-up years—he was away from us during the week and home on the weekends—so my mom was often like a single mom. During all those years, I never once heard her complain. She worked full-time as a teacher, walked home with us from school, cooked simple dinners, made homemade cookies, and even stayed up late to sew when we had to have certain outfits for school or a play we were in.

When my dad came home, she always welcomed him happily, made sure we kids stopped what we were doing so we could tell him all about our week and hear about his, and had a treat prepared so we could munch, talk, and laugh together.

When I was in middle school, there were a lot of activities to do on Friday nights, and I was constantly invited by friends to do things. But I'd tell them,

That It's Not "All about Me"

Every person in your home should have tasks that he or she is expected to do on behalf of the group as a whole. Being part of a family means working together and pulling your part of the load. It doesn't mean Mom or Dad becomes the servant and the kids get off scot-free. The first priority of the family should be the group as a whole, not merely the ease of one individual.

So let me ask you, does each family member have specific work to do that benefits all of you? Whether it's cleaning the refrigerator out once a week, making sure the dog has water, dusting the living room, washing the car . . . you name it?

Your job as a parent is not to entertain your kids through the hedonistic middle-school years and further enforce the concept of "it's all about me." So if you're running in circles trying to please your kid, making him feel like he's the center of the universe, you need to stop and reevaluate. There's nothing worse than feeling

"Thanks, but my dad's coming home, and I want to spend time with my family." The other kids would look at me like I was weird, but I didn't care.

My parents—my mom especially—set the bar high on gratefulness. She taught and modeled for both my sister and me how to be grateful for the little things . . . and to creatively use what we did have. Because of her always positive attitude, I decided that when I became a mom myself, I'd do the same things she did.

When my daughter was in middle school, my husband had to travel quite a bit too, and I soon learned how hard that was. I had even greater empathy for my mom, who parented two girls solo a great amount of the time for 10 years. I also gained an even deeper respect for her. But I knew how much her attitude of gratitude had been imprinted on my heart and my own parenting when my daughter said one Friday night, "Mom, I just want to be home with you and with Dad. That's all that matters."

Wow. Pretty cool to be your middle-school daughter's favorite people.

Carmen, Saskatchewan, Canada

that you're working hard on someone's behalf but not seeing any benefit from that work. *I'm breaking my neck to keep this kid happy, and I don't even get a thank-you for making dinner? Something's majorly out of kilter here. I'm doing all the giving; he's doing all the taking.*

Exactly. God did not put you on this earth for your kids to run over you. Your kid needs a large, healthy dose of Vitamin N—no. Yes, I know sometimes it's easier to do a task than to follow up with your child to do it, but keep the long-term goal in mind. The world is not about him. If he fails to do a task, there will be a consequence, and you shouldn't rescue him from that. Let him be the one to get in a bind if he forgets to tell you he needs black slacks for his band concert. If the ones he ends up wearing are high-water ones from last year and he gets teased, well, he'll remember to tell you earlier next time, won't he?

> Does each family member have specific work to do that benefits all of you?

Don't do things for your kids that they should do for themselves. Otherwise you create a child who says, "I need, I need, I want, I want," and expects you to always jump to fulfill those requests.

If your middle-schooler isn't "all about me," there's also a side perk: the cattiness and nastiness of others won't bother her as much. She won't think, *How could she do that to me? I've always been nice to her, and she dishes that out? How dare she?* Instead, she'll think, *Wow, that girl must be struggling with something to have to give me a piece of her mind like that. Especially since what she said wasn't even true. I wonder what's bugging her so much.*

See how the focus changes? When it's not "all about me," and your middle-schooler can think about an event from another perspective, the sting of changing peer emotions is dulled. During the wild solar flare-ups of Planet Middle School, that's useful indeed.

To Celebrate Others' Successes and Rally behind Them

Do family members naturally pull together, celebrating each other's successes and rallying in difficult times? If your son comes home to announce, "Hey, guess what? I made the honor roll!" or "I just got voted in as class treasurer," do you all gather around him to cheer and celebrate his hard work? Do you say, "We'll have to figure out a special dinner we can make on Friday night. . . . Hmm, what sounds good?"

> Being glad for each other should be a natural occurrence if everyone in the family is feeling loved, valued, and respected.

For the Leman family, a special meal is Swedish pancakes, minus the lingonberries. We make them four or five times a year together. Other times we skip dinner and search out the most calorie-ridden dessert we can find in town. Yes, our family is a little wacko, but we love being together.

Being glad for each other should be a natural occurrence if everyone in the family is feeling loved, valued, and respected.

What about when something difficult happens? The family should rally then too—whether that means respecting a person's privacy to veg out, process, or cry, or whether a hug or conversation is needed.

People who are successful in life are able to get along well with others, treat them with respect, and work as team players. The place children need to learn that is in their family.

Not to Equate Monetary Reward with Their Value as a Human Being

I really hate it when I hear parents say, "We've established a monetary system for grades, and here's how it goes: $10 for an A, $6 for a B, and so on." When you do that, what are you really teaching kids? That it's not about giving of themselves and their best efforts; it's about working in order to get something—money. They then begin to view reward as their right. "Okay, I got my grades, now gimme my money."

How much better would it be if you said to your son, who has spent a lot of hours studying for a class that's difficult for him, "Seeing that B has to make you feel great inside. You've worked so hard on history, a subject that I know isn't easy for you. And look at the results. I can't wait to see the happy look on your dad's face and your sister's when you tell them!"

What Worked for Us

My son, Daniel, is artistic and organized. Having things that look nice is important to him. He spends a lot of time picking out the right notebook for each class every year. But this year, my company downsized and my hours were cut to half-time. I told Daniel we had 15 bucks to cover his and his sister's school supplies. "But Dad," he whined, "the calculator for math costs over 200 bucks. And I also need . . ."

I let him finish his big, long list, then said, "I heard what you said, but 15 bucks is all we have."

He stomped off to his room and slammed the door. I could feel the bad attitude steaming from there.

A couple days later, I walked into the kitchen and saw Daniel and his little sister, Becky, working away on a project. There was a neat stack of school items on the kitchen desk. "Hey, where'd you get the calculator?" I asked.

He shrugged. "One of my buddies knows a guy who had the class a couple years ago and didn't need his anymore."

I noticed there was dragon-print duct tape adorning the bottom and top of the calculator.

"Yeah," my son said, "the calculator was a little beat up, but now no one will know the difference. And it looks cool."

He'd bought the duct tape at an office supply store for 75 percent off and spent $1.03 on it from his allowance money, he said. He'd also found

Rewarding kids with money for grades is never a good idea. Do you get paid every time you wash the dishes? When you scrub the potty? Then why should your kid get paid for grades? That's *his* work, just like you have your work.

Developing an Attitude of Gratitude

I'm convinced the single most important skill every person needs to learn growing up is an attitude of gratitude. Being grateful is

---

previous years' notebooks that still had lots of pages in them stashed in our basement, so he generated computer art for the covers and used the duct tape as a border. Even more, he was helping his sister do the same thing with her old notebooks, sharpening her colored pencils from the previous year for her, and decorating the used box with duct tape to make it stronger.

When I asked the kids what they still needed for supplies, my daughter said, "Nothing! We got it covered, Dad."

Stunned, I took the 15 bucks out of my pocket. "In that case, you two can split what I'd set aside."

My son and daughter exchanged a glance. "No, Dad, you keep it. We don't need it," Daniel said. "You do plenty around here for us. This is the least we can do. And we've got something for you too." He pulled out over 40 dollars in assorted bills and some change and gave it to me. "For groceries and school snacks."

He and his sister had bought three more rolls of assorted patterns of duct tape, canvassed the neighborhood for old notebooks, and started a small business making notebooks for friends. In just a couple of days, they'd made over 40 bucks already and still had a stack of orders to fulfill and hand-deliver before school started in a week.

I was shocked by the business they'd launched and that they were already seeing the reward from their hard efforts. But what impressed me most is the gratefulness I saw in my kids for what they had . . . and their ingenuity in repurposing old items.

Philip, Arizona

---

an art that starts with a realization of what you have, compared to others in the world, and that you should be thankful for it. If you're truly thankful for what you have, it changes the core of who you are inside. You can't help but have a giving heart toward others.

How do you encourage your child to have an attitude of gratitude?

Model Unconditional Love, Caring, and Gratitude

You can tell your child that he is supposed to love others, but if he doesn't feel unconditional love from you as a parent, he won't have a clue what loving others really means.

I have never had a conversation with any of my five kids over the last 40 years where I haven't closed the conversation with "I love you." My kids will text me and say, "I love you to the moon and back." Yet some of you reading this book have never experienced anyone truly saying "I love you" to you. That lack has set you up for an arm's-length relationship with your own kids. Now is the time to make a change—to deal with your own feelings about that lack of love—and to decide not to pass the broken baton on to the next generation.

You can tell your child that he should care about others, that he should have empathy toward them and invest in their lives. But if you aren't modeling serving others, you're merely a tin can clanging on the end of a car bumper as you speed away. Your words literally mean nothing. In fact, if what you say doesn't line up in your kid's mind with your actions, that disconnect will become a source of rebellion, driving him in the opposite direction you're asking him to go.

However, if your child is part of a family that models gratitude for things both large and small, a family that works together, learns together, and serves together, then wow . . . oh, the things you can do together!

Find Ways for Every Family Member to Contribute to Benefit the Family as a Whole

The Billings family has recently gone through a rough nine months of unexpected medical bills. Since the mother has been diagnosed with a severe case of MS and is now in a wheelchair, they have also lost her income. The father is taking on extra work to support the family and pay medical bills. His priority is to be home in the evenings with his family, but he often has to work on his computer and doesn't have as much time for regular life details.

The Billings family has always been close-knit, so the four kids—ages middle school through high school—brainstormed how they could help out and plunged in to do so.

- Megan, 11, already feeds and walks their dog, but now she whizzes home after school and helps her mother with life basics. Her mother directs the projects from her wheelchair—making dinner, doing laundry, cleaning, and other tasks that need to be done. They break down the tasks so Megan spends an hour or two helping, then can jump on her own homework.

- Elise, 13, loves to work outside. A widow from their church has a small farm nearby and picks Elise up after school. She spends two hours helping the woman with her chickens, gardening, and herding the woman's two cows into the barn. In exchange, Elise brings home eggs; milk; a variety of garden veggies; home-canned fruits, vegetables, and stews; and home-baked goodies like bread, cinnamon rolls, and pies. The widow gets needed help and company, and the Billings family's grocery bills have been cut greatly.

- Mark, 16, is a people person who likes things to be hopping. He just got his driver's license and is the family errand runner, using his mom's car. He picks up the grocery list from the fridge (everybody in the family adds items they see missing), shops at Aldi nearby, and picks up his siblings from rehearsals or practices and his older brother from work. He sorts the mail, pays bills online, and has developed an interest in accounting.

- Matt, 17, quiet and studious, works at a T-shirt shop, stamping logos two nights a week and every Saturday. He also works weekend shows once a month, where he can make a chunk of change. Thirty percent of what he earns goes in the grocery store jar, which Mark uses for his grocery runs. In between, Matt pounds away at his studies and runs on the inside track after school three days a week. He's determined to go after a sports scholarship at their state university and is well on his way.

Each of those kids is using their personality and skills to uniquely contribute to the family and is being raised with the value of hard work, responsibility, and accountability. No slackers there. In spite of their hard work on behalf of the family, each of the kids gets nearly all As, with an occasional B mixed in. They know that keeping up their grades will greatly help them with college once they're ready to start investigating. Those kids are succeeding in every area of life.

If you visited the Billings home today, you'd see a happy, healthy family who pulls together and laughs together. Even more, they're generous with the little they have. I'd be surprised if Megan didn't give you a canned item to take home with you.

The Billings family is a model for what can happen when members put the family unit first and brainstorm creative ways to meet any challenge. When I think of an attitude of gratitude, I think of the Billings family.

So let me ask you:

- Is your child a self-starter?
- Does he routinely do things around the house without you asking or adding them to his chore list?
- Does she frequently ask, "What can I do to help?"

If you are the average family with middle-schoolers, chances are, you've just answered no, no, and no. You're thinking, *Are you kidding? Surely you jest. My kid? The kid who resembles a bear in hibernation? Of course not!*

Then perhaps you're doing far too much for your kid that he could do for himself. In a family, no member is more important than the group. You're all in this together, and cooperation is necessary for the small corporation called "family" to function and survive.

What can your child do to serve others in the family? Help a younger sibling with homework? Prepare part or all of dinner? Clean out a closet? Research tire brands to find the most economical one for your car? All children need to contribute in order to feel they belong to the family unit. They need to problem-solve and work out differences too. Without developing those qualities, there is no respect for other family members and what they contribute, only the "it's all about me" attitude.

Treat Others—and Their Feelings, Thoughts, and Ideas— as Important and Having Value

One large family I know has a big, old chalkboard in their kitchen. In fact, it takes up most of one wall. As the parents and kids come and go, they write messages to each other. Sometimes those messages are:

- "At library. Back at six."—Suzanne
- "Family Fun Night on Friday: tacos! Bring funny of the week."
- "Have extra rehearsal Sat. at 2. Can anybody take me?"—Jan

Other times the messages are:

- "Having trouble in science. Can u help?"—Matt
- "Thought he liked me. I was wrong. Need choc. Having pity party in my room but welcome company."—Marcy

This family has six kids, but they're one of the closest-linked families I know, with siblings who truly care about each other's welfare and don't compete with each other. They came up with the chalkboard system because, as their mom would say, she's "technologically dysfunctional." The kids tried hard to teach her texting, to no avail. So they came up with the chalkboard method for swapping important info with each other every day. Nobody at their house ever has to wonder where someone is. They simply check the board. There's no "Does anybody know where your brother is?" or "Why didn't you tell me . . . ?" Their family news is streamlined, easy, and immediate. All they have to do is walk in the door and check the board.

Kids love things that are routine and predictable, because there is safety in the fact you can count on something not to change. The Williams kids know they can communicate anything on the chalkboard. They also know that Friday night is always "Family Fun Night." They not only respect that boundary, but they look forward to it.

As you develop time together as a family unit on a routine basis, it will make other discussions about respect easier as well. If you notice that your older son is saying mean things to your younger son and won't share with him, pull your older son aside. "Luke, I heard what just went on in there. I've got to ask you something. Do you think what you said to your brother was kind?"

You'll get the usual, "Well, he started it. He said . . ."

"I understand what both of you said. But I'm asking you, do you think that was a kind thing to say?"

"Well, no."

"Okay then, we both agree that what you did was mean. You're now 12 years old. I've seen you pick on your brother more and more. Evidently you're not happy about something, and you're choosing to focus on only how you feel and what you think. You're 12 and I'm 38. You have a lot of life to go between where you are and where I am now. So I'm going to ask you to listen to what I'm saying. If you treat your peers the way you do your brother, I've got news for you: nobody is gonna like you. They won't want a thing to do with you. That's not how the world works.

"I can't make you be kind to your brother. I can't make you not be selfish. You're going to be who you choose to be. But I know that you are capable of treating your brother right. Yet what I'm seeing now is that you have to be the boss. Other kids—whether your brother or your friends—have to play by your rules. I look around and see what happens to people like that—people who try to enforce the rules on others around them. So it's not as much this one thing you did to your brother that bothers me; it's the pattern I see in you.

"I need you to think these things through. It might be a good idea if you went to your room and spent time by yourself. When you get there, you can think about anything you want. You can blow off good ol' Dad, but I gotta tell you, I'm concerned. I love you, but I'm concerned about the selfishness I see in you. I believe you're better than that. I believe you can handle your brother and your friends better than how you currently are. Once you've had the opportunity to think all this over, I'd like to hear any thoughts you might have."

Kids will say and do stupid things all the time because they're kids. But if you see a pattern of selfishness, it's time to nip it in the bud with such a discussion.

Time goes by quickly. In these years, it's easy to become passing ships in the night, because activities outside the home increase significantly. But if you engage with your kids, you can make the best of these Planet Middle School years.

Keep in mind that every day your kids are asking, *Am I going to make it in this world?* What you do in your home—the way you treat your children, the way you allow them to treat others—gives them the answer to that question. So be an oasis for your kids—a place where they get food, water, emotional comfort, and whatever they need to pack in their bags to support them when they're away from you. If they aren't prepared, the desert parts of Planet Middle School can be dry, dusty, and rather terrifying, especially when hurricane winds blow through.

> Kids will say and do stupid things all the time because they're kids. But if you see a pattern of selfishness, it's time to nip it in the bud.

The attitude your child has now toward others has everything to do with whether he has learned to be grateful in life. Having an attitude of gratitude grows a resilience in children that many kids today don't have. Being grateful for what they have creates kids who don't crumble at the first whiff of failure. They have the drive and determination to power on. Why? Because they see what they have and what others don't, and they want to make the world a better place.

Remember the boy who threw his lunch at his mom at the beginning of this chapter? If your child has an attitude of gratitude, he won't be snarky about the lunch you packed in the reused, wrinkly paper bag. He'll think, *Wow, I have a lunch, and that lady I saw at the park yesterday didn't have any.*

Instead of treating you like a servant who is on earth to do his bidding, he'll think, *Mom worked really late last night on a project, yet she got up early and made me a lunch. That makes me feel special. She's right. We're all in this family thing together. I wonder what I can do to make things easier for her today.*

That's how an attitude of gratitude works. It can change a single heart, transform an entire family's interactions, and indeed make the planet a better place to live.

See why I call it the single most important character quality?

16

Raising a Giver
in a Gimme Generation

How giving without receiving can transform your child's
world . . . and his or her life.

A few years ago, I had the privilege to go with a team from Compassion International on a trip to El Salvador. On that trip I met a woman who lived in a mud hut with a dirt floor. She had a small piece of metal she'd bent so she could put a few pieces of wood underneath it to light a fire. On top she placed the one cooking utensil she owned—a pot—and stirred the thin gruel in it with a stick.

When the woman saw that we had a camera with us—we were shooting some video for Compassion International—she motioned that she needed to change. A nursing mother, she had wet spots on her shirt. She ducked inside her hut and emerged only a minute later with an equally filthy shirt, but it had no wet spots on the front. It also looked like she had attempted to comb her hair. And she was beaming, as if the small change meant the world to her. I thought of all the things I owned, and my heart broke on the spot. I had seen a lot of poverty before, but never in that desperate a form.

As I boarded the plane that would take me from El Salvador back to the United States, my pockets were empty. I had handed over all of the cash I'd brought to people who needed it far more than I ever could. But my mind overflowed with the stories of those people, and my heart was overwhelmed with gratitude for everything I had.

When your heart brims with gratitude, how can you not be generous to others?

How to Raise a Giver

You don't have to travel to other countries to become aware of people who have less than you. Just take a short jaunt to the poorer area of your town or a city near you. And a careful look around your own neighborhood will reveal those who are struggling—the elderly, the disadvantaged—and could use your assistance. Identifying needs is always the first step. But unless you go beyond that, actually stepping into a situation where you and your child can experience giving, talking about it is meaningless. Do your kids know what it's like to not have anything for breakfast? To wonder where lunch and dinner are coming from? To not be able to walk outside without assistance? To be so lonely the only person you can talk to is yourself? There are so many things we take for granted. Children have to see what it's like to live in that world and to be that person. And frankly, so do you. Only by experiencing firsthand that others live differently can you truly realize what you do have and develop an attitude of gratitude.

I can't tell you how many times I've talked with people who have gone on a mission trip and returned to say, "Seeing people live with so little, yet be so happy, has forever changed my perspective."

But has it changed their perspective long-term, or only when the experience is fresh in their minds? The truth is revealed in the outcome a month or two down the road. Does that person continue to have a heart for the poor? The homeless? The physically disadvantaged? Those suffering in the wake of the devastation of hurricanes? If so, that person is actively working in some area to make such a difference. If not, the trip was just a little time-out from the rat race, and it's back to life as usual.

> Only by experiencing firsthand that others live differently can you truly realize what you do have and develop an attitude of gratitude.

What you want to develop in your child is the kind of gratitude where giving is a natural response to someone in need. How do you raise such a giver?

Encourage Broad Relationships in Multiple Circles

In middle school it's easy for a child's world to shrink to only her and her friends. Children need to know people from outside their immediate circle—elderly neighbors and children who look different than they do, are from different backgrounds, and have various income levels. Your children need opportunities to serve those in need without getting paid. What's important is giving without expecting in return.

The little church I go to is amazing. Generosity is second nature to the people. Everybody pitches in to help when someone has a need. People bring in garden produce and give it away. Every Sunday the pastor says, "We need to make a difference in the community we live in." And the people of the church do. The kids go around the neighborhood and help others with whatever they can do for them for free. In the process, I watch as those kids grow generous hearts.

Sande and I wanted our kids to be acutely aware that others count in life—that their opinions and perspectives are valuable,

13 Creative Ways to Get out of "Me" and into "We"

1. Visit a senior center or nursing home. Give the gifts of smiles, conversation, board games, and music.
2. Research a country. Learn about the geography and how others live. Make a food that is served in that country. Invite an international student from a nearby high school or college or someone else from that country to share dinner with you.
3. Volunteer at a food pantry or soup kitchen.
4. Donate your time, food, and clothing to a homeless shelter.
5. Invite neighbors you don't know for a simple picnic or cookout.
6. Rake leaves, shovel snow, wash windows, and take in garbage cans for the elderly. Some who can no longer read may welcome you reading a book to them. Others may enjoy a home-cooked meal or simply your company to pass some lonely hours.
7. Host a free lemonade stand or a free car wash. Don't accept donations.
8. Ask a trailer park office if you could provide a free concert for the residents or organize some sports and games for the kids.
9. Pass on gently used clothes to people in need.
10. Offer to babysit for a single parent who could use a break.
11. Thank doctors, dentists, and nurses for their services.
12. Deliver groceries to a family in need.
13. Make a meal for a new mom or someone who has just lost a loved one.

and that people of all faiths and colors should be treated with respect and kindness. The Golden Rule still applies: "Treat others the way you'd want to be treated."

That's why it's so important that your child doesn't move only in one particular group but has the opportunity to interact with others from vastly different backgrounds, cultures, and economic levels.

When kids see those who live differently, they're prompted to think about their own lifestyle and future goals. They will develop gratefulness for items that they've otherwise considered as their right, such as cell phones, iPods, and three square meals a day plus snacks. They'll look at potential purchases in a different way. *Do I really need that shirt if I already have 10 other shirts in my wardrobe? Could I use that 25 bucks in a more useful way, to help someone?*

Raise Awareness of How Others Live

It's easy for kids to think, *Every family is like ours. We have a house, a dog, two cars, and a lot of cell phones.* But that's far from the truth. How can you raise awareness of how others live?

When our kids were young, we would pack them up in the car, go grocery shopping, and drop groceries off for a family who was in need. Seeing the gratitude in the eyes of the parents and the children stirred not only an awareness of what others don't have but a compassion and generosity in our kids that continue to this day.

You can also raise awareness by discussing issues as a part of your regular conversation. For example, you see an article about thousands of immigrants streaming illegally into Texas from Central America and Mexico. "I just read a fascinating article about . . . ," you say and share what the article was about. "It got me thinking, what would it be like to be so desperate that you left everything you knew behind? That the only hope you had not to starve was going to a completely different country? What do you think?"

Teachable moments arise naturally. So talk about what's happening in the Middle East and in Ukraine, and about the girls abducted in Nigeria. Ask, "Did you know that every Thanksgiving, the Salvation Army feeds several thousand people who live on the streets? Can you imagine not having anything for Thanksgiving dinner?" Even better, bring your entire family to serve turkey, mashed potatoes, and stuffing to men who haven't shaved or been near clean water for a month. Let them see the joy brimming in the eyes of the women and children. Our kids will never forget the trips we made to serve people at centers such as the Salvation Army ones.

Awareness can also arise through research projects. A homeschooling group decided to research one country a month for a year to find out what it was like for children to live in that particular country. They invited people who knew about the country to talk with them and researched the poverty level, what kids ate, what the medical issues were, etc. At the end of the year, the homeschooling group connected with various mission organizations, and the students had workdays to be able to contribute financially to the kids in those countries. The homeschoolers knew the poverty level and the issues involved, and they worked really hard because they could put themselves in those kids' shoes and wanted to help them.

Invest Time and Resources in Those Who Have Less than You

When my kids were growing up and we would see a destitute person on a street corner, I'd pull over, stop, and hand the person some food or some money. If I didn't see the person or was in a hurry, one of my kids would always prompt, "Look, Daddy, see that lady? She needs our help!"

Some of you are saying, "But what if that person used the money for a cheap bottle of wine or drugs?"

She might have. That's something I don't have control over. But what I do have control over is whether I will choose to be generous to someone in need. When you choose to be generous to others, your children will see that and develop generous hearts themselves.

If your child becomes interested in a specific cause and says, "Those kids really need help. Can't we do something?" you should say, "Maybe we can. Why don't you check out . . ." Suggest an assignment—some research your child could do to come up with some answers. Sometimes helping people isn't always about money. It's about investing time and taking risks.

Like the sixth-grade class who collected gently used toys and clothing to donate to a mission in El Salvador. Or the seventh-grade class who did work projects so they could purchase toothpaste, toothbrushes, and medical supplies for a children's orphanage

✓ What Worked for Us

The day my daughter Jamie whined when I told her I didn't have time to pick up the after-school snack she wanted, I decided things had to change. It was my fault. I'd spoiled her far too much.

The next Saturday I told her we had somewhere to go but didn't tell her where. We drove to a local food pantry and spent the morning stocking shelves and helping the families who came in load their bags with cans of food. Jamie's attitude stunk, until a young mom came in with two little girls.

"Thank you so much," the mom told Jamie softly. "This morning my girls had a can of green beans for breakfast, and they saved me some out of their portions. Then someone told us about this food pantry." The lady's eyes welled with tears as her children hugged her legs. "Tonight we will have rice . . . and even some tuna."

I looked at Jamie. She hated tuna—she made fun of it as only good enough for cats. Yet those two little girls' eyes glowed at the mention of tuna, as if we'd just given them a prize.

in Kenya. Or the eighth-graders who raised money for a five-day class trip before graduation but instead decided to give the money to a local farming family who had lost everything in a tornado, and then spent those five days helping the family with cleanup. They also went door-to-door in their community, asking people to donate water, sandwiches, and cleaning supplies. As a result of those middle-schoolers, an entire community was motivated to pitch in and help that family.

Millennials today are attending church in fewer numbers. Even many of those who believe in God would say they don't attend church because they have seen the hypocrisy and because church isn't relevant in today's world. But what do the millennials want to do? Be socially active people of faith. They want to provide clothes and other items to disadvantaged families. They want to

---

Jamie was quiet on the way home. She skipped lunch and later said she didn't feel like eating dinner. Instead, she went to bed early.

The next morning, a teary-eyed Jamie walked into the kitchen. "I couldn't stop thinking about what it would be like to have nothing to eat except green beans. I wanted to see what it felt like to be hungry. I couldn't sleep all night. I felt so bad for those kids." Then she asked, "Mom, do you think there's anything else we could do for them?"

That was two years ago. Jamie is now in high school, and we both help a full Saturday at the food pantry once a month. After school on Thursdays, she reads to and plays with a group of disadvantaged kids for two hours while their moms learn job skills. Recently she spearheaded an additional food drive when the pantry was especially low and needs were high. As she and I went in on a weekday to sort the bags at the pantry, Jamie called out, "Look, Mom! Tuna! Cans and cans of tuna!"

How things have changed.

Jocelyn, North Carolina

---

serve in soup kitchens. They want to build homes with Habitat for Humanity and refurbish ghettos into safe family climates.

Who you are is very important. However, others will judge who you are by what they see you do. So the real test of character is in what you do. How do you and your kids treat others who have no possible way of paying you back?

Step out of Your Comfort Zone

There's nothing like connecting with people who have less than you to realize how much you truly have. However, simply telling your son that you're going to sponsor a kid from Africa won't really teach him anything. Your child has to own that relationship. That means all of you should work together to come up with the money to support that child each month. Once you make the commitment, you sacrifice to meet it. You can also save money as a family to go on a short-term mission trip. There's nothing like seeing with your own eyes how others live to change your heart toward the poor.

> How do you and your kids treat others who have no possible way of paying you back?

My daughter Hannah worked for an organization called Spark, which organizes sponsorship for children in foreign countries. Seeing a photo of another child, being able to write a letter to that child, and finding out how he or she lives makes the experience more real. Hannah has always had a heart of generosity and the kind of personality to engage easily with those outside her comfort zone. She and her husband, Josh, are part of the Friday night "Warm-Ups" at her local church, where homeless people are welcomed, fed, and able to stay overnight in a warm location. Hannah's life work has been aiding nonprofits that work in countries on the African continent, most particularly Zambia.

292

One family I know is passionate about supporting Kenya Children's Fund. Each of the children exchanges letters with a child similar in age at that organization and learns how simply they live. Even more than that, the children donate portions of money they receive from odds-and-ends jobs, such as mowing lawns or making jewelry, to the KCF jar in their kitchen. At the end of the month, if the jar is short, the family brainstorms how they can make the money. Several times they have visited their local urban train station as a family and played music to raise the money as well as an awareness of KCF. The donations that came in exceeded what they needed for the month, so they were also able to donate money toward KCF's building fund.

Another group of families leaves the comfort of their own homes every February and takes their kids to Mississippi, where they all work for Habitat for Humanity. The kids are plunged into relationships with children and adults who have nearly nothing. These kids have the awesome experience of pouring their time, their resources, and their hearts into getting to know those people.

There's nothing like a little real-life therapy to pop the entitlement bubble, dampen middle-income-kid requests for more, and lessen squabbles between siblings over what they each have.

Kids at their core are self-centered and egotistical . . . until you teach and role model for them a different path, as well as provide opportunities for them to develop an attitude of gratitude.

> There's nothing like a little real-life therapy to pop the entitlement bubble, dampen middle-income-kid requests for more, and lessen squabbles between siblings over what they each have.

Sheila used one of her kids' days off from school to take them to work at a nearby mission that reached out to those who were homeless and/or recovering from drug and alcohol abuse. When the kids walked in, they were shocked by how dirty and smelly some of the people were when they came off the streets.

"My kids huddled in a group like they were lost and didn't know what to do," Sheila explained. "They didn't know how to relate to people who were so different from them. But as the day progressed and they cleaned floors, served lunch, and talked with the people who came in and out, my kids began to see the homeless as real men, women, and children. When I saw my daughter hugging one woman who was crying and later helping a four-year-old wash her hair and braid it, I knew the hard work I'd done to make the day happen was worth it."

Sheila's kids arrived home exhausted after their "day off." But the next time they had a day off, guess where they asked to go? To that same mission. And this time, they also brought gently used clothes they'd gathered from their own closets and from people they knew, and groceries they'd purchased with their own allowances.

That was one wise mom to take her kids from middle-class America, where they had all their needs covered and perhaps too many of their wants, into a situation where they realized what they had and what many people didn't. Each of those four children has developed an attitude of gratitude and now looks for additional ways to give to others—whether it's organizing activities for Salvation Army kids, helping a disadvantaged child who is struggling with math, or babysitting to give a single or working mom a break.

Take a good look at your kids. Do you see an attitude of gratitude in them for the most part? Do they think of serving others as a natural response to what they've been given? Or are they self-absorbed, drawn into the whirl of Planet Middle School, so the only thing that matters is that they come out on top?

You can't force your kids to change. But you can go out of your way to offer opportunities that provide the impetus for change. It all starts with teaching and role modeling responsibility, hard work, and a servant's heart—both at home and beyond your home.

A Word of Encouragement

If you're one of those parents who has lain awake many a night staring at that small crack in the ceiling, wondering if that kid of yours is ever going to turn around, take heart. You may have tried everything under the sun—including sending him to summer school, giving him a variety of rewards and punishments, and hiring a tutor. Sometimes it takes a long time for late bloomers to bloom. Take a look at this report card.

REPORT OF CLASS WORK AND ATTENDANCE	6 wks	6 wks	6 wks	Jan. Exam.	6 wks	6 wks	June Exam.
English	G	P	P	70	VP	3+8	67
Latin	P+	VP	P+	81	P+—F	P—	70
French							
German							
Spanish							
History							
Social Studies	F+	G—G	76	P+—F	VP	65	
Algebra	P+	VP	—P	57	VP	UP	VP 22
Geometry							
General Science	F	F	—F	65	P+	P	P 65
Physics							
Chemistry							
Earth Science							
Home Economics					G		
Art							
Industrial Arts							
Physical Education HEALTH	F—P	G—	61	VVP	P	P—66	
Half Days Absent, legal	4			8			
Half Days Absent, illegal	6						
Times Tardy, legal	2						
Times Tardy, illegal	3						

REGULAR AND PROMPT ATTENDANCE IS ESSENTIAL TO PROGRESS

E—Excellent—90-100%   P—Poor—60 to 70%
G—Good—80-90%   V. P.—Very Poor—Below 50
F—Fair—70-80%

Yes, this is my report card from ninth grade. I was blessed to have a mom and a dad who believed in me, despite all evidence to the contrary.

You are the best advocate your child will ever have.

I'm living proof that change is possible.

Conclusion

I guarantee you'll miss these days . . . someday.

My youngest daughter, Lauren, discovered Audrey Hepburn when she was in eighth grade. In fact, there's still a framed picture of the actress in her bedroom today.

She and her girlfriend were hanging out at our house on a Friday night. They'd already made and eaten brownies, discussed boys, and giggled a lot—all things that eighth-grade girls do as a matter of routine. Then Lauren said, "Dad, would you mind running to get us a movie?"

"Sure," I agreed. "What movie do you want?"

Lauren and her friend started talking about one of the really stupid movies that was quoted as a "great movie," yet it was anything but. It was adolescent slapstick humor at its worst and a total waste of any brain cells. To this day, I don't remember what movie it was. I just remember how stupid it looked.

If I were an authoritarian dad, I would have barked, "That has one of the stupidest movie trailers I've ever seen. There's no way I'm renting that for you!"

If I were a permissive dad, I would have simpered, "Oh, okay, honey, anything you want. I'll just go right now and get it."

But no, I was an authoritative dad. I pulled out my parent card, took a look at it, and decided I would rather my daughter watch something that had a bit more meat to it, was a classic, and was worth watching. I didn't demand, though. I merely suggested calmly, "Hey, would you ever want to watch some movies that your old dad thinks are great and even funny but that you've never heard of?"

And then, to sweeten the deal, I said, "Oh, and you want me to pick you up a pizza at the same time?" Remember what I've said all throughout this book about middle-schoolers and food? Well, you can use that to your best advantage.

That day started Lauren's love of old movies. I went to the video store and came back with a movie called *Charade*, in which Audrey Hepburn, Cary Grant, and Walter Matthau star in a murder mystery that's set in Paris and also filled with humor. Lauren's friend spent the night with us, and the girls promised to get to bed early. I was just glad it wasn't a school night, because I knew that "early" to middle-school girls on a sleepover meant about 3:30 in the morning.

Later I suggested to Lauren a bunch of other movies: *Vertigo*, a thriller starring Jimmy Stewart as a former police detective; *North by Northwest*, starring Cary Grant; and one that really made her shiver—*Wait Until Dark*, with Audrey Hepburn, Alan Arkin, and Richard Crenna. I also introduced her to *Paint Your Wagon*, a comedy Western with Clint Eastwood and Lee Marvin. And for Christmas, we watched *It's a Wonderful Life* with Jimmy Stewart, and *Miracle on 34th Street*, the original one made with Thelma Ritter and Anthony Sydes in 1947.

Lauren loved them all. And they also sparked in her an appreciation for the classic songs from the movies. That continues to this day.

Recently, when Lauren was visiting, she borrowed my car to run an errand. When she and I got back in the car later, she flipped the radio on.

"What the heck is that?" I said and grinned. She had Frank Sinatra on.

"Oh, Dad, I love Frank," she replied.

If you call her cell phone, the song that greets you is from the movie *Oklahoma*: "Oh, What a Beautiful Mornin'." Lauren is a very hip twenty-something, with a business of her own, but that song is as old as the hills.

One of the pivotal moments in her life was that day with her girlfriend in eighth grade on Planet Middle School. Yes, I could have just gone and rented that trashy movie for her. But I didn't. I played the role of the authoritative parent because I knew what was best for my daughter. Look at the ripple effects it's had since then.

You, parent, can create ripple effects too. If you take the information in *Planet Middle School* to heart and practice it with your kids, you'll be prepared for the changes you'll see in them—physically, emotionally, and relationally—and understand their expanding universe.

You'll have a sense of humor with the drama of solar-flare emotions, yet know when you need to step in to protect your kids or help them.

You'll find ways to shower your kids with acceptance, belonging, and competence so they can confront peer pressure and technology and take solid stands where things really matter and could impact their lives in the long run.

You will learn how to talk so they'll listen and how to use the power of positive expectations to prepare your children for high school and life beyond your mother ship.

You'll encourage their uniquenesses, whether or not their bents are "bent" in the direction you thought they'd go.

But most of all, you'll focus on building a relationship with your child. You'll believe in her and give her lots of Vitamin E. And in a time when love and acceptance are conditional, even moment by moment, within the peer group, you'll shower her with unconditional love and a 24/7 listening ear.

Is it any wonder, then, that home will become her favorite place to be? That her attitude will be gratitude? And that she'll grow a heart that is passionate about giving to others?

Isn't that the kind of child everyone dreams of? Well, you can have that. We have five of them.

Never sell yourself short. The words you choose do make a difference. Pair them with authoritative parenting, actions that match your words, and positive expectations, and you'll have a winning combo that will help you rear your child into an adult who will be a healthy, giving member of society—one who isn't "all about me" but "all about we."

A day will come all too soon when you wish you could hear the little giggles down the hallway again from when your daughter had an overnighter. When you long for the loud, testosterone-laden boasting of your son and his friends shooting hoops in your driveway. You won't even remember that the neighbor called to complain because they played past dark and interrupted her evening soap opera on television. Or, if you do, you'll chuckle about it. You will even think fondly of the pizza smears on your kitchen counter, the empty milk jug in the fridge, and the brownie crumbs in the crevices of your couch.

I guarantee it.

A Middle-Schooler's
10 Commandments to Parents

1. Let me spread my wings and try to fly, but keep me from falling too far.
2. Don't tell me what to do. Allow me to sort things out on my own.
3. Expect the best of me, trust me, and believe in me. Deep down I really want to please you.
4. Love me even when I mess up, and give me another chance. Some things I need to learn the hard way, but I will learn from my mistakes.
5. Talk *with* me instead of *at* me, and listen . . . always.
6. Say "Forgive me" when you're wrong, and you'll have my loyalty and gratitude forever.
7. Tell me what I did wrong, but never criticize me.
8. Realize I'm doing the best I can in a tough, intense world. I appreciate the freedoms you give me and the stop signs you

place along the way, because they keep me safe. Thank you for teaching me the difference between right and wrong.

9. Accept me for who I am . . . and who I am becoming.
10. Never forget how important you are to me. Even when I seemingly blow you off, I love you and need you in my life.

Notes

Chapter 1 Creature from the Black Lagoon

1. *Creature from the Black Lagoon*, YouTube, https://www.youtube.com/watch?v=svyPswixryM.

2. *Creature from the Black Lagoon*, YouTube, https://www.youtube.com/watch?v=lM1o1xe5FGE.

Chapter 3 All Flared Up!

1. ESA, "Super-Hurricane-Force Winds on Venus Are Getting Stronger," NASA, June 18, 2013, http://solarsystem.nasa.gov/news/display.cfm?News_ID=44053.

Chapter 4 Survival of the Fittest

1. Alex Rosenberg and Robert Arp, eds., *Philosophy of Biology: An Anthology* (Hoboken, NJ: John Wiley & Sons, 2009), 99–102.

Chapter 5 Walking on Polar Ice

1. *To Save a Life*, directed by Bryan Baugh (New York: Samuel Goldwyn Films, 2010), DVD.

Chapter 6 Confronting the Black Hole

1. Samuel Gibbs, "Facebook Patent Reveals Plans for Children to Join the Social Network," *The Guardian*, June 3, 2014, http://www.theguardian.com/technology/2014/jun/03/facebook-children-join-social-network.

2. "Bullying and Suicide," Bullying Statistics, 2013, http://www.bullyingstatistics.org/content/bullying-and-suicide.html.

3. Susan Donaldson James, "Teen Commits Suicide Due to Bullying: Parents Sue School for Son's Death," ABC News, April 2, 2009, http://abcnews.go.com/Health/MindMoodNews/Story?id=7228335.

4. Allie Bidwell, "Sexting and Sex Go Hand in Hand for Middle Schoolers," *U.S. News & World Report*, June 30, 2014, http://www.usnews.com/news/articles/2014/06/30/study-middle-schoolers-who-sext-are-more-likely-to-report-sexual-activity.

5. Jodi Mohrmann, "Excessive Texting Linked to Sexual Activity in Middle Schoolers," News4Jax, August 22, 2014, http://www.news4jax.com/news/excessive-texting-linked-to-sexual-activity-in-middle-schoolers/27686844.

Chapter 8 Becoming a (Gulp) Man/Woman

1. Zoe Williams, "Early Puberty: Why Are Kids Growing Up Faster?" *The Guardian*, October 24, 2012, http://www.theguardian.com/society/2012/oct/25/early-puberty-growing-up-faster.

Chapter 9 Blue Chip or Penny Stocks?

1. Stephanie Watson, "Teens and STDs: Get the Facts," WebMD, http://teens.webmd.com/features/teens-stds-get-facts.

2. "Four in 10 Children Are Born to Unwed Mothers," Familyfacts.org, 2011, http://www.familyfacts.org/charts/205/four-in-10-children-are-born-to-unwed-mothers.

Chapter 13 Raising a "Home" Boy/Girl

1. "The *Real* Value Meal . . . Eating Together," Rutgers: New Jersey Agricultural Experiment Station, http://njaes.rutgers.edu/spotlight/eating-together.asp.

Chapter 14 Life-Mapping

1. *Star Trek: The Next Generation* (1987–1994) Quotes, IMDb, http://www.imdb.com/title/tt0092455/quotes.

2. *A Cinderella Story*, directed by Mark Rosman (Burbank, CA: Warner Bros., 2004), DVD.

3. Michael Dunlop, "10 World Famous Companies That Started in Garages," Retire@21, http://www.retireat21.com/blog/10-companies-started-garages.

4. "Dropping Out of College Is Not a Good Idea, Says Bill Gates," *Economic Times*, April 22, 2010, http://articles.economictimes.indiatimes.com/2010-04-22/news/27576976_1_bill-gates-online-courses-students.

About Dr. Kevin Leman

An internationally known psychologist, radio and television personality, speaker, educator, and humorist, Dr. Kevin Leman has taught and entertained audiences worldwide with his wit and commonsense psychology.

The *New York Times* bestselling and award-winning author of *Have a New Kid by Friday*, *Have a New Husband by Friday*, *Have a New You by Friday*, *Sheet Music*, *The Birth Order Book*, and *Have a Happy Family by Friday* has made thousands of house calls through radio and television programs, including *Fox & Friends*, *The View*, Fox's *The Morning Show*, *Today*, Dr. Bill Bennett's *Morning in America*, *The 700 Club*, CBS's *The Early Show*, *Janet Parshall*, CNN, and *Focus on the Family*. Dr. Leman has also served as a contributing family psychologist to *Good Morning America*.

Dr. Leman's professional affiliations include the American Psychological Association, AFTRA-SAG, and the North American Society of Adlerian Psychology.

North Park University in Chicago awarded Dr. Leman the Distinguished Alumnus Award in 1993 and an honorary Doctor of Humane Letters degree in 2010. In 2003, he received from the

University of Arizona the highest award that a university can extend to its own: the Alumni Achievement Award.

Dr. Leman received his bachelor's degree in psychology from the University of Arizona, where he later earned his master's and doctorate degrees. Originally from Williamsville, New York, he and his wife, Sande, live in Arizona and have five children and two grandchildren.

For information regarding speaking availability, business consultations, seminars, webinars, or the annual Love, Laugh and Learn cruise, please contact:

Dr. Kevin Leman
P.O. Box 35370
Tucson, Arizona 85740
Phone: (520) 797-3830
Fax: (520) 797-3809
www.birthorderguy.com
www.drleman.com

Follow Dr. Kevin Leman on Facebook (facebook.com/DrKevin Leman) and on Twitter (@DrKevinLeman). Check out the free podcasts at www.birthorderguy.com/podcast.

Resources by Dr. Kevin Leman

Books for Adults

Have a New Kid by Friday
The Birth Order Book
Have a Happy Family by Friday
Have a New Teenager by Friday
Have a New Husband by Friday
Have a New You by Friday
Planet Middle School
The Way of the Wise
Be the Dad She Needs You to Be
What a Difference a Mom Makes
Parenting Your Powerful Child
Under the Sheets
Sheet Music
Making Children Mind without Losing Yours
It's Your Kid, Not a Gerbil

Born to Win

Sex Begins in the Kitchen

7 Things He'll Never Tell You . . . But You Need to Know

What Your Childhood Memories Say about You

Running the Rapids

The Way of the Shepherd (written with William Pentak)

Becoming the Parent God Wants You to Be

Becoming a Couple of Promise

A Chicken's Guide to Talking Turkey with Your Kids about Sex (written with Kathy Flores Bell)

First-Time Mom

Step-parenting 101

Living in a Stepfamily without Getting Stepped On

The Perfect Match

Be Your Own Shrink

Stopping Stress before It Stops You

Single Parenting That Works

Why Your Best Is Good Enough

Smart Women Know When to Say No

Books for Children, with Kevin Leman II

My Firstborn, There's No One Like You

My Middle Child, There's No One Like You

My Youngest, There's No One Like You

My Only Child, There's No One Like You

My Adopted Child, There's No One Like You

My Grandchild, There's No One Like You

DVD/Video Series for Group Use

Have a New Kid by Friday
Have a Happy Family by Friday
Making Children Mind without Losing Yours (Christian—parenting edition)
Making Children Mind without Losing Yours (Mainstream—public school teacher edition)
Value-Packed Parenting
Making the Most of Marriage
Running the Rapids
Single Parenting That Works
Bringing Peace and Harmony to the Blended Family

DVDs for Home Use

Straight Talk on Parenting
Why You Are the Way You Are
Have a New Husband by Friday
Have a New You by Friday
Have a New Kid by Friday

Available at 1-800-770-3830 • www.birthorderguy.com • www.drleman.com

Visit DrLeman.com

for more information, resources, and videos from his popular books.

Follow Dr. Kevin Leman on

 Dr Kevin Leman

 drleman

Revell
a division of Baker Publishing Group
www.RevellBooks.com

Available wherever books and ebooks are sold.

My child used to be normal.
What happened?

MORE THAN 100,000 COPIES SOLD

Have a New Teenager by Friday

From Mouthy and Moody to Respectful and Responsible in **5 Days**

Dr. Kevin Leman

New York Times Bestselling Author

"Congratulations! You have a teenager in your home. Life will never quite be the same again. . . . But it can be better than you've ever dreamed. I guarantee it."—Dr. Kevin Leman

Ω Revell
a division of Baker Publishing Group
www.RevellBooks.com

Available wherever books and ebooks are sold.

Boys will be boys—ALWAYS.
And no one has a more powerful impact on them than you, Mom.

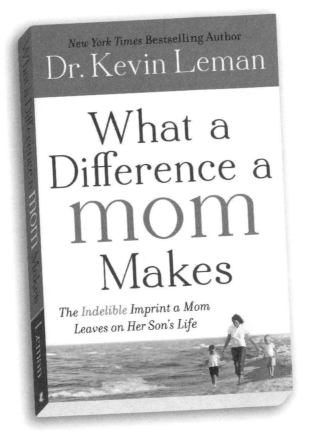

New York Times Bestselling Author
Dr. Kevin Leman

What a Difference a mom Makes

The Indelible Imprint a Mom Leaves on Her Son's Life

Want to capture your boy's heart? Want a man you'll be proud to call your son? You can make a difference, because you are the one who matters most in your boy's world.

Revell
a division of Baker Publishing Group
www.RevellBooks.com

Available wherever books and ebooks are sold.

Powerful kids
don't just happen.

They're created, and their power comes in different packages. Whether loud and temperamental, quiet and sensitive, or stubborn and manipulative, powerful children can make living with them a challenge. But it doesn't have to be that way.

Revell
a division of Baker Publishing Group
www.RevellBooks.com

Available wherever books and ebooks are sold.

Take the
5-day challenge

Family expert Dr. Kevin Leman reveals in this *New York Times*
bestseller why your kids do what they do, and what you can do
about it—**in just 5 days.**

Revell
a division of Baker Publishing Group
www.RevellBooks.com

Available wherever books and ebooks are sold.

New York Times Bestselling Author
Dr. Kevin Leman
Will Help You with Real Change

Use these easy action plans to improve your
communication and life in five days!

Revell
a division of Baker Publishing Group
www.RevellBooks.com

Available wherever books and ebooks are sold.

Find Out How Your Birth Order
nfluences the Way You React to Your World

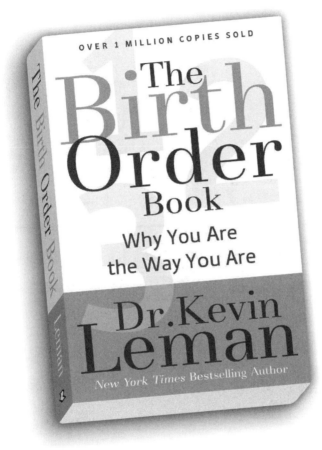

Firstborn? Only child? Middle child? Baby of the family?
Find out what your birth order means to you, your relationships,
and your career in this updated edition of the bestselling book.

Revell
a division of Baker Publishing Group
www.RevellBooks.com

Available wherever books and ebooks are sold.

No matter where you are on your journey in life, you can take *the way of the wise.*

New York Times bestselling author Dr. Kevin Leman reveals ten life-changing principles—all packed in six amazing little verses by the wisest man of all, King Solomon.

Revell
a division of Baker Publishing Group
www.RevellBooks.com

Available wherever books and ebooks are sold.

Make your marriage *sizzle!*

Creating Intimacy
to Make Your
Marriage Sizzle

Sex Begins *in the* Kitchen

Dr. Kevin Leman
AUTHOR OF **THE BIRTH ORDER BOOK**

Learn to build communication, affection, consideration,
and caring in your marriage to make it more
emotionally—and physically—satisfying.

Ϩ Revell
a division of Baker Publishing Group
www.RevellBooks.com

Available wherever books and ebooks are sold.

Be the First to Hear about Other New Books from REVELL!

Sign up for announcements about new and upcoming titles at

RevellBooks.com/SignUp

Don't miss out on our great reads!

Revell

a division of Baker Publishing Group
www.RevellBooks.com